Writing Mothers, Writing Daughters

Writing Mothers, Writing Daughters

Tracing the Maternal in
Stories by American Jewish Women

Janet Handler Burstein

University of Illinois Press
Urbana and Chicago

© 1996 by the Board of Trustees of the University of Illinois
Manufactured in the United States of America
1   2   3   4   5   C   P   5   4   3   2   1

This book is printed on acid-free paper.

Library of Congress Cataloging-in-Publication Data

Burstein, Janet.
    Writing mothers, writing daughters : tracing the maternal in
stories by American Jewish women / Janet Handler Burstein.
       p.   cm.
    Includes bibliographical references and index.
    ISBN 0-252-02252-1 (cloth : alk. paper). — ISBN 0-252-06555-7
(pbk. : alk. paper)
    1. American literature—Jewish authors—History and criticism.
2. American literature—Women authors—History and criticism.
3. American literature—20th century—History and criticism.
4. Mothers and daughters in literature. 5. Jewish women in
literature. 6. Motherhood in literature. 7. Women and literature—
United States—History—20th century. I. Title.
PS153.J4B87   1996
810'.98924—dc20   95-50191
                                                CIP

For my mother,
Fan Handler,
whose memory has become a blessing

A Woman and a Jew, sometimes more
of a contradiction than I can sweat out,
yet finally the intersection that is both
collision and fusion, stone and seed.
—Marge Piercy, "The Ram's Horn Sounding"

Where is the angel
to wrestle with me and wound
not my thigh but my throat
so curses and blessings flow storming out
and the glass shatters, and the iron sunders?
—Denise Levertov, "Where Is the Angel?"

Contents

Acknowledgments

More thanks than I know how to say

to students: Amanda Johnson, Dale Peck, Helen Thow, George Mitsis, Brenda
Koenig, Patti Palermo, Sylvia Skaggs McTague, and Heather Stewart
—who searched, gathered, duplicated, and read proof;

to book people: Josie Cook, Ruth Friedman, Bruce Lancaster, and Liz Heusler
—who found the impossibles;

to friends and colleagues: Judith Baskin, Jacqueline Berke, Delight Dodyk,
Diane Lichtenstein, Nadine Ollman, Marion Powell, Riv Ellen Prell,
Ann Saltzman, Lynn Seligman, Carl Sheingold, Merrill Skaggs, John M.
Warner, and most of all, Mark Burstein
—who read, and reread, and said truly what didn't work;

to Robert Ready (Chair), Paolo Cucchi (Dean), and the Drew faculty in
English
—who allowed time to write;

to Gladys Rosen and Yehuda Rosenman
—who turned my attention to the Jewish family;

to Carol Orr
—who first dignified this project with her interest;

to Judith Arcana
—who showed me the path to an ending;

to Joyce Antler
—who helped me understand the ending when I got there;

to Ann Lowry and Terry Sears
—who made a book out of a manuscript;

and to my dearest ones: David Calle and Mark Maben, Julie, Mark, and Bob
—whose love sustains.

Introduction

When I was a little girl, "Jewish" meant the feel of the fringes on my father's tallith[1] and the light of sabbath candles on the back of my mother's hands. Softness, light, and warmth: those Jewish memories abide. But they were shadowed, even then, by puzzling undertones. I always knew, for example, that my mother didn't like rabbis. She listened intently to our rabbi's sermons; she spoke of him with affection and respect. But she wouldn't let us attend the Hebrew school he supervised. Instead, devising her own curriculum, she hired a series of rabbinical students to teach us. She didn't like the rules of observant Judaism either, even though she practiced many of them. Scrupulous about kashrut at home, she raged nevertheless against Orthodox women who insisted on keeping kosher, at great expense, the fund-raising luncheons she ran for the rescue of Jewish children during the war. Contemptuous of women who were willing to sit in the women's section in shul, separate from their sons and husbands, she attended regularly a synagogue that let her sit beside my father. But her synagogue called only men to say blessings over the Torah, counted only men in the quorum (minyan) needed for communal prayer, elected only men to govern the congregation. Hers, not my father's, was the passionate commitment to Jewish history, Jewish practice, Jewish survival. But when she sat beside him in shul she was institutionally invisible, voiceless, uncounted—almost like me: a little girl braiding the fringes on her father's tallith.

As a child, I often wondered why my mother was angry at rabbis and their rules, but I never asked. What she did and thought were the givens of my world, the norms by which I judged other women—and myself. At the beginning, I accepted her inconsistencies without understanding them. Now, when they no longer organize the world for me, they have become the warp and woof of her image, running like colored threads across and beside one another as they texture my memories of her. Jewishly uneducated, the child of secularist parents, she studied Bible and Hebrew all her adult life. The eldest of five children in a poor, immigrant family, she became an expert American consumer. She loved to buy things, but she also admired fiercely the ethic of austerity that animated Zionist pioneers in Israel.

She was antagonistic to rabbinic authority as long as she lived. But after her death, when I lifted down from their hooks the iconic paintings that had always hung in my mother's house, I realized how many of them portrayed male authority figures: there were an eighteenth-century male teacher at a high desk; a visionary Abraham, staring anxiously past his wife and son into a covenanted future; five rabbis seated around a shabby wooden table, disputing a Talmudic text. There was also, however, a splendid portrait of her, with the hills of Judea painted into the background at her request. Circumscribed in the larger world by forces beyond her power to change or control, she had exercised in that painting both the subject's and the artist's prerogatives. Strong and beautiful, her image dominated entirely the space within the frame. My mother didn't match the mothers of my Jewish friends. Like their mothers, she shopped a lot and got her hair done, but they played cards in the afternoons while she went to meetings and study groups. Accommodating and rebellious, compliant and willful, self-indulgent and self-disciplined, materialist and intellectual: my mother fascinated and confused me.

As I grew older, I sometimes ignored and sometimes tried to confront these confusions. I always suspected that they were connected with my sense of myself as both a woman and a Jew. But eventually, dissuaded by a male advisor from entering a graduate program in Jewish studies—"You are a woman," he said; "there will be ten men ahead of you for every job"—I put aside the Jewish issues and turned myself into a professor of English literature. For many years, I retained only the most superficial, conventional connections to Jewish life and thought. But on the first Shabbat after my daughter's bat mitzvah in 1971, she asked me why no one from the shul had invited her during the week, as the boys in her class had been invited, to join the morning minyan. Hearing my daughter's question, feeling the pain of her exclusion from the community of worshipers that she had worked hard to enter, wondering why I had never noticed that pain before, I knew it was time to try to understand my mother.

Research for this book actually began with that effort to understand.

The connection between the book and my mother was not immediately apparent. My mother was, inimitably, herself. And she was mine. Thus, learning to understand her required for me, as it requires for all children, the deeply inward work of searching out and untangling observations, feelings, memories, and beliefs. In time, I learned to distinguish her from me, to see the differences between us as Jews and as women, and to identify the ways in which her sense of herself as a Jewish woman had shaped my own. In the years after her death, however, my reading and thinking began to move deliberately toward this book. I wanted to clarify the social and historical forces that had acted upon my mother—and that connected both her and me to other American Jewish mothers and daughters.

In the 1970s, scholars had begun to study the givens of history, class, and culture that shaped Jewish women. These writers showed me that many vectors of my inimitable mother's behavior also moved other Jewish women of her period and class. Their work revealed what my mother and I owed to our time and place in the world, to the circumstances of our families, and to the cultural and religious tradition in which we knew ourselves to be Jews. Even the roots of my own gendered and ethnic self-awareness began to stretch beyond the personal, into collective social experience. Thus, the inward work of understanding my mother merged almost imperceptibly with questions about the extent to which other Jewish women shared my confusions, about the way in which other Jewish women understood their mothers, about the process that constructs us all as gendered and ethnic creatures—as American Jewish women.

I put these questions to literary texts because I trust storytellers to render the kind of truth that is faithful to both facts and feelings. One needs to be very careful about linking literary portrayals of mothers and daughters to either writers or their families. Literary texts offer images of human experience—verbal constructs, not historically verifiable human beings. However, what we know about mothering and being mothered moves, unbidden, not only into our dreams and conversations but also into the stories we tell about ourselves and others. In the features and expression of what we imagine—as in the scholarly projects we design—traces of our own felt experience often surface. Thus, however far removed from verifiable "fact" a literary image may be, it can tell truthfully some portion of what a writer "knows" of maternal and filial experience. The critical effort in this study to recover such partial, subjective, imaginative understandings has, if anything, reinforced my predisposition to respect these qualities of literary images. They reflect accurately the fragmentary, intermittent, emotionally laden, personal awarenesses that always seem to construct our "understanding" of our mothers and ourselves.

Recent work on the value of literary texts as both agents and reflectors of their culture has reinforced this predisposition. From scholars like Nina Baym, Ann Douglas, Jane Tompkins, Madonne Miner, Janice Radway, and Suzanne Juhasz I have learned that literary texts are not just "works of art" but also attempts to do "a certain kind of cultural work within a specific historical situation" (Tompkins xi, 200). The effort to see stories about mothers and daughters as a kind of cultural work has become the leading intention of this study and has largely determined its principle of inclusion.

One important cultural function performed by the stories of American Jewish women is to recover, to dismantle, and to reconstruct the mother—to clarify her voice so that the daughter may hear it separate from her own. Therefore, without considering canonical status, I have selected works that treat in some detail the mother/daughter portion of the family dynamic, written in English by twentieth-century American women who identify themselves, in one way or another, as Jews. That these writers derive mainly from Eastern Europe and belong for the most part to the middle class says more about the availability of texts than about my intention. But the ethnic and gender specificity of the study reflects my assumption that specific tendencies within Jewish culture and tradition, as well as social pressures, opportunities, and attitudes toward Jews and women in America, have created a cluster of issues for Jewish women that are distinctive.

I have not sought here to test that initial assumption by systematic comparisons. To be sure, although the mother is as important a figure for her sons as for her daughters, her male and female children tend to portray her very differently.[2] Maternal images are also likely to resemble in some ways and to differ in others among women writers of different ethnic groups.[3] Given the limitations of space and the state of research in the field, such comparisons have had to be less important here than the effort, first, to discern the issues that American Jewish women's stories share with one another and, second, to analyze the forces that give emphasis to certain issues, that shape both the ways they are perceived and the responses they evoke. Gender and culture play obvious roles in this process. Perhaps one comparative example will clarify the role of gender. In his autobiography Alfred Kazin recalls that his mother's "fantastic capacity for labor and her anxious zeal" gave a special character to his life; she worked all day in the kitchen "because the law of her life was work, work and anxiety; she worked because she would have found life meaningless without work" (67). The sight of his mother on her knees scrubbing the dining room floor before the Sabbath made him feel great "tenderness" for "every single object in our household" (52). But Anzia Yezierska's *Bread Givers* develops more emphatically the sources of one immigrant mother's anxiety, the hardship of her impoverished, workful life, and her daughter's defiant determination not to replicate her mother's situation. In these texts, gender seems to work with other factors—like class—to shape the image of the immigrant mother and her relation to her child. Similarly, the interplay of such circumstances helps to account for the particular ways in which these stories render and respond to the issues that emerge from the experience of American Jewish mothers and daughters.

Among the messages that people of different races, classes, and genders always hear in their mothers' voices, I have tried to listen to the particular messages of American Jewish mothers and to understand the ways in which daughters have sorted them out. The structure of this study reflects one complexity of that task: the mutual resonances of daughters' and mothers' voices. In this literature, mothers both empower and restrict the efforts of their daughters to become subjects: to speak themselves as both women and Jews. A woman may be not only energized but also enraged or inhibited by the voice of her mother. Thus, the effort to hear a daughter speaking her own story calls for some understanding of the way her mother has enabled and/or constrained her. A mother's voice may be similarly mediated. Her sense of herself may be distorted by internalized cultural assumptions and expectations. Or, if she speaks through the narrative of her daughter, her story may be distorted by the stubborn residue of a child's old frustrations and disappointments. Thus in many respects, the effort to hear a mother's story is complicated by the need to unburden her image: to dismantle it, stripping away the accretions that distort it. Awareness of these complexities led me to "listen" in separate chapters to the voices of daughters and mothers.

Some concern with the tension between theme and chronology in the analysis of women's literary work also complicated the task of listening to mothers and daughters. In this study I needed to foreground the thematic interest of stories in order to identify what appeared to be the major developmental issues belonging to mothers and daughters. But I also wanted to discern the social forces that make this relationship a kind of elaborate dance. In order to contextualize historically as well as developmentally the pattern of engagement and separation that the stories represented, I let chapters proceed roughly in step with chronology. I attended first, for example, to developmental issues that rose out of the gender imbalance within immigrant families and, in subsequent chapters, to issues that emerged later in the experience of American Jews. Within most chapters, moreover, I arranged stories chronologically, to catch change or development in the ways particular issues were conceived. Throughout the study, I tried to clarify the social and historical conditions that seemed to influence writers' perceptions and treatment of issues. But the issues themselves determined the placement of stories within one chapter or another and even, in the last chapter, overrode my concern with chronology and shifted my interpretive bias—like the turning of a kaleidoscope—from psychology toward politics.

This tension between theme and chronology often appears in scholarly work on women's experience. Gerda Lerner's *Female Experience*, for example, groups its texts under headings that represent phases of "the female life cycle." Similarly, Susan Glenn's *Daughters of the Shtetl* discusses the history of American immigrant Jewish women under headings that represent major issues that confronted them. I share this privileging of theme over chronology also with Mary V. Dearborn, whose study of ethnic women's literature (*Pocahontas's Daughters*) is organized thematically. Here, one virtue of this approach is its power to delineate, chapter by chapter, salient and persistent features of a relationship that is always in motion.

The persistence of these features in stories that differ in so many other ways surfaces the subtle but distinctive likeness among them—like the resemblance that exists among people whose hearing has become attuned to the sounds of a common language. Speaking that language can enhance such a likeness, for the effort to pronounce certain sounds develops certain throat and mouth muscles, and the words that give form to experience also shape imagination. In much the same way, the treatment of mother/daughter issues in these stories reflects the influence of a common experiential "language" of shared stress and opportunity. In part, it reflects the ethnic experiences and memories of immigration, anti-Semitism, assimilation, "traditional" gender imperatives, and the legacy of devalued but sometimes radically rebellious European foremothers. In part, it reflects the familiars of American culture: consumerism, secularism, individualism, social mobility, "experts'" dominion over family life, rapid change in economic status, and the reawakening of feminist consciousness.

As the stories attend to and represent the richly problematic intricacies of motherhood and daughterhood, they reveal a characteristic cluster of issues shaped partly by gender, ethnicity, and history. The issues themselves are neither resolved nor erased as time passes, but the responses they evoke show the effects of increasingly sophisticated personal insight and social change. For example, mothers in Grace Paley's stories of the sixties remain as sensitive as immigrant women to cultural imperatives that subordinate their needs to the needs of children and men. But their attitudes are vastly different. Thus, in general, this study suggests that mothering and daughtering do not get simpler as time passes; instead, protagonists learn new ways of moving through the ancient, filial dance.

Emphasis on the issues called up by mothering and daughtering does vary, however, as American Jewish women move forward in time—beyond traditional boundaries, social restrictions, and the deliberate or helpless silences of earlier generations. Chapter subjects attempt to follow this changing emphasis. For example, chapter 1 considers stories published between 1912 and 1986 by daughters of immigrants whose protagonists confront the effects upon their own development of the gender imbalance within the immigrant family. These writers translate into English immigrant mothers and daughters who remain connected even though their lives diverge from one another. Despite the social and/or historical forces that encourage such divergence, Mary Antin, Anzia Yezierska, Emma Goldman, and Kate Simon write about daughters whose struggle to become subjects reflects the impaired subjective status of their mothers. Avoiding the tendency to either romanticize, satirize, or demonize the immigrant mother, these women writers recognize in her the scars of poverty, cultural dislocation, and domestic subordination that sometimes disfigure her image, sometimes alienate her daughters. Their stories also reveal, however, the immigrant mother's achievement of a manifold self that becomes her legacy to her American daughters.

Chapter 2, on the consequences of disconnection from home and mother, begins with works of the twenties and thirties by Tess Slesinger, Edna Ferber, and Fannie Hurst and continues with more recent novels by Jo Sinclair, Marjorie Duhan Adler, and Lynne Sharon Schwartz. In this chapter, the earliest works identify the issue of differentiation as both social and psychological. In psychological terms, as Jessica Benjamin explains, women must "overcome their primary identification with their mothers and replace it with more generalized gender identifications that do not equate all feminity with the mother" (*Bonds* 168–69). That task is both complicated and intensified for Jewish women who grow up in a culture—like that of the twenties and thirties—that devalues their mothers not only as women but also as Jews. If a woman, attempting to define herself in terms more acceptable to her culture, repudiates the mother who seems to embody characteristics that the culture defines as unworthy, she never achieves the sense of difference that "exists in tension with likeness" (*Bonds* 169). Such a failure, these early stories suggest, impairs her sense of herself as both female and Jew.

After recognizing the persistence of this thematic issue in works by Ferber, Hurst, and Slesinger, I looked for stories by later writers to see what would happen to the issue over time. But the perspective of American Jewish women writers on "leaving home and mother" remains fairly constant. Throughout the period, as protagonists attempt to become themselves by growing away from their families and, in some cases, "passing" beyond ethnic boundaries, they discover the power of their identification with their mothers to sustain their ethnic and gender identity.

Because this literature privileges the mother's—as well as the daughter's—voice, the first two "daughter-centric" chapters[4] are followed by chapter 3, which focuses on works in which mothers develop the power to speak for themselves. Chronology is particularly important in this chapter because it allows us to follow that development. Stories by Rebekah Kohut, Leah Morton, Emanie Sachs, Hana Stein, Jo Sinclair, Violet Weingarten, Tillie Olsen, and Grace Paley re-vision traditional imperatives by drawing the mother to the center of her own narrative. The importance of "centering" the mother as narrator of her own story becomes particularly apparent in light of ethnic imperatives that both silence and subordinate mothers, relegating them to the margins of their husbands' and children's lives.

That similar imperatives affect women in many cultures is generally acknowledged by feminist scholars who attempt to understand what Marianne Hirsch and others have called "the profound and pervasive cultural fear and devaluation of the mother" (18).[5] Particularly in patriarchal cultures, which expect women to serve others, daughters learn from their mothers, as Karen Horney observed, to devalue their own needs, seeing them as less important than the needs of others. If negative effects of the cultural devaluation of women's needs have long been particularly evident in American Jewish literature,[6] however, one reason may be that silence and service were virtually mandated by tradition for Jewish women who were both subjected to less-than-adult religious status and denied access to education by the androcentricity of Jewish tradition.

One important caveat: in this time and place it is virtually impossible to define with any specificity the nature or influence of Jewish "tradition." Descended, for the most part, from immigrants who were neither pious nor learned, American Jewish writers come "after the tradition," to use Robert Alter's words—or in its "twilight," to use my own. Among American Jewish women who write stories for publication in English, moreover, only a few are either religiously observant or highly educated as Jews. And yet, the residue of a religious "tradition"—particularly its attitudes toward women—persists in the consciousness of many contemporary Jewish women and in the unconscious roots of their behavior and emotional lives as well. As Susannah Heschel has observed, "Although most American Jews today define themselves as non-religious, the traditional attitudes of classical Judaism remain strong, particularly in terms of gender roles and family structures. . . . It might be argued that traditional Jewish views of women and men have persisted with greater tenacity than classical religious beliefs in God, revelation, and observance" ("Jewish Feminism" 31).

Three examples will clarify Heschel's sense of "tradition" and its aftermath. First, many Jewish women who rarely participate in Jewish rituals, who do not belong to Jewish communal institutions or seek to perform mitzvoth, are aware nevertheless that Orthodox Jewish men thank God in their morning prayers that they were not created women. Second, a *rebbetzin* who was asked by her Reform congregation to become their rabbi after her husband's death refused because she felt constrained by a tradition that would not have applied to her as a Reform Jew even if she had understood it correctly. "I didn't think I should read from the Torah," she said, "if I were menstruating" (Umansky, "Spiritual" 281). Third, in a recent interview with the *Forward*, Wendy Wasserstein recalled an entirely secular character of hers who swore that no matter what she did with her life she would "never be exiled to the balcony" of a synagogue where Orthodox Jewish women must sit. Wasserstein observed that "somewhere we do come from that. It's there. I don't quite know what to do with it but it's there" (11, 19). Thus, "tradition" in this sense survives among us—its origins in rabbinic Judaism scarcely visible to many of these writers, yet strangely potent in their minds and feelings.

Therefore, until chapter 5, in which feminist writers assert their sense of what tradition means, when I speak of tradition here, I refer not to Orthodoxy or to any other specific branch of Judaism but to a cluster of ideas and attitudes that can be traced to the teachings, texts, and practices of East European Jewry, whose memory endures. I choose Tevye's word, "tradition," rather than Arthur Hertzberg's phrase "folk religion" to identify the body of laws, liturgy, commentary, and custom against which many of these writers react, for which some of them long, and toward which many of them look when they want to assess Jewish authenticity.[7]

In this sense, Jewish tradition has silenced Jewish women by omitting their voices from its canon, by denying them formal religious education and spiritual authority, and by recognizing them not primarily as subjects but as relative creatures whose experience became significant only when it affected men (Ozick, "Notes" 124).[8] Jewish law did not accept the testimony of a woman, child, or slave (Rachel Adler 13). Jewish women's bodies at certain times of the month were considered sources of contamination to men (Heschel, *On Being* xxii); and women in public were seen as "dangerous temptations to men" (Ozick, "Notes" 140–41). Used to perceiving herself through traditional maternal images, the Jewish mother may have been extraordinarily active and verbal in the home or the marketplace. But, like my mother, she dwindled into invisibility in the communal space and activities most highly valued by her culture and therefore reserved for men. Moreover, her role demanded that she enable male performance of those activities (Berman 118–22).

Texts discussed in chapter 3 suggest that when the Jewish woman begins in the twentieth century to tell her own story she achieves a perspective from which she can see herself as a central—rather than a subordinate—figure in the family narrative. From that perspective, she confronts at first the residue of "traditional" imperatives that have silenced her and shaped her sense of herself as an enabler of men and children. Later works by Adrienne Rich, Jane Lazarre, and Phyllis Chesler not only continue to re-vision these imperatives from a maternal perspective but develop more fully the mother's voice by recovering her power to "think through the body."

Chapter 4 returns to the daughter's point of view in stories of the sixties and seventies by Cynthia Ozick, Anne Roiphe, Alix Kates Shulman, Erica Jong, Shelley Steinman List, Rosellen Brown, Camille Baum, and Daphne Merkin. These stories begin to show the influence of the feminist movement on women's work. On the whole, they emphasize the daughter's awareness that her image and story are not her own but mirror reflections of her mother's. I grouped these stories under the heading of "narcissism" because that issue becomes so prominent in them. The pervasiveness of mirror imagery alone signaled the presence of an issue that social critics had already named and linked to this moment of American experience. These stories, then, develop a Jewish woman's "take" on an American phenomenon. They also probe the particular tangle created in mother/daughter relationships by the inability to see one's mother as separate from oneself. And they show how hard it is for women to develop when they cannot look away from their mirrors.

Chapter 5 expands the definition of "tradition" by considering works by Jewish feminist writers of the seventies, eighties, and early nineties who see from a fresh perspective the role of Jewish mothers in the development of their daughters, who connect themselves to activist Jewish women who came before them, and who confront in their work the conflict between feminism and Judaism. This chapter devotes more space than others to history, introducing the long tradition of Jewish women's activism that may be unfamiliar to many readers. As writers in this chapter recall that tradition, they shift the perspective of this study from psychology to politics, demonstrating that the personal really is the political. These writers—Vivian Gornick, Judith Plaskow, Adrienne Rich, Irena Klepfisz, Evelyn Torton Beck, Melanie Kaye/Kantrowitz, Judith Katz, Blu Greenberg, Nessa Rapoport, E. M. Broner, and Kim Chernin—are also keenly aware of the power of "storying" not only to reveal but also to shape the emergent self. "Re-storying" is for them the process that connects them with their mothers and foremothers as they not only recall but also transform the narratives they inherit, penetrating their silences and through them speaking new stories of their own.

Indeed, as the title of this book suggests, all of these chapters deal in one way or another with the power of storytelling and its connection to the discovery of the self. Although both gender and ethnicity conspire against the Jewish woman's telling of her own story, many contemporary American Jewish women writers identify their narrative gifts as part of their mothers' legacies. Thus, the Jewish mother seems to persist in her daughter's memory very close to the roots not only of gender and ethnic identity but also of language. Different contexts, as always, afford different insights into this phenomenon. In a personal, domestic context, Kate Simon and Vivian Gornick recall that Jewish mothers at their kitchen windows interpreted the neighborhood, making narrative sense of tenement babble, stilling desire for the world beyond the kitchen. From an ethnic and historical point of view, Jewish women historically found their public voices outside of the study house and synagogue as they addressed the needs of others. In businesses that supported their families, in unions that sought to empower workers, and in communal organizations that tended to the poor, sick, and homeless, since the early decades of the century American Jewish women have spoken boldly of both their womanly and their Jewish commitments (Umansky, "Spiritual"). This study suggests, however, that self-forgetfulness and denial of their own needs often accompanied this public emergence from silence into speech.

Current feminist theory suggests yet another dimension of the mother's link to language. According to Bella Brodzki, "As the child's first significant Other, the mother engenders subjectivity through language; she is the primary source of speech and love. And part of the maternal legacy is the conflation of the two." In Brodzki's view, women's writing "variously seeks to reject, reconstruct, and reclaim—to locate and recontextualize—the mother's message" ("Mothers" 245). Brodzki is speaking specifically of autobiographical writing, but at different levels of explicitness the same effort can be seen as well in many novels and stories by Jewish women. As the novelist Tova Reich recently affirmed, "My mother had been my muse. She had fed me the words" ("Hers").

Connected, then, from a child's earliest memory with both "speech and love," a mother's voice can empower the daughter who recovers it, can help her both to conceive and to articulate herself as subject of her own experience. But in her daughter's memory the Jewish mother is also connected with the ways in which she has reacted to social and cultural forces that would deny her subjectivity. Therefore, recovery of her voice can reconnect her daughter not only with "speech and love" but also with the sources of maternal silence—or with the sacrifices mothers have made to speak as both women and Jews. Thus, a mother may not only empower a woman writer to find her own voice but also reinforce the cultural influences that would either keep her mute or turn her story into a battle cry.

For example, my mother's accommodations were as much a part of her legacy to me as her passionate commitments and self-assertions. Having found her own voice through service to other Jews, she saw my profession of literature as self-indulgent. And the deference toward Jewish male authorities that kept her silent in synagogue, even during the Holocaust when she spoke tirelessly on behalf of European Jewish children at women's meetings all over the country, also became part of my inheritance from her. Before I understood the authoritative male images that presided over my childhood home, one of the first painted images I hung in my own house was of another Jewish male authority figure: not Abraham but Moses; he was not looking forward to the fulfillment of a divine promise but getting ready to smash the tablets of the Law. I didn't question or understand his attraction for me until I was able to see him as a descendant of my mother's icons. I unraveled his attraction for me by seeing clearly his significance for her. In much the same way, the texts studied here indicate that recovery of the mother's image and voice is part of a larger task. These stories write clearly the labor of both dismantling and reconstructing the mother's image and story that is vital to the daughter who would know and speak herself as subject.

As American Jewish women writers inscribe both their mothers' and their own voices, they work against powerful forces that inhibit women's subjective self-awareness. The energy they summon to that complex task transgresses conventional genre boundaries and calls for the inclusion in this study of autobiographical as well as fictional writings. My decision to include autobiography and memoir with prose fiction owes much to the work of feminist theorists who argue persuasively for the continuity of genres in which women inscribe female identity. In a time when postmodernist thought renders problematic the very status of the self, feminists have become increasingly attentive to the ways in which conventional genre boundaries blur as women writers record the construction and emergence into awareness of the female self.[9] Because many works by American Jewish women in both genres are preoccupied with the "female self in process" (Schenck 286) and because their "strategies of representation" (N. Miller, "Writing" 58) are often so similar, I take the liberty here of working with fiction and autobiography as though those genres were, as the theorists suggest, continuous or coextensive, supplemental to one another.[10] Following the path recommended by Mary V. Dearborn and taken recently by Diane Lichtenstein, I believe we benefit in the study of ethnic women's literature if we "relax our standards and expectations of genre itself" (Dearborn, *Pocahontas's Daughters* 15) and ask what writings of different genres "have in common, particularly in regard to their shared 'themes, topics, and tropes'" (Lichtenstein, *Writing* 9).

I decided to treat both fictions and autobiographies as "stories" because I believe that genre boundaries have softened between the cultural pressures on women to be silent, to be objects or commodities, and the equal and opposite pressure of their need to become subjects by writing "the female self in process." Nancy K. Miller and others suspect that "the textualization of a female 'I' means escape from the sphere inhabited by those 'relative beings' . . . who experience the world only through the mediation of men" ("Writing" 54). Whether a woman speaks of her subjective experience in fiction or in autobiography, she engages in a particular kind of struggle—against both the culture that works to silence her and the cultural assumptions that she (and her mother) have internalized. That struggle to "verbalize the vast areas of feminine experience which have remained unexpressed, if not repressed," engages the woman writer "in an attempt to excavate those elements of the female self which have been buried under the cultural and patriarchal myths of selfhood" (Lionnet 260). Thus, the magnitude of a woman writer's effort to give birth to her own subjectivity, by telling the manner of her origin and growth, effaces, in my view, the importance of genre distinctions that would constrain the form and manner of her telling.

A Jewish woman, of course, shares that effort with other women. She remembers the particular burden of silence and exclusion from the ritually active community of male subjects imposed on her by traditional laws, texts, and customs; she knows the sacrifice of communal approval her foremothers have often made to develop their public voices;[11] she works, like other women, toward the recognition and expression of herself as subject. In that work, her most powerful ally and antagonist is her mother. Having known a daughter's ordeal, a mother bequeaths to her own daughter a complex image of the problem they both confront and a sometimes confusing assortment of accommodations, subversions, and rebellions.[12] "Discussions of female identity thus inevitably return," as Judith Kegan Gardiner has noted, "to the special nature of the mother-daughter bond" ("On Female" 356). This study examines that bond as it has been configured by the writings of twentieth-century American Jewish women.

What I have been able to see in their writings depends heavily upon the last two decades of work by feminist scholars who have taught women new ways of looking at themselves and their mothers. By 1971, when my daughter's question set this research in motion, the feminist movement had shown women how to connect the personal with the cultural and political, had fashioned a perspective from which my daughter's exclusion from the morning minyan, my mother's complexities, and my own confusions could reveal a logic of their own. Since 1971 woman-centered scholarship in several fields has prepared the critical lens through which this book examines mothers and daughters in American Jewish women's literature. The work of social historians, psychologists, feminist theorists, and critics of culture, literature, and language have influenced the shaping and the insights offered by this project.[13] Because it attempts chiefly to read literary texts, however, it depends upon but does not deal centrally or systematically with the ideas of historians and psychologists.

On the whole, this study seeks to clarify the work of recovery, dismantling, and reconstruction that the writings of American Jewish women perform as they attempt to hear their mothers and to speak for themselves. I have tried to demonstrate here the representation of this task in Jewish women's stories. I have contextualized literary representations in several ways, using not only the insights of literary critics and theorists but also the work of social historians and feminist psychologists to interpret family interactions in fiction and autobiography. Having augmented in this way a more strictly literary perspective on mothers and daughters in American Jewish women's literature, I can see now what I suspected long ago: that gender, psychology, and ethnicity are powerfully shaped by family experience; that families function partly as agents of their culture; and that for Jewish daughters the family figure closest to the nexus of those fateful forces is the mother.

I am sad to have to exclude from this study not only many writers of memoirs and prose fiction whose works touch just slightly the central issue of this study but also poets who have taught me much of what I needed to know about mothers and daughters, about Jewish women, about language and the process of self-discovery. Though their poetry cannot, for reasons of space, be discussed critically here, phrases, lines, and insights drawn from Adrienne Rich, Muriel Rukeyser, Marge Piercy, Irena Klepfisz, Denise Levertov, Maxine Kumin, and others appear, as I need them, to say the things they have enabled me to hear.

I would close where I began, with what I know about my mother. For a long time, only poets and novelists could tell me anything. Beloved to two generations of Hadassah women as speaker and mentor, my mother could never find the right words for me. But her voice never faded, either. Eventually I began to listen to her again: when I could hear that voice as hers, not my own, and when I could discern what lay within her silences. She told me all the stories I have never forgotten—her own, submerged, among them. I hear that narrative more and more clearly as I read the writings of other American Jewish women. It acquires resonance and dignity as I listen to other women working—like her, like me—to find their voices as women, as Americans, and as Jews. Both within and at the margins of what has been traditionally central to Jewish life, in activities long considered peripheral to the study of Jewish law and the performance of Jewish ritual, that work continues.

Notes

1. See the glossary for translations of Hebrew and Yiddish words used in the text.

2. See, for example, two essays by Fisch: "Fathers, Mothers, Sons and Lovers" and "The Crisis in the Jewish Family." See also Gollin's response to Fisch in "Understanding Fathers in American Jewish Fiction."

3. One early comparison of black and Jewish mothers is Zack's "Deification and Disdain." Several recent studies of African American mothers in literature include Bell, *The Afro-American Novel and Its Tradition*; Collins, "The Meaning of Motherhood in Black Culture and Black Mother-Daughter Relationships"; Davies, "Mothering and Healing in Recent Black Women's Fiction"; and Wade-Gayles, "The Truths of Our Mothers' Lives."

4. "Daughter-centric" was coined by Daly and Reddy and appears in their introduction to *Narrating Mothers*.

5. Some American feminist theorists suspect that the mother has been muted as a literary subject partly by the daughter's guilt at separating from her and partly by the assumption that adulthood requires separation from her. At a deeper level, the powerful Freudian myth that recognizes separation from the mother as the cornerstone of adulthood also explains why she has been deprived of subjective status and why "writing . . . and motherhood . . . [have become] not merely incompatible but antithetical" (Reimer 208). In Jacques Lacan's reading of Freud, according to one feminist critic, "maternal discourse" becomes "a theoretical impossibility" (Reimer 208). For a more detailed reading of this theoretical construct, see Homans, *Bearing the Word*. See also Dinnerstein, *The Mermaid and the Minotaur*.

6. See, for example, Friedman's study of negative images of Jewish mothers in fiction by Philip Roth, Herbert Gold, Bruce Jay Friedman, and others. For negative images of Jewish women that persist in popular culture, see the special issue of *Lilith* on JAP baiting (Fall 1987); Schneider's earlier es-

say on negative images of women that persist in Jewish jokes, "In a Coma!" (*Jewish and Female*); or Prell, "Rage and Representation."

7. Perhaps the endurance of "tradition" in this respect is not surprising when one understands that, as Wegner points out, "the legal-cultural-social system now called rabbinic Judaism, which developed in Palestine and Babylonia during the first six centuries C.E., was . . . normative for virtually all Jewish communities for the next twelve hundred years" (69–70). From 600 C.E. till the sixteenth century, Baskin observes, the code of rabbinic law called Talmud "provided a uniform pattern for family, business, community and religious life," no matter where Jews lived. Even while they assumed the dress, language, and mores of their gentile neighbors, they endeavored "to maintain . . . allegiance to the guidance and demands of Jewish legal dicta and rabbinic leadership" ("Jewish" 95). Three hundred years of relative emancipation have eroded but not entirely cancelled the normative power of this tradition for the modern Jew.

8. According to Ozick and others, under Jewish law (halacha), "The male is the norm, and the female is a class apart" ("Notes" 124).

9. Whether that "self" is called fictional, autobiographical, or some mixture of the two, attempts to record its coming into being and into self-consciousness commonly transgress genre boundaries. Exploring the interface between autobiography and other genres, Nancy K. Miller, Sidonie Smith, Germaine Brée, Celeste Schenck, Carolyn Heilbrun, Francoise Lionnet, Mary G. Mason, and others have demonstrated a range of formal and technical conventions that apply to fiction and poetry as well as autobiography (see their essays in *Life/Lines*, ed. Brodzki and Schenck). See also S. Smith, *Poetics* (45).

10. The reasons that women writers transgress genre boundaries when they try to speak as subjects of their own experience connect Jewish American women's writing with the larger enterprise of women's literature. Perhaps, as Heilbrun has argued, some elements of female self-awareness are so disturbing that they can at first be only fictionally—rather than autobiographically—embodied ("Non-Autobiographies" 68). When Edna Ferber, for example, develops in fictional non-Jewish mothers and daughters the filial tensions concealed in her autobiography but acknowledged in her journals, she may fictionalize to avoid the pain of both disloyalty and the self-exposure that would inhibit autobiographical expression. Or perhaps the very difficulty of articulating female subjectivity makes the act of self-writing intrinsic to self-realization for women writers in every genre. In cultures that silence women and see them always as not-men, the act of naming the self and its manner of coming into being may infiltrate many genres because it underlies the power of a woman writer to enter the world, to speak for, of, and as herself.

11. Sochen notes, "It was very difficult for Jewish women to identify themselves in ways other than the traditionally prescribed one. Jewish American women writers faced the additional identity crisis of entering the male domain of literature and creativity. While women writers have always been part of the American cultural landscape, Jewish women writers became a sociological phenomenon only in America and largely in the twentieth century. Because they did not enter a socially acceptable identity role, they had to define themselves and create their own identity" ("Identities" 6).

12. Perhaps this confusion accounts for both the plentitude and the disparity of mother images in fiction by Jewish writers. See, for example, Ruth Adler, "Mothers and Daughters," and Mintz, "The Myth of the Jewish Mother."

13. Social history is one of the contexts widely recognized as constitutive of mothering in particular and of individual identity in general. See, for example, the introductions to Ginsburg and Tsing, *Uncertain Terms,* and O'Barr, Pope, and Wyer, *Ties that Bind.* For a sense of the important work that has been done to contextualize in this way the dynamic of the Jewish American family, see especially Baum, Hyman, and Michel, *The Jewish Woman in America.* See also Glenn, *Daughters of the Shtetl;* Kramer and Mazur, *Jewish Grandmothers;* Krause, *Grandmothers, Mothers and Daughters;* Kuzmack, *Woman's Cause;* Meyerowitz, *Women Adrift;* Moore, *At Home in America;* Shepherd, *A Price below Rubies;* Sochen, *Consecrate Every Day;* and Weinberg, *The World of Our Mothers.*

In the last decade, feminist psychologists and psychoanalysts have revised conventional assumptions about the family, insisting on the importance of pre-oedipal experience, enabling insight into facets of the mother-daughter relationship that were earlier obscured. See, for example, Benjamin, *The Bonds of Love;* Chodorow, *The Reproduction of Mothering;* and Gilligan, *In a Different Voice.*

On language, see especially Dinnerstein, *The Mermaid and the Minotaur;* Gardiner, "On Female Identity"; and Hirsch, *The Mother/Daughter Plot.*

1

Translating Immigrant Women: Writing the Manifold Self

We are translations into different dialects of a text still being written in the original.
—Adrienne Rich, "Sibling Mysteries"

From where we are, in the last decade of the twentieth century, the Jewish women who came to America from Europe look like heroic beginners. Founders of our families, the matrix that nurtured our mothers and/or grandmothers, to us they seem pioneers: intrepid adventurers who move always forward, setting in motion the long process that produced us. From a less self-centered point of view, however, these women who began Jewish life in America were also part of a much longer process. Caught in a moment of radical change, they were also shaped by ancient influences that resisted change. Thus, they lived at the confluence of powerful forces that moved in different directions. Out of the tensions created by their situation as immigrants, as Jews, and as women, they fashioned a distinctive—if not always heroic—sense of self. Their daughters' stories not only translate that achievement but also record its effects upon their own efforts to become Americans.

Bearing featherbeds and samovars from Eastern Europe to make home-like the new world, Jewish women also brought to America an assortment of disparate self-images.[1] These working-class immigrants differed from one another in countless ways, but as Jews they had all seen themselves reflected in the prejudices of gentile Europe.[2] By reflection in the teachings of traditional Judaism, moreover, they knew themselves as women to be secondary creatures. Within their own communities they were excluded from authority in communal and religious life and denied the education enjoyed by their brothers, fathers, and husbands (Baum, Hyman, and Michel 3–16; Glenn 8; Weinberg 6, 9, 14). Thus, they were accustomed in Europe to subordinate status as both Jews and females. However, they were also responsible for the sustenance of their families. Husbands and older children might help to earn the bread and maintain the "fundamental religious rituals of private life"[3] but, in a world where most Jews were poor and politically impotent, women's work at home and in the marketplace was acknowledged as an "essential component of physical and cultural survival"—even though women themselves "were considered inferior to men" (Glenn 8). Such discordances between their actual accomplishments and their subordinate cultural status probably toughened (when it did not erode) their confidence in their own skills, strengths, and wisdoms.[4] Acquainted with what Patricia Waugh has called "the provisionality and positionality of identity" (13), they stabilized their sense of self by doing, working, giving, caring for others.[5]

In America, their work remained essential to the survival of their families, but their lives changed. As Jews began to "conform to modern, not traditional, understandings about women's roles" (Glenn 77), married women withdrew from the marketplace into the home. Unfamiliar with the new language, they were insecure in streets beyond the neighborhood. They were also barred by the proprietary sexual protectiveness of their husbands from work in factories and shops—marketplaces of the new world that accelerated their children's and husbands' cultural adaptation. Shut away in urban tenements, married women are said to have measured their housework by higher standards and performed even more complex domestic tasks in America than they had known in Europe (Glenn 71).[6] Like their neighbors, they worked at these tasks alone, having left in Europe the relatives who might have helped with housework and child care.[7] Thus, the scope and status of the Jewish mother, whose economic and domestic prowess had been widely acknowledged in Europe, whose work had given her "some family authority, a knowledge of the marketplace, and a certain worldliness" (Glenn 14), were often diminished rather than enlarged by her emigration to America.[8]

In America, immigrant daughters entered an even wider world than the European one in which their mothers had labored. As an unmarried Jewish woman's economic responsibilities and social opportunities expanded, she benefited from the tradition of women's work in Eastern Europe that had empowered and validated her mother. Because her sexuality escaped ritual notice, she was also freer than her mother had been to work for and with men (Glenn 81). Politically and socially sophisticated by work in the factories and shops of the American marketplace, some Jewish daughters transformed themselves into union organizers; others found ways to become teachers. But the malaise of the newly sequestered mother and the disjunctions between the lives of mother and daughter troubled the Jewish immigrant daughter and complicated her development.

These developmental complexities are often submerged in historical accounts of immigrant women that necessarily concentrate on achievements rather than the subjective issues that inspire or accompany achievement. They are muted also in many oral histories, which implicitly encourage inexperienced informants toward versions of their experience that suit the scholarly agendas and listening skills of their interviewers.[9] Then too, memory often obscures difficulties unresolved by time—or delivers them transformed by resignation. But the stories of several Jewish immigrant daughters surface the complex issues they confronted as they turned themselves into American women.

Mary Antin, Anzia Yezierska, Emma Goldman, and Kate Simon are prominent among writers whose stories probe these complexities. Their stories set forth the needs of young protagonists in terms quite consistent with historical accounts: to meet both their own and their families' expectations, unmarried fictional protagonists and autobiographical personae need to become active subjects in a public world where their mothers once flourished but from which they have virtually withdrawn. To accomplish that task, immigrant daughters in fiction and memoir accommodate themselves to the changes in their mothers' lives and to the increasing disparity between their mothers' experience and their own. Without maternal models of even limited "worldliness," moreover, some daughters in these stories require—more than ever—fathers who can be for them what psychoanalysts believe fathers have always been: their "way into the world" (Benjamin, "Alienation" 122).[10] Like the disparate self-images that toughened their mothers' confidence, the tension between such needs and their uncertain gratifications tempers, where it does not subdue, the strength and self-awareness of immigrant daughters in stories by these writers.

The first fruits of that tension are the stories themselves, which translate into the language of America the experience of women born in Europe. Immigrant daughters knew the fascination of the story from the novels they read to their mothers and from the tales their mothers told of their own pasts, of the neighborhood, or of people who wrote letters to the Yiddish newspaper. Unlike the Jewish women who continued to write in Yiddish after they came to America,[11] these writers tried to tell for the first time, in a new language, stories of mothers that carried the European past into the American present and stories of Jewish girls who became women as they became Americans. In these stories, one can see the tensions that strained relations between mothers and daughters, as well as the differing strategies of connection and differentiation that continued to bind them to one another. One sees also the emergence into awareness through storytelling of an American Jewish woman who knew several disparate versions of herself. This sense of a manifold self—and the power to formulate it in stories—may have been the immigrant mother's most distinctive legacy to her American daughter.

The work of translation that these writers perform by writing in English was familiar to East European Jews who had always needed several languages to manage their everyday lives. Translating an exchange with peasants in Russian into an anecdote in Yiddish, for example, acknowledged the simultaneous existence of two modes or versions of experience. One version did not become or replace the other. Consistent with the Freudian assumption that dream images translated psychic messages, or that the "talking cure" translated affects into words (Hunter 111), the work of translation always implied that the original was alive and well. Moreover, Jewish women were often accomplished literary translators whose work, according to Naomi Shepherd, played a very important part in the diffusion of Marxist culture in Eastern Europe (124). Thus, the choice of English may raise many questions about the relationship of these American Jewish women writers to both their Yiddish-speaking families and their own ethnic identities. But that choice need not suggest that these writers either converted away from or rejected the experiential "text" that inspired their translations.[12]

Indeed, the translator's attentiveness to her original may testify to its enduring vitality even though, like the work of writing itself, translation also attenuates the bond between the original and its transcriber. As she concentrates—to hear more clearly the meaning of an event in her family, for example—and as she searches for language appropriate to its retelling, this effort differentiates her family, as object, from her self as subject. The work thus distances the writer from her "original" but also affirms the power and endurance of the bond between them. Perhaps more vividly and more self-consciously than is common for native-born writers, the immigrant writer who is also translator experiences both attachment to and alienation from her subject.

No single story represents more clearly than Mary Antin's *Promised Land* (1912) this tension between attachment and alienation in the immigrant writer/translator's work. Indeed, in Antin's memoir, negotiating that tension becomes an analogue for her own development as an immigrant daughter. If, as one critic has suggested, Ludwig Lewisohn's autobiographical persona is "born" out of the opposing versions of himself that his memoir enunciates (Sollors 198), Antin's persona is created by the disjunctions and connections her memoir manages to embody. Her story presents duality as the developmental puzzle that her persona must solve as she becomes both an American and a woman.

From the memoir's two beginnings, dichotomy constructs this narrative, offering divided images of both self and world. First, the autobiographer divides her adult self from her childhood self: "I am absolutely other than the person whose story I have to tell," she insists (xix). Then, almost immediately, the child/"person" speaks, denying the autobiographer's detachment by connecting the adult's creation of a divided self to the child's perception of a world "divided into two parts": the shtetl and everything beyond it. In some ways, the child's vision both reinforces and interprets the adult's. What the child first saw in the world, the adult still feels in herself. That sense of duality in experience will develop as the narrator records other disjunctions she perceived as a child: between mother and father (xix), Jews and gentiles (5, 17), men and women (33–37), reality and imagination (132).

Antin—the adult persona created by this narrative—is always *both* the adult who distinguishes herself as subject and the child she has objectified as "the person." While the narrator denies this child's subjectivity, the story itself immediately confirms it. Antin's representation of the uneasy, unstable connection between these two personae reproduces inadvertently one facet of a developmental process that, in D. W. Winnicott's theory, validates an individual's sense of her own subjective authenticity (Benjamin, *Bonds* 37). According to Jessica Benjamin, Winnicott calls this process "recognition" and believes that subjective self-realization depends upon one's ability to both recognize and be recognized by an "other" who is experienced as entirely beyond the control of the self: an "entity in its own right." Moreover, the "other" has to survive as an independent entity one's attempts to "destroy" or negate it—by trying to control it. In its earliest form, a mother and her nursing infant demonstrate this process most clearly. As the child nurses, its gaze recognizes the mother as subject. When the child looks away, a mother who is not an independent entity may withdraw or seek to attract the child's attention back to herself. Either way, she acknowledges her inability to survive as a subject without her child's recognition. Thus, she subverts the child's awareness of her as an "entity in [her] own right," for her subjective status can be "destroyed" by the child who controls her attention. Similarly, the child's sense of herself as subject depends upon her mother's recognition and her own capacity to survive her mother's distractions (Benjamin, *Bonds* 24–27).

In Benjamin's and Winnicott's view, the sense of oneself as a subject depends upon a process that originates in a child's earliest experience with its parent and that is repeated in every phase of development. By alternately denying, attempting to subvert, and experiencing the independent reality of other subjects, Winnicott's individual discovers again and again, in each new phase of her life, that she is neither solitary nor omnipotent—but companioned in the world by others both like and unlike herself.

This early drama is replicated in the shifting mode of relationship that Antin's memoir creates between her child and her adult personae. As Antin's child tells her story, the adult narrator clarifies and confirms her own sense of self by identifying likeness or difference between them. The adult heightens awareness of difference by "destroying" the child as subject: objectifying, evaluating, judging, criticizing her. But her text also sustains the child's subjective authority and demonstrates likeness between them. The unstable yet undeniable mode of connection this memoir creates between these divided personae thus becomes a metaphor for the self-creating American Jewish woman who was once a Russian immigrant child. The memoir embodies the narrator's validation of two editions of herself: the Russian original and the American translation.

In this narrator's efforts to differentiate herself from the child she was, readers often perceive the displacement of an immigrant by an American self-image. But the memoir suggests that differences are no more important to Antin than similarities. Among the likenesses that connect these two personae perhaps the most significant is their identical response to the massive dissonances produced by their experiences of poverty, of prejudice, and of dislocation. Both personae become writers/translators partly in response to the disintegrative power of those experiences.

For both, writing/translating serves the survival of the self. By the time she is ten years old, Antin masters potentially disintegrative anxiety by translating feelings into words. When government agents invade her fatherless, impoverished home, she retires to a "quiet corner" to "grapple" with the "oppressive fear" that threatens to overwhelm her: "I was not given to weeping," she writes, "but I must think things out in words" (147). She has already learned the power of words to overcome separation. Her letters to her father in America and the ones she writes later from America to her uncle in Europe not only bind absent people in far places to one another but also join past to present. The letters find their way into this narrative where—in translation—they draw the impressions of the child into the narrative of the adult.

The double vision of self so pronounced in the adult narrator is apparent also in the child/writer, who uses metaphor self-consciously to connect subjective to objective perceptions of herself. On the journey across Europe the child sees herself from two perspectives: subjectively, she is one of a group of bewildered emigrants, terrified by treatment they cannot understand. Objectively, she and other emigrants appear "like dumb animals, helpless and unresisting" (175), "a flock of giant fowls roosting, only wide awake" (176), or "a picture of woe, and yet so funny" (177). These images catch the double vision of the immigrant whose journey constructs her as "other" even to herself.

One reader identifies Antin's "distance from her old self" with her "rebirth" as an American (Sollors 32). But division within this narrator's self-image appeared long before her American experience began.[13] As a Jew in a non-Jewish culture, as a female in a patriarchal religious tradition, and as an immigrant among people who are at home in the world, this child knew very early what Elaine Showalter called the dual languages and paradigms of both the "muted" group to which she belonged and the "dominant" groups within which she had to function ("Feminist" 261–62). Her writing is itself a strategy of negotiation between such groups: of adaptation by translation.

In the memoir, adaptation is always in process, for the text contains without resolving the tensions created by such dualities. The most sustained source of tension for this immigrant daughter, for example, is created by the ethnic and gendered dichotomies that shaped her parents. Antin's father and mother can and do sustain her work of self-creation. But they cannot give the recognition she needs to take her place as a subject outside the text, in the world. Benjamin believes one becomes such a subject by identifying with parents who are subjects in their own lives and who can recognize one as a subject like themselves. But both ethnicity and gender prevent Antin's immigrant parents from fulfilling these requirements.

As a student, Antin identifies most explicitly with her father, whose male privilege entitled him to the education her mother longed for, but was denied. Her father's intellectuality, stimulated but not satisfied by Jewish learning, makes him restless within the shtetl and ultimately drives him to America. Here, as in Europe, his economic skills are weaker than her mother's. But his daughter models herself on him nonetheless. Like him, she would be an intellectual, a writer, a teacher, a doubter of conventional pieties, an adaptor to modernity, and an unquestioning believer in the virtues of learning. He affirms these shared characteristics in his daughter. By his unwavering support, he recognizes Antin as a being like himself. His recognition confirms her as an active subject in the world. Indeed, as she reckons his deprivations and failures beside the successes he empowered her to achieve, she recognizes herself as an instrument of his ultimate achievement. Through her, she believes, he "took possession of America" (203–5).

Recognition of this sort between shtetl father and American daughter is rare in stories by immigrant Jewish women. Its value to this daughter is augmented by her mother's generous encouragement and worldly status as breadwinner. The strength, competence, and resourcefulness of Antin's mother make her in her daughter's eyes a worker in the world rather than a domestic nurturer. In good times and bad, she runs the businesses that liberate this daughter from economic responsibility. In her work, moreover, she thrives—learning English rapidly and making herself at home in the American store (196) as she was in the European marketplace. Unlike her, Antin never excels at women's work; indeed, from her earliest years she is alienated by it. She knows the heaviness of women's burdens (311) and the emptiness and narrowness of women's lives (95–96). But she also knows that her escape from this treadmill is made possible only by the work of her mother and elder sister. Unlike them, she will neither sew nor cook nor clerk in a store. But from their unfailing and unselfish support she draws the strength to carry out her own and her father's agendas.

Mother and sister thus help Antin to become her father's active, intellectual daughter. But the traditional self-subordination of even this powerful and generous mother limits her ability to validate her daughter as subject of her own life. From her mother, Antin inherits not only the image of woman as worker in the world but also—less advantageously—the image of woman as secondary creature, whose power as a subject is traditionally limited by her subordinate status. This mother's story makes her subordination very clear. After defying unsuccessfully the parents who would rather marry than educate her, Antin's mother not only submits but also clings for the rest of her life, respectfully and obediently, to powerful conventions and prejudices. When her child is abused in Europe by a peasant boy, this mother teaches resignation: "The Gentiles do as they like with us Jews" (5). Because the mother is "one of those women who always obey the highest law they know, even though it leads them to their doom" (64), in America Antin's mother follows her husband's orders, painfully divesting herself of the "mantle of Orthodox observance . . . that . . . was interwoven with the fabric of her soul" (247). Seeing her pain, Antin praises her mother's "native adaptability, the readiness to fall into line, which is one of the most charming traits of her gentle, self-effacing nature" (246). The narrator does not acknowledge such "charming traits" in herself. But they affect her sense of her own subjective authority.

In Benjamin's words, "only a mother who feels entitled to be a person in her own right can ever be seen as such by her child, and only such a mother can appreciate and set limits to the inevitable aggression and anxiety that accompany a child's growing independence. Only someone who fully achieves subjectivity can survive destruction and permit full differentiation" (*Bonds* 82). Despite her physical strength, her economic prowess, and her resourcefulness in her husband's absence, Antin's mother only partially achieves subjectivity in this memoir, for her daughter records the obedience exacted of this mother by parents and husband, as well as her submissive acquiescence to the assaults of non-Jews. Thus limited by gender and ethnicity, Antin's mother transmits to her daughter her own limitations.

Antin rejects them, in part, by identifying with her father. In her defiant assertions of equality with George Washington, her embarrassingly self-celebratory claims to success as a student, and her insistent refusal of "woman's work" that might liken her to her mother, one also hears echoes of that rejection. But her defiance betrays the insecurity that makes defiance necessary. Like both parents who subordinated themselves to the will of the gentiles, she is a Jew (18). Like her mother, moreover, whose story recalls defiance but whose behavior models obedience, Antin becomes obedient to a fault to the non-Jewish authorities who dominate the world she seeks to enter.

Of course, this habit of obedience complicates her sense of herself as an active subject, for it undermines her self-esteem. As she idealizes and exaggerates her gratitude toward those subjects who command her obedience and upon whom she depends (cf. Sollors 45), she becomes, according to Benjamin, like a child who "idealizes the father because the father is the magical mirror that reflects the self as it wants to be." Indeed, such idealization "can become the basis for adult ideal love, the submission to a powerful other who seemingly embodies the agency and desire one lacks in oneself" (*Bonds* 100). But the one who loves in this way also harbors anger toward those to whom she submits. Anxious about her own unacknowledged and dangerous hostility toward subjects who command her obedience, she then defends them against herself, enlarging their virtues and magnifying her gratitude toward them. As Benjamin reminds us, Freud believed that "obedience . . . does not exorcise aggression; it merely directs it against the self. There it becomes a means of self-domination, infusing the voice of conscience with the hostility that cannot be aimed at the 'unattackable authority'" (*Bonds* 5). Thus, as Antin yields, always gratefully, to the power of various mentors in this memoir, she acknowledges them—but not herself—as subjects.

Beneath the surface of this American success story, an undercurrent of insecurity persists. Antin fulfills her intellectual father's ambitions but remains her subordinate mother's daughter. Embodying not only her achievements but also the unresolved tensions of her own development, Antin's memoir becomes an eloquent translation into English of the gendered and ethnic strengths and restraints carried by one immigrant daughter from Europe to America. The narrative strategies and complexities of her story carry into the public world the manifold persona of an American Jewish woman writer who remains, in her complexity, very like her European mother.

Anzia Yezierska lived and wrote much closer than Mary Antin to the emotional turbulence of self-creation. In her changes of direction one discerns the uncertainties that often divided her against herself and frustrated her development as both a woman and a writer. Marrying twice but unwilling to live with either husband, bearing a daughter whom she could not raise by herself but to whom she was devoted, forging and reforging fictional versions of her own story whose imperfect untangling kept her at work for nearly a decade on her own autobiography, and creating a series of narrator/protagonists whose relationship to their creator defies clarification (Schoen 15; Sullivan 60), Yezierska's life and work, like cloudy mirrors, reflect the uncertainty of her sense of herself as a subject. But they also reflect her powerful drive to satisfy her need for recognition. If, as Thomas Ferraro persuasively argues, Yezierska's *Bread Givers* chronicles the reinscription of traditional Jewish patriarchy in ethnic American middle-class culture (76), then the novel identifies the daughter's attempt to be "recognized" by a powerful male figure as the motive force behind that dynamic—and as an imitation of her mother.

Both parents shaped the quest for recognition that dominates Yezierska's life and work. Although many readers have identified hunger as the crucial issue in Yezierska's stories (e.g., Duncan, "Hungry" 231–41), her protagonists—like Yezierska herself—are driven by longing not for food or money but for the regard of powerful subjects. The intensity of that longing owes much to the relationship between the traditional Jewish patriarch and his immigrant daughter.[14] Yezierska's novel, *Bread Givers* (1925), portrays the gendered imbalance of subjective authority that seemed to her to characterize such relationships. In this work the father, Reb Smolinsky, knows that

> the prayers of his daughters didn't count because God didn't listen to women. Heaven and the next world were only for men. Women could get into Heaven because they were wives and daughters of men. Women had no brains for the study of God's Torah, but they could be the servants of men who studied the Torah. Only if they cooked for the men, and washed for the men, and didn't nag or curse the men out of their homes; only if they let the men study the Torah in peace, then, maybe, they could push themselves into Heaven with the men, to wait on them there. (9–10)

Spiritually dependent, traditional women had to serve the patriarch who could study and speak for them before God, who could embody what Benjamin calls the agency and desire that women lack. Yezierska's Reb Smolinsky thus commands obedience and enjoys the fruits of his daughters' labor until husbands replace him in their lives.[15]

The father is also moral arbiter and judge. Economically incompetent, he demonstrates powerfully by his devotion to study and his control of his daughters' wages a value system in which money serves chiefly to foster intellect. In this respect, this traditional father inspires his youngest daughter, who has always hated him, to imitate him and to seek his recognition. Against his will, Sara struggles to set her own feet upon his path—to follow his way into the world. But after leaving home to go to school, and after rejecting a suitor too materialistic to value her commitment to study, she longs for her father's validation of her as a being like himself: "A sudden longing to see my father came over me. I felt that my refusal to marry Max Goldstein was something he could understand. He had given up worldly success to drink the wisdom of the Torah. He would tell me that, after all, I was the only daughter of his faith. I had lived the old, old story which he had drilled into our childhood ears—the story of Jacob and Esau. I had it from Father, this ingrained something in me that would not let me take the mess of pottage" (202). Like a child seeking the confirmation of its mother's recognition as it takes its first independent steps away from her, Sara is drawn to her father "in my great spiritual need, *as a person is drawn to a person*" (202, my emphasis). Having demonstrated her ability to exist as a subject beyond her father's control, she needs him to recognize her as a subject like himself.

But in this novel—as often in works by Jewish immigrant daughters—the father withholds what he has primary power to give: moral and intellectual validation of his daughter's effort to become, like him, a powerful, authoritative subject. He comes to her door to disown, not to recognize her. To him, she is neither student nor writer, but woman: "A woman's highest happiness is to be a man's wife, the mother of a man's children. You're not a person at all," he scolds (206). This daughter knows herself to be her father's child and thus a subject in the world beyond the family, but that knowledge is not secure until her father confirms it.

The situation of this protagonist parallels in some ways Yezierska's own family situation and helps to explain the radical insecurities that made her, in her daughter's words, "an explosion to everyone" (quoted in Kessler-Harris xii). She was, of course, seriously handicapped by poverty and by unfamiliarity with the language and customs of America. But beside the hindrances of class and culture, her insecurities reflect the developmental dilemma of a woman whose studious rabbinical father never affirmed, or encouraged, or supported her desire to study: never recognized her as a subject like himself.[16]

Yezierska's response to this dilemma constitutes the distinctive drama of both her life and her work. The key to that response, her stories suggest, is furnished not by the father but by the mother, who transmits the habit of idealizing love. Beyond the habitual deference to the patriarch that was common in traditional Jewish homes (but cf. Weinberg 16), the mother in *Bread Givers* teases, blames, and complains about her husband; she even occasionally subverts his authority. But—most memorably for her daughters—she adores him as what Benjamin calls "an other who is what she cannot be" (*Bonds* 86). When he tells stories, "Mother licked up Father's every little word, like honey" (12). When he touches his wife kindly, her daughter notes, "Mother's sad face turned into smiles" (11). Even when she is dying, "the touch of his hand was like magic. Her whole face softened. A beautiful look came into her eyes as she gazed at Father, undying worship in her face" (248). By idealizing in this way the husband who has lost her patrimony, doomed the family to poverty, and wasted the lives of three daughters, this mother acknowledges him as a powerful subject and demonstrates to her daughters her own inability to achieve such status for herself. She requires his touch, his glance, his voice to bring her to life.

From her mother, therefore, Sara Smolinsky learns the habit of idealizing the "other who is what she cannot be" and whose recognition enables her to realize herself. This daughter's achievements will feel empty to her until her father recognizes them. Other protagonists demonstrate again and again this fateful tendency toward idealizing love that confirms their need of recognition as subjects by powerful—usually male—"others." But these other men are not generally Orthodox Jewish patriarchs like Reb Smolinsky, for Yezierska suspected that the culture he represents could not satisfy his daughter's need.[17] Instead, Yezierska's protagonists—like Yezierska herself—seek validation by male surrogates who are not handicapped in America by Orthodoxy or immigrant poverty but possess the traditional patriarch's power to recognize immigrant daughters and to help them become active subjects in the new world.[18]

Yezierska's brief but intense relationship with the educator John Dewey furnishes the prototypical love affair in which a whole series of her protagonists enjoy, momentarily, the recognition that transforms and confirms them as subjects in their own lives. Sometimes the transformation has spiritual overtones. More often, the effect of the idealized male gaze upon the woman who lives only to be seen by him is psychological. Fanya's mentor/lover in Yezierska's novel *All I Could Never Be* (1932) exemplifies this effect: "'You desire to be. You are: but you do not yet fully know that you are. And perhaps I can have the happiness of help-

ing you realize that you are and what you are'" (208–9). An earlier protagonist, Sonya in *Salome of the Tenements* (1932), knows the "fire of
worship" is "roused" in her by her mentor/lover's "unconscious air of superiority" (7). "It's my worship for him that lifts me out of myself!" she
cries (25). As Yezierska herself was urged into becoming a writer by Dewey's recognition of her talent, Sonya is fired by her lover's regard to create of her shabby self a stylish, silken creature capable of winning and
holding a Protestant American millionaire. In her later memoir, *Red Ribbon on a White Horse* (1950), Yezierska clarifies the source of the father/
mentor/lover's power to transform a woman by his gaze into her better
self: when she meets the figure called in this work John Morrow, she says,
"I had found some one who saw me, knew me, reassured me that I existed" (108). Although several of her protagonists suspect that their inability to become and to sustain themselves as subjects is related to
their cultural alienation from family and ghetto, these protagonists—like
Yezierska herself, one suspects—actually seek throughout their lives
confirmation of themselves as subjects in the regard of powerful men.

   In the background of these endless quests in Yezierska's work for recognition by an idealized male figure lies the felt loss of something beautiful and precious that once belonged to the protagonists' mothers in an
earlier phase and mode of being. Sara Smolinsky's mother, for example,
recalls a particular hand-crocheted tablecloth with "all the colours of the
rainbow" in it; "there was a feeling in my tablecloth—" she says, as she
mourns its loss (32–33). Similarly, the protagonist of Yezierska's memoir
mourns the loss of her mother's wonderful flowered shawl that "had been
her Sabbath, her holiday" (*Red Ribbon* 26). Without these lost remnants
of an earlier time that carry echoes of the mother's story into the daughter's life, the world feels ugly and empty for Yezierska's protagonists. Like-
wise, Antin's "mother," whose girlhood is also symbolic of beautiful
promises and lost romance and whose efforts to sustain her family in
Europe are as heroic as Mrs. Smolinky's in *Bread Givers*, recedes into the
background of the memoir after she brings her children to their father
in America. These mothers exist now only to sustain others, but their
own brief stories speak of early promise, agency, and desire. Thus, they
model the womanly energy, strength, and generosity that will empower
their daughters. But as they defer to their husbands, obeying their orders
and seeking their confirmation of their value, mothers transmit also the
sense of subjective impairment and the compensatory habit of idealizing
love.

The mothers' lives, moreover, offer no current image of work in the world as a source of the recognition the daughters seek. Many of Yezierska's protagonists are fervent workers, but the value of their work is always entangled with their need for its recognition by the loved one. An early protagonist, Sonya/Salome, briefly sees her work as sufficient to this need. But the later protagonist of Yezierska's memoir is more typical, for she knows that success as a writer will satisfy her only when her former mentor recognizes and responds to it. As she waits for the train that will take her to fame in Hollywood, "every man I saw seemed John Morrow coming to see me off. . . . He must know *Hungry Hearts* was written for him" (*Red Ribbon* 34). Like Yezierska herself, who was both personally and professionally confirmed by Dewey's regard for her attractiveness and her talent, her protagonists' pleasure in their work when their idealized lovers are gone always feels incomplete.

Thus they become, like Antin, both proud achievers and dependent, clinging lovers of powerful men. Threatened by what W. H. Auden in his preface to Yezierska's memoir called "the abyss of nonentity" (*Red Ribbon* 16), her protagonists whip back and forth between the poles of excessive humility (Henriksen 269) and gratitude toward privileged benefactors on the one hand (cf. Dearborn, *Love* 108) and outraged rebellion against powerful philanthropists, social scientists, and filmmakers on the other. As familiar with self-assertiveness as they are with obedience, these protagonists—like the writers who created them—replicate the disparate modes of self modeled by Jewish immigrant mothers. Ironically, the replication of the mother's life that both Antin and Yezierska's Sara seek to avoid, becomes, by translation into narrative, an imitation of her way of being herself.

That irony is deepened in the writings of Emma Goldman, who knew—like Antin and Yezierska—the family imbalance that diminished the mother and enlarged the patriarchal father. Like many other immigrant daughters, however, Goldman was also keenly sensitive to the social conditions that surrounded and intensified the family dynamic. Memoirs, oral histories, and autobiographies provide plentiful evidence of those conditions, clarifying from a social perspective the desire of daughters to avoid living their mothers' lives.

Well-acquainted with loss, for example, many immigrant Jewish mothers knew first the departure of their husbands and children for America (Hasanovitz 10–12, 194) and later their own separation from families left in Europe (R. Cohen 149). They knew the sudden or gradual erosion of customary habits of dress and behavior that had sustained generations of Jewish women in Europe (R. Cohen 152–53). They were dispossessed of both language and familiar environments. Their responsibilities were often unimaginably compounded by such losses. For example, Rose Schneiderman's mother had to accompany her sick child to the hospital only a few days after their arrival in America but could neither find her way "home" again nor remember her new address when the child recovered. Lost in an alien world, her condition was reflected in her daughter's memory of that first separation from her mother as "the saddest, loneliest time of my life" (24–25).

Other daughters also record in terms of their own deprivations their mothers' experience of poverty and childbirth. Among Sydney Weinberg's informants, for example, one woman remembers: "My mother had nothing to give us." Another generalizes her mother's inability "to express love" because "their life is such that they have to take it out on somebody" (37). One woman explains: "My heart knew that it was not my mother beating me but her ill fortune" (31). Another blames herself for needs her mother couldn't satisfy: "I held it against her that she never got up to make breakfast. The poor woman used to get up and run to work. But she came home to make me lunch every day, ran up four flights of stairs. And she would stand there with her hat, making me a hot lunch. She was a very good mother[;] How dare I resent that she didn't make me breakfast" (139).

Whether these mothers succumbed to or triumphed over their trials, their malaise spoke vividly to their daughters. Most graphic are the daughters' memories of bad marriages, too frequent childbirths, and abortions. "My mother told me she had twelve abortions!" one of Weinberg's informants recalls, "and I saw one that she herself aborted" (220). Lucy Lang, on the other hand, remembers the pregnancy that destroyed her mother's "beauty and buoyancy, which had survived so many hardships," the callous indifference of the doctor and nurse who humiliated her mother during the childbirth, and the change in her mother after the baby was born: "Her body was contorted, and in place of the smile that her lips had so constantly worn was an expression of vague, dark regret." Lang traces her first "stirrings of revolt" to this memory (20–21).

Like other immigrant daughters who remember their mother's pain and their own deprivations as two facets of the same condition, Goldman describes in her autobiography, *Living My Life,* her mother and her own childhood self as victims of the same oppression. Goldman's violent, sexually demanding father frequently beat his daughters and held their mother in an "iron grip" (61). The adult narrator attributes her mother's lack of "warmth" (11) and insufficient "affection" (59) to the death of her first, beloved husband (447) and to her withdrawal from the "insatiable" sexual "hunger" of her second, Goldman's father (448). Each childbirth, Goldman remembers, nearly brought her mother "to the grave" (448). Sexually abused as an adolescent by both a teacher (117) and a young male friend (22), frequently beaten as a small child by her father (59–60) and her uncle (66–67), and longing for the affection her depressed mother could never give, Goldman understood her mother's plight through the medium of her own pain.

And she never forgot. Partly from that understanding, one suspects, grew the adult opposition to conventional marriage, the concern with children's health and safety, the work of midwifery among the poor, the fight for birth control,[19] and the "passionate maternal spirit" (Falk 175) that led Goldman to "mother" several lovers and a multitude of friends. Goldman's memory of her mother's pain remained vivid even when it worked its way into generalizations:[20] "The old-time motherhood to me is the most terrible thing imposed upon woman," she wrote. "It has made her so unspeakably helpless and dependent, so self-centered and unsocial as to fill me with absolute horror" (Falk 121). Ultimately this horror nourished an ideological conviction: "Modern woman cannot be wife and mother in the old sense," Goldman insisted, "and the new medium has not yet been devised" (Falk 208).

From the pressure on both her mother and herself to marry, and from the givens of their married lives, she grasped the logic that could transform "strong and self-assertive" women capable of love into feeble, damaged creatures. Lacking an "outlet" for energetic spirits (Goldman 301), "cut off from all intellectual contact" (305), women like her mother, her niece, and even herself, she believed, were overwhelmed at times by depression. In lectures on "The Hypocrisy of Puritanism" and "Marriage and Love," she argued against the conventional restraints on women's sexuality and intellectuality that had condemned her mother and countless other women whose "dull and inert submission to their lot" and "fierce, blind struggle . . . against frequent pregnancies" intensified her own determination to address "the entire social problem" of which their suffering was one part (185–86).

Alienated from the women's movement of her own time by its concentration on the suffrage issue, Goldman's feminism searched for more

radical, more idealistic solutions to the suffering of women, addressing
not their political handicaps but the harshness of their submission to the
conventional family. As she translated her mother's gifts as a storyteller
and her mother's eloquence as public advocate on behalf of others (Goldman 27; Falk 11–12) into a command of language and emotion that filled
large lecture halls,[21] she won from the public the recognition denied her
at home. She also created a heroic persona that revised and idealized the
maternal image she knew best[22] and attempted to reshape the circumstances that had constricted her mother's life.

Beside the revisionary impulse that appears in Goldman's devotion to
revolutionary change, however, the child's anger at the mother who
failed to protect her from sexual abuse and paternal violence is also per-
ceptible in the memoir. Goldman's most vivid childhood memory of her
mother is mysteriously linked with her earliest image of revolutionary
heroism. "Always very vivid when she related stories of books she had
read," Goldman's mother captivates her daughter's imagination when she
tells the story of revolutionaries who tried to kill the czar. Her mother
condemned the would-be assassins: "'Coldblooded murderers . . . they
ought to be exterminated, every one of them!'" she cried. Her violence
"terrorized" her daughter. At first she shared her mother's feeling, but
later, "something mysterious had awakened compassion for them in me.
I wept bitterly over their fate" (Goldman 27–28). Years later, Goldman
leaped at the throat of a woman who called for the hanging of anarchists
in Chicago. And the next morning, she "woke as from a long illness,"
suddenly, incomprehensibly free of the depression that had immobilized
her, feeling in her soul the birth of "a great ideal, a burning faith, a determination to dedicate myself to the memory of my martyred comrades,
to make their cause my own" (Goldman 10). In that impulsive, liberating attack on a sneering woman who would, like Goldman's mother, have
cruelly punished resisters of tyranny, one hears echoes of the child's anger at the mother who failed to protect her from a tyrannical father.[23]

That anger accounts in part for the ways in which Goldman's adult
career diverged from the pattern of her mother's life. Denying her likeness to the mother who bore many children to a man she did not love,
Goldman refused to bear a child. And denying her likeness to a mother
so depressed by the death of her first husband that she became both
emotionally and sexually unresponsive, Goldman lived her life as a sexually and emotionally generous—and demanding—woman. But the heroic model of the idealized mother that Goldman's career created ironi-

cally affirms the identificatory likeness with her mother that called forth such denials.

As she translated herself into a heroic mother, Goldman also appears to have fashioned herself in part on a male model, for—like her father and the men who had abused her—she accepted sex as an attribute of her own nature and as an element of the social ideal to which she committed herself. Recognizing in herself her father's turbulent sexuality (Goldman 447) and ultimately idealizing sexual passion as vital to a creative personal and social life (Shulman, *Red Emma* 154–57), Goldman seems to have identified with the man who dominated her mother and drove Goldman herself first from Europe to America (Goldman 12–13) and later from her family home into an impossible, short-lived marriage.

Goldman's many love affairs translated her father's most problematic attribute into a source of intense personal gratification—as well as pain— and transformative social energy and vision. Thus, like Antin's autobiographical persona and Yezierska's Sara, who identify their intellectual strengths with their fathers, the "self" created by Goldman's writings[24] owes much to what Benjamin has called the child's "identificatory love" of a powerful father (*Bonds* 100–114). Like a child who needs most urgently to grow beyond her own infantile dependence, Goldman's need to be independent drew her in some respects toward—rather than away from—the abusive father whose beatings scarred her childhood. He was the dominant, more powerful parent; thus he commanded his small daughter's admiration even when he abused her: "I loved him," she writes, "even while I was afraid of him. I wanted him to love me, but I never knew how to reach his heart" (Goldman 60). Needing him to recognize her likeness to him so that she could grow beyond her own childhood weakness and her mother's subordination to his will, Goldman's desire for his love and recognition nourished both her compassionate understanding of him (60–61) and her lasting sense of resemblance to him.

Her tendency to idealize this hated father in later surrogates accounted also for her passionate devotion to a series of male lovers for whom he was the prototype (Liebowitz 165) and who invariably failed to satisfy her needs (Falk 224). In love, she knew herself to be "weak and dependent, clinging to the man" she loved (Falk 5). Aware of the ways in which successive lovers first obsessed and then disappointed her by their "inability to give what she needed" (Falk 224), Goldman not only "hid her personal failures and pain" (Falk 97) but also began to believe that "'a personal love is not for one who dedicates himself to an ideal. Somehow it is like serving two Gods'" (Falk 175). Goldman's use of the masculine pronoun and her periodic lapses into affairs that first confirmed and later subverted her sense of herself suggest the residual uncertainties about her subjective status as a woman that sought resolution in the attempt to both identify with and idealize what she wasn't sure she could ever be.

The persistence within Goldman of the abused, unloved child kept separate her personal and public personae and gave her, as one biographer notes, "something to hide" (Falk 1–8). Personally and politically, moreover, Goldman's passionate devotion to people and to causes that she idealized both trapped her in cycles of expectation and disappointment that repeated themselves throughout her life (Liebowitz 157, 168) and prevented her from healing the division between the heroic mother she became in public and the child whose passionate need for love dominated her private life. In the shadow of Goldman's public persona, as in the interstices of Antin's self-celebratory American narrator and Yezierska's rebellious protagonists, the unresolved developmental issues of immigrant daughters and their mothers assert themselves. Handicapped like all immigrants by class and culture, these women experience also the gendered ambiguities of Jewish daughters. Empowered by their mothers' considerable strengths, they are also confused by their mothers' submissiveness to male authority. They respond in different ways to this confusion. Antin denies her likeness to her mother, masking insecurity by self-congratulation. Yezierska's protagonists imitate one of her fictional mothers, dramatizing the maternal strategy of seeking ideal lovers to confirm themselves as subjects. Goldman revises her mother, dividing the fragile self who needs to be loved from the heroic self who fights and gives to others, sustaining in disjunctive private and public lives two versions of herself—neither of which can translate fully the abused European child into the powerful American woman. Driven by the need to resolve the gendered ambiguities transmitted by their mothers, the formidable talent and energy of these immigrant daughters—like their mothers before them, one suspects—develop multiple modes of being themselves as they translate themselves into publicly productive American women.

Like them, Kate Simon knew the domestic imbalance of the immigrant Jewish family and the gendered ambiguities of women's status in it. But the narrative persona of Kate Simon's memoirs neither denies, nor imitates, nor revises her mother. Instead, she is maternally groomed to defy her mother's fate, tuned in by her own experience to the adversaries she must overcome, and made aware by her mother's story of the weapons most effective in a woman's hands. Simon is blessed with a strong, independent mother who sustains her own subjective authority and empowers her daughter to become herself. Nevertheless, Simon develops the manifold sense of self that seems to persist in these immigrant daughters.

Power, rather than negotiation, imitation, or revision, is the central issue in these memoirs. The earliest and most fruitful sources of power are first revealed to Simon by her mother. Impressed in early childhood by her mother's verbal skill in both argument and anecdote, Simon recalls—like Goldman—her mother's power to give or withhold sympathy from certain characters (*Bronx* 4–5). The romantic story of her mother's independent girlhood in Warsaw, replete with a gentile lover, lends depth and perspective to her image and weight to her lectures on "female independence" (*Bronx* 17). Even in America, Simon's mother demonstrates her power to be an active, self-determining subject in the world. Never an advocate of "the overrated charms of marriage" (*Bronx* 17), this mother succumbs to neither domestic responsibilities nor her husband's authority. She sings, laughs, and studies, insisting she would always rather study or work than clean house (*Wider* 64). Unlike other women in the tenement, she "didn't accept her fate as a forever thing. She began to work during our school hours after her English classes had taught her as much as they could" (*Bronx* 48). She dresses differently than her neighbors and will not gossip in the street. She is "the only mother who went out alone at night to join her mandolin group" (*Bronx* 48). Remembering the mysterious and beautiful complexities of her mother's "talented sewing machine," whose treasures of little drawers and colored silk threads animated Simon's happiest childhood hours (*Bronx* 6), she portrays this mother not only as a creature "so beautiful that I couldn't see her; her radiance blinded me" (*Bronx* 109), but also as a creative person whose work is a source of power and pride to herself. Simon's early financial independence and adventurous, self-sustaining career as a travel writer testify to her early familiarity with work as a source of independence, authority, and self-realization for her mother.[25]

This mother's resistance to the temper and stinginess of her husband also confirms for her daughter a woman's power to exist as a subject independent of male regard. When she ignores him, muttering under her breath as she walks out on one of his monologues, she demonstrates to her daughter that "she was not afraid of my father, nor particularly in awe of him" (*Bronx* 47). When she refuses to respond to him, when she teases or argues with him, when she protects her children from him, she writes large her power to be herself. Rejecting traditional ritual (*Bronx* 90), she even exemplifies to her children a generosity of spirit that elevates her moral authority above her husband's: when he complains of her willingness to help neighbors, her answer is "short and always the same,'*Es is doch a mench*,' yet these are human beings, the only religious training we ever had, perhaps quite enough," Simon remembers (*Bronx* 51).

Work, silent withdrawal, and moral self-assuredness are the strategies this mother employs to empower herself as an independent entity. But her most powerful resource is her sexuality. Although parental sex is a carefully kept secret in this memoir, a secret that both tantalizes and terrifies this immigrant daughter, its presence is powerfully felt. Behind the memorable sewing machine, Simon recalls, looms "the dignity of the parental bed" (*Bronx* 6). On one level, the parents' sexuality guarantees the children's domestic security. After one extended silence between warring parents, in which the children expect "to be swept away . . . separated, to starve and burn alone in a desert" (*Bronx* 53), Simon finds their apartment door locked, hears unfamiliar sounds through it, and later finds her father washing her mother's feet while she splashes "him a little. They were making jokes, lilting, laughing," she remembers. "Something, another branch in the twisted tree that shaded our lives, was going to keep us safe for a while" (*Bronx* 54).

On another level, however, parental sex becomes more threatening. Ignorant at first of the link between sex and pregnancy, Simon blames herself and her baby sister for her mother's suffering during childbirth. She knows the power of heterosexual love to punish and transform women even before she associates these consequences with their natural cause. Of her pregnant mother, she remembers, "I hated this swollen person who used to be as lively as jumping rope and never scared. Now she was scared when she stepped off the sidewalk, scared of the boxes flung around in the market, scared of crippled people. . . . She was becoming a big ugly crybaby, and lazy" (*Bronx* 61–62). Only later will Simon learn to connect sex with the bearing and birthing of children. Once she grasps the connection, she is delighted with its power: "All that day I could feel the laughter bubbling in me, I could see the whipping bodies of the dogs and the people mixed up with the swell of my mother's body. . . . The tall door to their secret gardens was beginning, maybe just a crack, to open to me" (*Bronx* 67). Discovering much later that her mother had thirteen abortions, Simon concludes that her "mother enjoyed sex and was fatalistic and stalwart about abortions" (*Wider* 142). But awareness of sex as both pleasure and pain comes to her much earlier in the sensuality and suffering of her mother.

Ultimately, this mother presides over Simon's own transformation into a sexual being, slapping her face when menstruation begins and then surprising her with a "woman's dress" (*Bronx* 178) that makes this newly adolescent daughter feel "ready" for sexual combat. Thus, punishment and power are always tangled in Simon's experience of sexuality. Furtively exploited in her girlhood by assorted relatives and neighbors (*Bronx* 123, 125, 159, 160), Simon knows she is a woman when she feels ready "to play, to tease, to amorously accept, to confidently reject" men (*Bronx* 178).

But she also recognizes in herself a longing for male regard that she associates with her father's long absence in America and with his harshness toward her when they were reunited. Desiring his affection and admiration, she receives from him only punishment, criticism, deflating sarcasm, and a readiness to absorb her into his own fantasies. Because of him she will, like Goldman, always find it hard to believe that she is lovable (*Etchings* 9). Babysitting for another family she learns to generalize paternal abuse of daughters and male lust and anger toward the women who serve them (*Wider* 44, 48). But she blames her father for failing to protect her from sexual exploitation (*Wider* 71–72) and also for damaging her confidence as a woman. Both the mother's readiness for sexual pleasure and the father's rejections and deflations of this immigrant daughter participate in Simon's characteristic acceptance of the many brief sexual adventures that she enters with a shrug and leaves without regret.

Unlike Goldman's autobiography, Simon's memoirs embrace her private as well as her public life. Her story includes the personal, developmental issues that Goldman hid from the public in her letters. But Simon's sense of self remains as bipolar as the narrative persona of Antin, as fluid and driven as the protagonists of Yezierska, as divided as the heroic persona of Goldman. As an adolescent, driven by guilty self-doubt and courageous self-assertion, Simon creates different versions of herself in every situation. Within her adventurous adult persona modeled on her mother's strengths and strategies, moreover, her father's critical image of her persists as a "doppelganger companion" who always mocks the "twin me" (*Etchings* 11). Because of him she knows in herself an "other" who seeks in many lovers the "father who left" even though she knows the search is futile. She confesses at the end of her memoirs that "little more than I knew at seventeen do I surely know who I am at seventy-five" (*Etchings* 238).

By the end of her memoirs, however, the writer persona has become central to her self-image. To be sure, she carries with her "an envelope of earlier shapes": the child she "would never again be," as well as all the people who hurt or helped her to become an adult. But the writer/self translates these other personae into her own story where they become "immutably mine" (*Wider* 186). Assuming, like her immigrant mother, the storyteller's superior power to mock, to mourn, to "destroy" other subjects, Simon achieves a public self by re-presenting them—and herself. She shares with Goldman, Yezierska, and Antin the verbal power that allowed them and many lesser immigrant women writers to be recognized, to stand firmly at what Francoise Lionnet called "the confluence of different cultures" (262) and to become there—themselves.

Ironically, some of these writers discovered this power reflexively, through the recognition of strong male figures. "I did not even discover my own talent. It was discovered first by my father in Russia," Antin reports, "so what is there left for me to do . . . but put my grandfather's question into words and set to music my father's dream? The tongue am I of those who lived before me" (214). Her talent dependent on his recognition, Antin's persona justified herself as a writer by her usefulness to male ancestors capable of confirming her value.

Yezierska's initial sense of herself as a writer was similarly dependent on male recognition and similarly validated by her usefulness to others. After her first meeting with John Dewey, she sent him this message: "Generations of stifled words—reaching out to you—aching for utterance—dying on my lips unuttered—" (*All* 41). Dewey's poetic response caught both Yezierska's power to give voice to others and the curious interweaving of her own sense of self-worth with her function as their translator:

> Generations of stifled words, reaching out *through you*
> Aching for utterance, dying on lips
> That have died of hunger,
> Hunger not to have, but to be.

> . . . In you I see them coming to be, . . .
> You shall not utter them; you shall be them.
> (*All* 43)

Yezierska's consciousness of her connection to other immigrants—noisy at home and in their neighborhoods, but voiceless in the larger world—governed both her choice of subject and, to a large extent, her style.

Other writers discovered their power through the response of their audiences. On the lecture platform, Goldman realized that she "could sway people with words! Strange and magic words that welled up from within me, from some unfamiliar depth" (Goldman 51). Feeling the audience's response, Goldman became aware for the first time of her articulate self: "I was conscious only of my own words, of my ecstatic song," she reports (51). Like the women whose passionate utterances stirred vast crowds to demonstrate or to strike, Goldman found her own voice as she used it for others. Although Simon's work privatized and professionalized this "ecstatic song" of the self, she also extended the range of the Jewish woman's voice into the world of travel and sexual adventure—away from the public meeting, the lecture hall, and the needs of ancestors, immigrants, and the poor.

By the power of the word and by their skill at translation, these and other Jewish women writers of the immigrant generation earned the recognition they required and rendered into English lives publicly silenced by tradition and made otherwise inarticulate by poverty, by cultural dislocation, and by the thousand insecurities common to the immigrant experience. They spoke not only for and of themselves but also for those whose voices were not supposed to be heard outside the home and marketplace and had never reached beyond Yiddish to non-Jewish readers. Thus, like the Jewish women whose words energized workers in the union movement and entered into American social history, these writers of stories projected the Jewish woman's voice into the public American world.[26]

As storytellers, some of them identified the mode of narrative with their mothers: "The voices that filled our world were those of women, the Mothers," Simon recalls (*Bronx* 36). Barred by traditional restrictions from the ingenuities of the study house and by middle-class pretensions from the American marketplace, Jewish mothers had focused their verbal wit and wisdom, their considerable interpretive and analytical skills, on human interactions. In the "Bintel Brief" columns, in novels bought and read by their daughters, and in the inadvertent dramas of their neighbors, Jewish mothers attended to the stories of men and women rather than to the politics of the shop, the rules of rabbis, or the ordinances of God. Thus, beside the political utterances that moved multitudes to change the world, the familiar, homely, maternal mode of the story became central to the literature of American Jewish women writers. In the process, they translated the disparate, manifold selves of European mothers and American daughters into the vernacular of the new world.

Notes

1. Hyman observes that "East European Jewish culture offered women contradictory messages" ("Gender" 224). These are Ashkenazi from Eastern Europe, not Sephardi Jews from Spain or the Orient.

2. Thus, as Glenn argues, they knew they weren't going home again (64). But Hyman cautions, "It is as rash to generalize" about them "as about immigrant men" ("Culture" 157).

3. Weinberg writes, "Although the great majority of men worked, helping to earn a livelihood was frequently considered a woman's job and an extension of her work in the home. This meant that working for money was not a source of shame for Jewish women as it would be among cultures where a man's status depended upon his ability to support his family. Throughout most of preindustrial Europe, non-Jewish women also shared this burden with their husbands, but only among the Jews of Eastern Europe was it accepted practice that some women would provide the sole means of support" (6).

4. Other, potentially toughening, discordances include the cultural image of the Jewish woman as both "inherently close to the physical, material world" and "endowed with an exceptional capacity for moral persuasion" (Baum et al. 12).

5. Echoing Weinberg's informants, who talk about their lives in terms of what they did instead of what they had or were (252–53), Barbara Myerhoff described the elderly Jewish women she studied as communicating "a quiet conviction and satisfaction with themselves, perhaps because they did what had to be done, did it as well as it could be done, and knew that without what they did there would be nothing and no one" (quoted in Weinberg 257).

6. It is hard, however, to imagine a more complex domestic task than the washing, bleaching, starching, and ironing of the family laundry described by Rose Pesotta in her memoir, *Days of Our Lives* (154–56), a process that

began at the local river, progressed to a hollow tree trunk filled—pail by pail—with cleaned ashes from the kitchen fire and boiling water, and ended in the muddy yard where a stray animal, rubbing itself against the drying clothes, might render the entire process futile.

7. But see Hyman on the functions of "female friendship groups" and the use of the "neighborhood and the public spaces of markets, shops, and stoops" as the locus of immigrant women's "communal Jewish identity and of their political activism" ("Culture" 164).

8. When daughters of these women speak to contemporary interviewers, they often stress the hardships and deprivations of their mothers' lives (Weinberg 36, 38, 45, 74). More important, perhaps, is Weinberg's comment that "mothers could not provide role models for their teenage daughters on the Lower East Side of New York any more than they could in the working-class areas of Bialystok or Odessa. Urbanization and industrialization had altered life in both places, and their mothers' homebound lives offered no clues to behavior" (118).

9. According to Anderson and Jack, "women often mute their own thoughts and feelings when they try to describe their lives in the familiar and publicly acceptable terms of prevailing concepts and conventions" (11).

10. According to Benjamin, even fathers who do not triumph—or even go "into the world"—can look as though they do to children whose mothers are most familiar with the child's dependent needs. To such children, the father's relative distance from that intensely intimate relationship appears to give him the key to the child's independence or freedom from that primary bond ("Alienation" 123–25).

11. See Pratt, "Culture and Radical Politics," for more information on these writers.

12. Klein has suggested that literary portrayers of the ghetto benefited by paying their literary respects and thus assuaging their guilt; by mythicizing and thus further emigrating from it; or by teaching "official Americans" that the ghetto, too, constituted a "home town" (184). See also Sollors, *Beyond Ethnicity*, in which he describes Antin's grammatical treatment of her two "subjects" as evidence of a "conversion" experience (32–33).

13. Composed, translated, and inserted into her adult memoir, the child's images of alienation from herself as traveler attach themselves to and help to explain the adult narrator's euphoric celebration of America as journey's end, as home. Thus, the images link child to adult as effectively as they once overcame the distance between the child/writer and her relatives and between Europe and America.

14. Weinberg's informants emphasize male assumption of superiority in the shtetl (16) but note as well that even in Europe women made the important decisions in the home (24) and, in America, commonly deferred to

their husbands in public in order to uphold the mainly "ceremonial" authority of their men (132–33). Weinberg also reports that fathers were less likely
than mothers to encourage their daughters toward an education. In the
workplace, Glenn notes, the lack of male encouragement for women's efforts
reflected "the status anxieties of immigrant men": as Jewish men experienced
the downward social mobility common to immigrants, "women became the
victims of men's efforts to assert, or perhaps reclaim, their masculine dignity" (116).

15. Weinberg reports that working daughters were initially expected to
turn over all their wages to their family but, in time, customarily kept a
portion for their own use (187–202).

16. Regenbaum also develops the consequences for Yezierska's work and
self-image of her father's failure to "recognize" her (55–66).

17. Ammons has called attention to the Orthodox father's life-sustain-
ing recognition of several of Yezierska's protagonists. As her Sophie in an
early short story is literally fed a sacramental meal by Shmendrik, the old
man who is her neighbor (164), so Sara Smolinsky in *Bread Givers* is re-
deemed from dissatisfaction and despair by her Orthodox father's willingness
to live with her. But the gift these fathers possess is not, strictly speaking,
"the nourishment to be received from traditional patriarchal culture" (Ammons 165). In both the early novel, *Bread Givers* (296–97), and the late
memoir, *Red Ribbon on a White Horse* (216–18), protagonists recognize that
the culture of their fathers will not validate women as subjects.

18. Henriksen, Yezierska's daughter and biographer, has called attention
to the resemblance Yezierska noted between one beloved man and her father: "The feeling of familiarity shocked and amazed her. Absurd! Her father had lived . . . in the ghetto of Poland. This man was a Gentile, an
American. And yet for all their difference, there was that unworldly look
about [his] eyes that made her feel her father . . . as he might have been in
[the] new world" (111).

It is important to note that Yezierska was mentored by women as well as
men. Sullivan describes, for example, the liberating effect of Henrietta Rod-
man's encouragement as an "emissary from the American world ready to
meet [Yezierska] as she was, accept her goals as she expressed them, and help
her find what she was looking for" (54).

19. Wexler describes the complex and sometimes ambivalent roots of
Goldman's work for birth control (210).

20. Falk, another biographer, often notes Goldman's tendency to "uni-
versalize" personal conflict, pain, and anger in letters and lectures that formulate her ideal vision (75–76, 140, 233, 282).

21. But to Johan Most, Goldman's earliest mentor, Wexler gives credit
for teaching Goldman her early rhetorical style (53).

22. Wexler argues that Goldman's public persona may have been her most original creation (xviii).

23. The autobiography reveals the residue of that anger as well in Goldman's patronizing recollection of her mother's belated "proof" of maternal love: the gift of assorted medals she had received from various charity organizations (Goldman 697). "I assured her that I had already received too many medals of my own," Goldman remembers. Even grammar betrays the persistent ambivalence of this immigrant daughter's attitude toward her mother. "She was the *grande dame par excellence*," Goldman insists, "more careful of her toilet than her daughters" (696). More careful than her daughters were? or more careful of her appearance than of her daughters? One cannot tell. The confused comparison suggests deeper confusions in the relationship between this immigrant daughter and her mother.

24. Contemporary theorists address the generic problem of autobiographical literature by recognizing at the outset the creation of a "self" as the chief function of the narrative. In this genre, as in the personal narratives offered to oral historians, narrative unreliability is not optional—as in a novel—but inevitable, for the self is partly discovered and partly created by the autobiographer as she remembers and composes the story of her life (cf. S. Smith 45).

25. Another source of the aggressive pursuit of work and education, according to Glenn, was the "drive for accomplishment for its own sake" (124) that differentiated Jews from other immigrant women.

26. Glenn observes that the union movement revealed "women's evolving awareness of the power of their public voice and political agency" (169): "The authority of radical women in the factories derived from their ability to articulate in clear and sympathetic ways ideological tenets that were part of the cultural milieu of the immigrant communities" (184).

2

Leaving Home and Mother: Dramas of Differentiation

From where does your strength come?
—Adrienne Rich, "Sources"

Her words were: "Find a place where
you are happy." But the sound of those words had
the mourning of separation.
—Irena Klepfisz, "A Visit"

In the writings of its daughters, Jewish immigrant culture waxed parental. It nourished and constrained. It stoked the energies of its offspring
and shaped their Jewish self-images even when it failed to satisfy their
needs. When its children left home, they knew the experience was both
cultural and familial. In their stories, two familiar American dramas
merge: the attempt to "pass," a deliberate, often reactive form of cultural assimilation, becomes linked with the developmental dynamic of differentiation and individuation. Both processes mingle in a single theme
that dramatizes a daughter's struggle to become herself by way of separation: by leaving home.

Like slamming a door on a quarrel, however, leaving home relieves
one sort of stress but provokes another. As protagonists in American
Jewish women's stories walk away from homes that seem too close, too
confining, they discover the power of cultural and familial connections to define them as women and as Jews. Jewish women's stories often inscribe that power in the figure of the mother and explore the
malaise of daughters who believe they must leave her in order to become themselves.

Mother images in these stories vary with the changing circumstances and preoccupations of writing daughters. Daughters of German American, middle-class Jewish mothers in the twenties and thirties, for example, knew little of the East European immigrant woman's struggle against poverty and patriarchy. Thus, in stories by Edna Ferber or Fannie Hurst, mothers and the reasons for leaving them differ from Sara Smolinsky's in Yezierska's *Bread Givers*. Although images of mothers vary as they absorb the emotional residue of different social and historical stresses, maternal images throughout the century are also continuous with one another. That continuity reflects an ongoing effort to clarify the cultural-cum-developmental processes in which mothers and daughters were—and are—involved.

In stories that explore the strategy of separation, mothers play an ambivalent role for both cultural and developmental reasons. From a developmental point of view, the mother's power as a conduit of both ethnic and gender identity[1] appears to limit the benefit to her daughter of separating from her. But from a cultural point of view, disconnection appears to offer certain advantages.[2] First among them might be the illusion that a daughter could find, at a distance, a quiet place to either sort out or dismiss the babble of often conflicting cultural imperatives. Culture speaks as loudly as family to the woman bent on finding her own voice, and American messages about gender before World War II were particularly mixed. As one historian puts it, from their predecessors in the fight for suffrage and reform American women of the twenties inherited both "freedom of choice" and the right to concentrate on "'the psychological development of themselves as individuals'" (D. Brown 249–50). Although women of the thirties continued to attend college, to serve in government, and to work outside the home, their newly won freedom to choose themselves was curtailed by the traditional role they were expected "to play in holding their families together" in the midst of the depression (Ware 199). Like other American women, Jewish women before World War II heard the voices of their time first calling them away from "home" and traditional female roles and then summoning them back again to the domestic tasks they were needed to perform.

As Jews, moreover, they heard other mixed messages as well. Diane Lichtenstein has shown that late nineteenth-century Jewish women writers attempted to synthesize two models of womanhood: the "true woman" who defined herself domestically in pious, submissive service to her family, and the "mother in Israel," whose strength preserved the home and whose home preserved Judaism (*Writing* 17–19, 30). Lichtenstein's Jewish women writers took themselves seriously as Jews and tried in their stories to reconcile that sense of themselves with the demands their culture made upon them as Americans.

But in the first three decades of the twentieth century, America's messages to its Jews subverted in many ways Jewish women writers' determination to "preserve Judaism" by foregrounding it in their stories and their lives. During this period, American Jews felt keenly the pressure to assimilate. In Arthur Hertzberg's analysis, efforts to restrict Jewish immigration, fears of Jewish radicalism, educational quotas, and job discrimination during the depression combined to make clear to American Jews that they were second-class citizens. Their "morale was lower in the 1930's," Hertzberg writes, "than at any time ever" (279).[3] Thus, Jewish women writers who concentrate on the daughter's drama of disconnection knew what Paula E. Hyman has called not only the limits of gender and class that circumscribed women within the Jewish community but also the "disability conferred by their ethnicity" in "society at large" ("Gender" 223). In the early twentieth century, an American Jewish woman's effort to develop her own voice was complicated not only by general social pressures and by "traditionally" Jewish inhibitions, but also by American social animus toward Jews.

Given these complications, it is not difficult to imagine at least some of the reasons why three Jewish writers of the early decades, Edna Ferber, Fannie Hurst, and Tess Slesinger, courted American readers with stories primarily about Americans, not Jews.[4] In their works, explicitly Jewish themes and issues that had figured prominently in immigrant stories and writings of the nineteenth century receded, as regional and other social issues moved to the foreground. But some stories that appear to have lost specifically Jewish resonance acknowledge the role of ethnicity in individual development. And other stories—in which ethnicity never becomes an issue—allow these writers to explore filial tensions and developmental strategies at a distance, as it were, from their own situations as American Jews.

Ferber and Hurst came from similar ethnic backgrounds. Of German Jewish descent, raised in the Midwest, minimally educated as Jews, relatively unfamiliar with home or synagogue ritual, and exposed in childhood to anti-Semitism, both women were encouraged as children to think of themselves as Americans and to mix socially with non-Jews. Beneath these similarities, however, are some striking differences. For example, Ferber resolved the tension between her American and her Jewish identities by insisting they were complementary. As early as 1938 she declared publicly that she was proud to be a Jew.[5] Her Jewish characters, moreover, are few but heroic. They owe to their ethnic inheritance their human and artistic sensitivities (*Fanny Herself*) and their moral fiber (*Cimmaron*). Acknowledging their Jewishness becomes for them an act of both self-acceptance and self-realization ("Girl Who Went Right"). In her non-Jewish stories and characters, as Lichtenstein has demonstrated, Ferber encoded the ethnic issues she knew best, transforming "the 'other' (the Jew and the woman) into the 'one' (the insider)" and embodying "the myths of True and Jewish womanhood into the fearless, invincible pioneer woman" (*Writing* 130–31).

Hurst's sense of herself as a Jew was both more complicated and more ambivalent. She remembers her own and her father's "furtiveness" as Jews (*Anatomy* 17–18). She records his explicit command that she be proud of being a Jew, but she notes as well his failure to defend Jewish colleagues attacked by non-Jews. And when she speaks of her husband's likeness to her father, recalling the quietness and gentleness of both men, she mentions also her father's unyielding objection to her marrying an East European Jew, one of those he called "kikes" (*Anatomy* 22).

Her father's contempt for East European immigrants was fairly common among German Jews, who had come earlier to America and whose speech, dress, and ritual customs seemed less obviously foreign. Whatever Hurst shared of that attitude, together with the unresolved tensions in her own ethnic identity, probably account for the stereotypically negative ways in which her early fiction represents Jewish characters. Accentuating the coarseness of immigrant speech, the vulgarity of immigrant behavior, the intensity of immigrant feeling, the claustrophobic tightness of immigrant families, Hurst draws her ghetto Jews as clowns whose painted faces write large essential human emotions. The narrator of "Humoresque," for example, demonizes one Jewish father's physical appearance in peculiarly racist terms: "With his son's little pulling wrist still in clutch, Mr. Kantor regarded his wife, the lower half of his face, well covered with reddish bristles, undershot, his free hand and even his eyes violently lifted. To those who see in a man a perpetual kinship to that animal kingdom of which he is supreme, there was something undeniably anthropoidal about Abrahm Kantor, a certain simian width between the eyes and long, rather agile hands with hairy backs" (*Humoresque* 8). Hurst ultimately regretted such portrayals. In her autobiogra-

phy she confessed: "I am not proud of my mental processes or the lack
of them concerning the long body-and-soul flagellation of another race—
my own" (*Anatomy* 350).

Ferber and Hurst differed not only in the ways they resolved tensions
within their ethnic identities but also in their personal and professional treatment of mothers. In a period "dominated" by psychological ideas,
as one historian notes (D. Brown 18), popular images of mothers were
shaped partly by behaviorists who found mothers "dangerous" in their
ignorance and incompetence (Margolis 51) and partly by Freudians who
conceived mothers as potentially formidable obstacles to their children's
development. In Marianne Hirsch's words, "the story of individual development, as Freud tells it, rests on a process of separation from the
mother" (169). In 1937 one Freudian said, "It is by turning away from
our mother that we finally become . . . grown men and women" (quoted in Chodorow 82). Hurst's stories—like her life—conform to this popular assumption about mothers. But Ferber resists such an assumption.

Ferber heard so clearly her own mother's story that she devoted her
life to compensating for her mother's early deprivations. But she needed first to build a life apart from her mother. Thus, her work emphasizes
both the incompatible, divisive needs of mothers and daughters and the
importance of sustaining the bond between them. Ferber's version of her
mother's story, recorded in a letter to her sister just after their mother's
death, reveals her compassionate awareness of her mother's struggles.
Ferber remembers that her mother

> married in her very early twenties. She married a man she did not
> love. She didn't mean to. She didn't know how not to. She mar-
> ried Jacob Ferber, a decent dull rather handsome man because her
> mother said she must. She was in love with a man named Will
> English, and he wanted to marry her. He was not a Jew, there was
> the most terrible brouhaha, she was bullied and threatened and
> browbeaten. Will English became a nationally known figure of his
> day, wealthy and distinguished. Mother would have made a won-
> derful wife for him, high-spirited, intelligent, quick to learn and
> evaluate. Jacob Ferber failed in his business, became blind, lost
> everything, his life insurance and his shop goods were mortgaged,
> there were two small daughters. Julia Ferber took over somehow,
> there was no one to whom she could turn for help. Her life, from
> the time she was twenty until she was about fifty-seven, was a tragic
> thing. (quoted in Gilbert 198)

For Ferber, hearing this story meant taking on the burden of restitution. After she became a writer, she chose to live "in tandem" with her mother—sharing a home and social life despite her mother's intrusions, demands, and jealousy (e.g., Gilbert 382–83, 392–93, 401).

Her letters and journals speak both the anger and delight engendered by her life with her mother. But her "Jewish," quasi-autobiographical novel, *Fanny Herself* (1917), makes audible only the delight. Remembering Adrienne Rich's observation that the mother/daughter relationship offers the possibility of the "deepest mutuality" (*Of Woman* 226), one senses in this novel the magnitude of Ferber's pleasure in having had for so many years her lively, vital—though difficult—mother all to herself. *Fanny Herself* describes the female journey toward self-realization as a process in which daughters first leave and then return home. Grown strong and capable to compensate for her husband's weakness and early death, the mother, Molly Brandeis, is "extraordinarily alert" (*Fanny* 3–4)—not only to the vicissitudes of business but also to the subtleties of her relationship with her daughter Fanny (40). This mother prods her daughter, like herself, to toughness and self-denial. They commit themselves mutually to the sacrifices required by Fanny's brother's career (42). The bond between them is nourished by shared deprivations as well as respect and love.

Beside these positive connections, however, the novel suggests another, less explicit dimension in this mother/daughter relationship. Believing that "sores displayed in the market place are seldom fascinating or even interesting" (*Peculiar* 5), Ferber concealed in this "Jewish" novel her own awareness of tensions between devoted daughters and their mothers. Like other twentieth-century women writers who "symbolically 'kill' their mothers in order not to have to take their places" (Gardiner, "Wake" 146), Ferber "kills" Molly Brandeis very early in the story, giving vent in this way to what her biographer calls her "maternal death wish" (Gilbert 407).

Within the novel, Fanny speaks the rage that may have lain behind Ferber's symbolic "murder" of the mother by expressing, first, anger (like Ferber's) at her mother's deprivations and then determination not to suffer her mother's fate: "'I'm through being sentimental and unselfish. What did it bring her? Nothing!'" Fanny declares (*Fanny* 106). Though this sentimental daughter cherishes for months a faded apron stained by many years of its—and her mother's—kitchen service, rejection of her mother's deprivations leads immediately to denial of her mother's emotional style and spirit. But susceptibility to emotion is part of the heritage Fanny carries within herself, a likeness to both her mother and her race that will endure despite her best efforts to deny it. "Generous, spontaneous, impulsive, warmhearted, she would be cold, calculating, deliberate, she told herself" (108). Thus, Ferber's narrator surfaces the irony within the daughter's rejection of her mother's identity, suggesting that the denial of the mother in oneself is also denial of one's self.

Furious and defiant, Fanny silences her mother's voice and leaves home. Before she can become *Fanny Herself,* she will have to affirm the qualities that liken her to her mother and link her to her Jewish identity. Thus, Ferber insists on both the gendered and the ethnic continuity between mother and daughter that remained problematic for the Jewish protagonists of some other women writers in this period. Leah Morton's pseudonymous, supposedly autobiographical narrator, for example, accepts estrangement from her beloved mother as the price of her maturation. Yezierska's Sara Smolinsky in *Bread Givers* assumes her mother's burden but worries that it will subject her again to the hated restraints of traditional Judaism. Ferber's Fanny, however, becomes most fully herself as both a woman and a Jew when she grows into likeness to her Jewish mother.[6]

Ferber's compassion for mothers bears fruit in later works with non-Jewish characters and settings, where she explores more fully the struggle for individuation that vexed mother/daughter relationships and threatened to culminate in the daughter's leaving home. These works, whose non-Jewish contexts allowed Ferber both to conceal her personal associations with mother/daughter conflict and to portray that conflict more explicitly, insist on the deep, mutual complicity of mother and daughter in the difficult process of a woman's growth. Remembering her mother's story, Ferber portrays women who have been dominated and deprived by their mothers and who become, in turn, oppressive to their daughters. Unable to satisfy their own needs, they deny the needs of their daughters. But even the worst of these terrible mothers does not "dream that she had blocked her daughter's chances for a career or for marital happiness. Neither did she know that she looked down upon that daughter for having failed to marry" (*Girls* 240). Entirely unaware, mothers in these works become creatures trapped by their own deprivations, snarling at the offspring born into their cages. Instead of "dangerous" mothers and victim-daughters, Ferber sees two women caught in webs of mutual deprivation and frustration.

Ferber's life and work formulate a decisively negative response to the appeal of separation from home and mother. She rejects not only the temptation to become herself by leaving her mother but also the conventional illusion that getting married would define her as an adult. She left home early and then returned, as both a daughter and a Jew. She restored and transformed both the ethnic and the filial connections that she had once disregarded. Having heard her mother's story, she rescued its protagonist and rejected its plot for her own life. She never married, and in her stories women who do marry to get away from their mothers turn into their mothers instead of becoming themselves. Thus, Ferber denies the value of leaving home and rejects the literary trope in which "marrying out" fosters a woman's individuation.[7]

Hurst, on the other hand, left home and never returned, though she lived to express remorse for her filial and ethnic disloyalties. Her work achieves insight into neither the cultural givens nor the maternal deprivations that alienate mothers and daughters. Instead, her novels portray filial separations that always end tragically and always feel like betrayal or abandonment.

Hurst's relationship to her own mother helps to explain why her female protagonists so often leave home only to fall into bondage to lovers, husbands, children, or jobs. The opening lines of Hurst's autobiography contain the initial clues:

> From the hour I gave Mama my first stare from her bed of my birth, I must have braced my new spine against being overpowered by the rush of her personality.
>
> When Mama walked into a room filled with ladies, she doused them like so many candles blown out on a birthday cake.
>
> Yet, on the other hand, no sooner had I left the warm cove of her body than we committed the anachronism of becoming one again.
>
> Despite the fact that we had neither temperamental nor intellectual compatibility, I loved her in a deep uncomplicated way that was never to waver throughout storm and stress.
>
> And storm and stress it was. (*Anatomy* 3)

Dizzying in its rhetorical indirections, its multiple negatives, its holding in tension of emotional oppositions and contradictions, this series of one-sentence paragraphs frames the salient data of Hurst's relationship to her mother. As rich in conflict as in pride and devotion, Hurst's feeling for this powerful, beloved, but uncongenial mother probably nourished the portrayals of mothers and daughters in her fiction. Out of this well of strong but confused feeling came story after story about women who, like herself, left home to avoid "becoming one again" with their mothers but remained all their lives "wonderers, in search of themselves"—the subtitle of Hurst's autobiography.

Some of Hurst's protagonists attempt to "find" themselves romantically. Like films of the period (Ware 187), many of Hurst's early short stories celebrate the poor working girl who marries the "right" man. But in her novels Hurst writes the story of romantic love as a tragedy of womanly abjection and self-denial. Her protagonists give themselves sexually, emotionally, and financially to men who reject, exploit, and abandon them. The kept woman in *Back Street* (1930), for example, nearly starves to death when her lover goes to Europe with his family; she has quit her job, at his request, but cannot ask him for money. The heroine of *Anywoman* (1950) devotes her life to nourishing a man who stays with her only after a crippling injury makes it impossible for him to run away. The central character of the late novel, *Family!* (1960), generously sustains with her sexual and emotional vitality several generations of a family. All of them need her, use her, and abandon her. At the end of the novel this protagonist, named—significantly—"Virgie," bathes the bleeding feet of an alcoholic who is stigmatized by nails that have worked their way through his battered shoes. The spiritual elevation of these "romantic" protagonists is directly proportional to their social, financial, emotional, and sexual exploitation. They are horribly ennobled by their sacrifices. They "find themselves" only by giving themselves away to men who need them but whose fear and hatred of that need turns into contempt for the women who can satisfy it. Thus, romantic love in Hurst's novels caricatures the infuriating imbalance of powerful, would-be mother and needy, rejecting child.

That imbalance leads Hurst's protagonists away from home and mother but toward other kinds of suffering. In these stories too, mother-love is the origin and end of the protagonist's ordeal. The mothers of Lilly Becker in *Stardust* (1921) and Bea Pullman in *Imitation of Life* (1933) prod their beloved daughters toward marriage, betraying them into connections that cannot satisfy their sexual and emotional needs. Hurst is very graphic on the subject of sexual repulsion: these protagonists notice and recoil from tiny details of their mates' appearance and behavior—from the ways they chew their food or touch their clothes. The domestic intimacy of the mothers and fathers lacks sexual excitement; in the daughters' marriages, intimacy provokes dismay, disappointment, and finally disgust. Newly wed Lilly in *Stardust*, for example, is repelled by the sound of her husband making his morning toilet:

> He gargled. It is . . . ignominious . . . to narrate Lilly's kind of anguish during this matinal performance of her husband. She suffered a tight-throated sort of anguish that could have been no keener had it been of larger provocation. Her toes and her fingers would curl and a quick ripple of flesh rush over her. Mornings, when he departed, his kiss which smelled of mouth wash, would remain coldly against her lips with the peculiar burn of camphor ice. All her sensibilities seemed suddenly to fester. (84–85)

Once liberated from their early marriages, such protagonists become successful career women and devoted mothers. But their devotion denies them the lovers they desire. As these women develop financial power, Hurst exacts from them the sacrifice of their own sexuality. Lilly Becker, guilt-ridden all her life because she has disappointed her mother, returns home to that overpowering embrace once her own daughter's career is launched. And both Lilly and Bea Pullman lose to their daughters the lovers they themselves desire. Two popular movie versions of *Imitation of Life* change this ending; both films allow the mother to keep her lover without alienating her daughter. But Hurst's fiction absolutely denies that satisfaction to these two businesswomen who pay for leaving home by living without romantic love.[8]

Hurst's own, publicly acknowledged, regret for the unhappiness her choices caused her parents may contribute to the punishments and deprivations her protagonists experience when they leave home. But her fictions punish mothers as well as daughters. Her own mother furnished the prototype in Hurst's fiction for other materialistic mothers who alienate or lose their children. Mama Hurst, the American-born daughter of a silent, overworked, immigrant mother (*Anatomy* 30) whose energies were entirely spent satisfying the material needs of her family, developed her own mother's role by becoming a critic and consumer, rather than a producer of material things. In this respect she resembled other immigrant daughters, transformed in America by an industrial culture whose "factory-made goods aroused and reinforced" the immigrant woman's belief that "the ability to buy goods" was "an act of transcendance, the realization of a new social status" (Ewen 64, 67). Hurst's mother remained obsessed with money and the material things it could buy as well as the status that money and things conferred. She lived, Fannie remembers, in a world of "bric-a-brac and realities. My laundress steals soap. Fannie is hard on pantywaists. Fifteen cents a dozen for 'cooking eggs,' but Mr. Hurst doesn't believe in them. Says they go into our stomachs even if they are in a cake, the same as better grade eating eggs. I always say it doesn't pay to economize. It's the extravagant women who are most respected by their husbands. You can't tell me she keeps a clean kitchen. She has ants." Alienated by her mother's "realities," Fannie simply denies their value: "Mama's world was composed of tiny mosaics, seven days a week of things you could eat and touch and smell and do. On the other hand . . . I moved in a world you could not see" (*Anatomy* 4). Daughters of materialistic mothers in *Five and Ten* (1929), *Mannequin* (1926), and *The Man with One Head* (1953) replicate Fannie's alienation. More severely punished mothers in *Imitation of Life* (1933), *Back Street* (1930), *Lummox* (1923), *Family!* (1960) and *The Lonely Parade* (1942) either die young or go mad—liberating their daughters as they disappear from the story.

Hurst's most ferociously punished and deprived mother figure is the saintly black Delilah in *Imitation of Life*, whose portrayal—considered racist by some readers—encodes Hurst's awareness of both her own filial and ethnic disloyalties and her mother's partial responsibility for them. In Delilah, Hurst represents the silent, self-destructive rage that flourishes within women who accept and pass on their subordination by class, race, and gender. She portrays as well the ways in which that rage—audible to daughters even when unexpressed—contaminates the mother/daughter relationship.

Delilah "mothers" virtually everybody—white and black, male and female—in the novel. When her own daughter leaves home to "pass" into the white society Delilah has always humbly served, she succumbs to a cancer concealed throughout the novel. Films based upon this novel and earlier critical readings have attributed Delilah's death to a broken heart (Wilentz 38). But in the novel she is devoured from within—as if by repressed rage at both her daughter's disloyalty and the racism that provoked it.

Delilah's malignancy achieves symbolic resonance as it transforms this abandoned mother into a grotesque. Her sufferings lose their dignity as her obesity renders her horribly comic. Her white mistress discovers her writhing on the floor, overcome by pain, wearing "a clean red-and-white striped bungalow apron that evidently served as a nightgown and gave her something of the appearance of a bathhouse on a beach. Manipulating her vast hulk to the living room couch reminded Bea rather grimly of motion pictures of whales being hauled ashore after a catch" (*Imitation* 319–20). Like her dying, Delilah's funeral further elaborates the grotesque, carnivalesque elements of her portrayal.

One theorist recently argued that in literature "the carnival of the dead body of the 'great mother' reveals a dark form of dealing culturally with fears of the female body and with the threatening aspects of femininity" (Schwab 209–10). Hurst's representation of the death and funeral of this black woman, servant and nurturer to all who need her, calls up specifically the negative feelings associated with mothering. In her last moments Delilah appears to her mistress, ironically, pregnant with her own death, like "a woman carrying the protuberance of something growing" (321). Indeed, Delilah's daughter has herself sterilized when she leaves home.

Stories like this one interpret their own writers. By setting the issue of maternal compliance, rage, and abandonment within the context of African American rather than Jewish experience, Hurst avoided confronting the personal and Jewish implications of Delilah's fate. But the parallels are clear. One critic has noted that, like Delilah's faithless daughter, "Hurst . . . denied her identity" (Wilentz 40). The novel heaps scorn upon Delilah's daughter for abandoning her mother and for refusing to shoulder with pride the burden of her racial identity. But the novel also punishes the mother, Delilah. It embodies in her the impotent and grotesque suffering of mothers whose submission to ethnic, racial, and gender deprivations devours them with silent rage and drives their daughters to leave home.

A third writer of the pre–World War II period, Tess Slesinger came, like Ferber and Hurst, from half-assimilated, middle-class parents. But they were East European, not German Jews, who sent Tess to school at the Ethical Culture Society with other children of assimilated Jewish families (Sharistanian 359, 362). Unlike Ferber and Hurst, Slesinger neither demonized nor idealized Jews in her stories, but she was keenly interested in the effects of assimilation. Like the second-generation New York Jews of this period who, as Deborah Dash Moore suggests, created and institutionalized "a form of liberalism as a distinctive American faith" (5, 15), Jewish and non-Jewish characters in Slesinger's *Unpossessed* (1934) are equally distant from ethnic roots. They busy themselves about the work of intellectual liberalism. Unaware that they may be

engaged in a process of ethnic redefinition (Moore 4), Slesinger's characters reveal the anguish experienced by people of different ethnic groups
at a preliminary stage of that process. Indeed, Slesinger's intellectuals
celebrate their detachment from bourgeois ethnic affiliations even as
their sterility and pain manifest the deprivations associated with leaving home.

Like Ferber and Hurst, Slesinger links the drama of ethnic disconnection with the figure of the mother. Her intellectuals, for example, are not
only uprooted from ethnic sources of collective faith, warmth, and vitality[9] but also alienated from mother-love and motherhood. Slesinger's
male characters, cut loose from the conventions and beliefs that now
seem "bourgeois" to their enlightened minds drift, argue, and betray one
another. Unable to respond to the maternal kindnesses of their women,
they conceive maternity itself as the enemy. In the final chapter, one
female protagonist, whose mother's voice and image were previously clear
and formative, returns home with her husband after an abortion to realize that—despite their intellectual and political commitments—"in
each of them the life-stream flowed to a dead-end" (*Unpossessed* 350).
This woman had always defined herself by her power to nurture, to protect, to love. But now that she has followed her husband's lead, refusing
parenthood in order to avoid becoming "bourgeois," she sees herself "as
a creature who would not be a woman and could not be a man" (357).

The novel remembers an ethnic past in the German grocers, Italian
landladies, Greek householders, and others who surround these intellectuals. In the final chapter the cabdriver's immigrant German mother is
linked with the fruitfulness of childbearing. But the protagonists are only
intellectuals: degendered and deracinated. Slesinger calls them "unpossessed" because they no longer belong to an ethnic community or respond
to the gendered imperatives that shape individuals in such communities.

Slesinger's treatment of mothering in this novel critiques a Freudian
image of the mother that was as familiar in Slesinger's time as in our own.
Many psychological theorists then, as now, conceived children's hostility toward their mothers as a response to excessive maternal control or
inadequate maternal attention and sympathy (Chodorow 119).[10] Freudians speculated that children, in order to become themselves, had to
separate from the mother who seemed too powerful, too familiar with
their dependent needs, too intimately beloved to let them grow easily
away from her. But Slesinger, like Ferber, rejected that popular conception of the mother, concentrating instead on the daughter's continuing

need of connection with her mother and on the ways in which an androcentric culture subverts that connection.

Her best-known story, "Mother for Dinner" (1935), probes the negative image of the mother to reveal at its source the cultural bias that conceives maturity in exclusively male, rather than female terms. The "world" of this story is deeply split, to suggest a dichotomous culture that polarizes male and female qualities.[11] For example, as Slesinger's newly wed protagonist, Katherine Benjamin, returns to her new apartment, she passes under an awning very like the birth canal, "stretched like a hollow wrinkled caterpillar to the curb" ("Mother" 144). Here she lives with a husband who is a "stranger to me, but I put away his male-smelling underwear" (145). Their apartment is a place of hard edges and shiny new appliances; and Gerald's intelligence is likened to a "beacon" that probes the darkness. Katherine's mother, on the other hand, is associated with images of warmth, softness, and containment. In her daughter's mind she evokes the womb-like image of a "cushioned rocker which is too large for the body but provides, nevertheless, a warm and comfortable harbor" (148). Slesinger contrasts maternal and marital worlds not only sexually but also emotionally and intellectually. Gerald considers Katherine's conversations with her mother "insignificant" (148); to him they are useless "gossip" (150). But Katherine both yearns for and recoils from hours of anecdotal talk with her mother that creates, for the two women, intimately shared patterns of thought.

This daughter's ambivalence reflects the cultural dichotomy she confronts. Now, when Katherine hears herself adopting her mother's way of talking to merchants and servants, she hears simultaneously Gerald's criticism of her mother's simplicity and sentimentalism. At first, she defends to herself her imitations of maternal rituals: they "made doing the things fun. . . . They gave meaning to what would otherwise be just marketing; they formed a link not only with yesterday and tomorrow, but with other women squinting at scales and selecting dinners for strange men to whom they found themselves married" (144–45). But the rituals that order a woman's world—deepening and enriching simple, repetitive individual tasks by linking them to the larger web of female experience—do not belong to the hard, pragmatic, rational furnishings of the value system articulated by Katherine's husband.

Slesinger suggests that Katherine has left home to marry Gerald partly out of her own "growing need of him" (153). The source of that need, however, critiques the conventional psychoanalytic paradigm. In popu-

lar Freudian terms, daughters turn their affection toward their fathers—
and later male surrogates—to define themselves as heterosexuals and to
break the stifling bond with their mothers. Katherine's turning appears
to have less to do with sexual orientation or with breaking a restrictive
mother/daughter bond than with developing her intellectual power. She
admires Gerald's mind; his judgments seem sound to her. She can see,
with him, that her mother really is stout and sentimental—even though
she cannot bear his ridicule of these features.

Unable to reconcile her continuing love for her mother with the rational, judgmental mode of seeing that Gerald represents and that her
culture privileges, her turning is further complicated by a terrible residue of both fear and guilt: "She hated herself for thinking of her mother. But not to think of her demanded a complete uprooting, demanded
a final shoving off from a safe dock into unknown waters. Besides, she
felt guilty toward her mother, she brooded over her as one does over a
victim, pitying him, resenting him and utterly unable to forget him"
(152). Slesinger identifies here not just a daughter's fear of leaving maternal support but also her dread of disloyalty toward the mother, an
anxiety that contemporary feminists recognize as "the most dreadfully
painful problem" (Baruch and Serrano 360–61).[12]

Both the gender and ethnic issues here are very explicit. Slesinger's
Katherine cannot differentiate herself from her mother without repudi-
ating the values that connect them, for the story's culture—like the cultures of traditional Jews and Americans in the thirties—polarizes male
and female values. If she repudiates her mother to conform to Gerald's
judgments, she loses the loving warmth, the power of relatedness that her
mother represents. But if she repudiates Gerald, she gives up an opportunity to improve her cultural status.

As the story defines Katherine's malaise, it shifts the provocation for
leaving home and mother from sexuality to gender. Katherine cannot
grow up to be a man; she can only learn to see women, pejoratively, from
an adult male perspective. Thus, Slesinger demonstrates that repudiat-
ing the mother in a culture that devalues females leads a woman not to
maturity but to the loss of self-respect. Unable to leave home and mother, frantic as she tries to hear both her mother's and her husband's voices, Katherine wishes only that one or the other would die.

Before the war, then, three American Jewish women writers not only
link a daughter's separation from her mother with the erosion of both
ethnic and gender identity but clarify as well the daughter's need to hear

her mother's voice despite the contempt of a culture that devalues women's stories. Ferber and Slesinger create protagonists who can discern in the story of their mothers' lives a legacy that will enrich their own. But in Hurst's novels the mother's story is silenced by death or madness, distorted by submissiveness and rage, or muffled by the listener's own inadequacy. Unlike Slesinger and Ferber, Hurst was never able to sense—beneath the endless materialities that disfigure maternal narratives in a culture that values mothers only as consumers—the unsatisfied hunger that can no longer even recognize its appropriate food. In the theme of leaving home, Slesinger and Ferber portray some of the forces that unravel the mother/daughter bond, as well as some of the needs that braid it smoothly again. But Hurst reveals the fate of the daughter who turns away from her mother's gifts because they appear inadequate or contemptible, only to discover after leaving home that growing up will be impossible without them.

In stories on the theme of leaving home published after World War II, mothers continue to embody, like Hurst's Delilah and Ferber's Molly, the ethnic cultures whose limits they define as well as the gender strengths and handicaps that they, like Slesinger's mother who comes for dinner, transmit. But in the wake of the Holocaust these stories develop more fully the image of the mother as silent victim. Whether she is abused because of her race or because of her gender, she cannot speak the story of her own suffering. Her silence afflicts her children more subtly but no less painfully than the harangues of the comic, overbearing Jewish mothers who populate the stories of their sons.[13]

In Jo Sinclair's *Wasteland* (1946), for example, the silent mother's plight both drives her daughter across the boundary of gender to assume her father's responsibilities and alienates her son, who tries to pass into gentile society. This silent mother, broken by her husband's insensitivity and selfishness, engages the pity of her children. She also starves them emotionally because she is herself sexually and socially famished. Erika Duncan suggests that "the holocaust in all its horror has become the ultimate expression of the violence done to [Jewish women]; the concentration camp, the black barred cage which locks us all from our own nurturance and warmth" ("Hungry" 234). This metaphor is reversed in *The Wasteland*, Sinclair's first novel. Her image of a silent, abused American immigrant mother articulates, in part, the voiceless suffering of the Jews in Europe, whose experience she can hardly grasp through newspaper accounts—for she reads, as she speaks, with difficulty.[14]

The mother's silence is powerful in Sinclair's novel. Like the Holocaust survivor in Philip Roth's "Eli the Fanatic," whose inarticulate wit-
ness to unimaginable suffering draws an assimilated American protagonist into reluctant identification with him, Mrs. Braunowitz's withdrawals
pull her children into identificatory bonds that cramp their own development. Her son Jake, torn with pity for her, enraged at his abusive father, and emotionally deprived by her unresponsiveness, unconsciously
assumes the impossible burden of compensating this wounded mother for
her suffering. Physically bent by this burden and psychically disabled by
shame at his own inadequacy, Jake becomes Jack, casting off his connection to his family as he tries to make his separate way in the gentile
world.

But leaving home is impossible for him. He remains bound by his love
for his mother and by the rituals through which she has expressed her
love for her children. In the food she prepares for the Sabbath meal
(*Wasteland* 15–16), in her whispered blessing as she "prayed [the candles]
into light" (37), and in the cleanliness and order of the Passover celebration, this helpless, silent woman becomes emotionally present to her
son.[15] However severely he limits his contact with the family, however
shameful or confused his feelings about being a Jew, his psychiatrist notices that the family's Jewish practices are "one of his very few possessions of security, stability" (44). He recalls his mother's silence at crucial moments of his life: when his father badgered him into leaving
school, his mother "hadn't said a word, not the picture of one word in
her eyes, on her lips to curve or narrow them" (84). But the comfort of
her concern denied him by her wordlessness exists in the image of her
at home in the kitchen on Friday nights: "There was reason (but God
knows what it was!) only to go home on Fridays, to eat the holiday meal"
(113). Jake thinks he goes home to eat his mother's special Sabbath
foods; in fact, the nourishment she provides in that kitchen is more essential than food to his well-being.

For Jake, his mother is a silent, wounded nurturer who sustains his
identity as a Jew by channeling into her ritual preparations the maternal feeling she cannot otherwise express. The one scene in which she
speaks her love changes entirely Jake's attitude toward himself. As her
husband reads to her in Yiddish the newspaper account of the destruction of the Warsaw ghetto, she assents to the fate of her generation but
demands a kinder destiny for its children: "'All right, all right, I'm glad.
I want to be a Jew. I'm glad. I'll go, a Jew, to my grave. But let my chil-

dren live! Let their children!'" (118). Overhearing this singular, oblique expression of maternal love, Jake conceives for the first time the possibility of relating to her as one adult to another, of growing up within his childhood home rather than leaving it.

Jake's sister's story highlights the wounded mother's effect on the gender, rather than ethnic, identity of her daughter. By assuming "more and more male characteristics," by virtue of her "greater strength and sensitivity" (123–24), Deborah shoulders effectively, like Ferber, her father's burden. She sustains her mother financially and emotionally, working with an analyst to accept both her role in the family and her lesbian identity. She threatens Jake's manhood by assuming male responsibilities and privileges in the family and at the seder table. She confuses him by her boyish appearance. But ultimately she shares with her brother a vision of the future in which both of them become themselves without leaving home.

In a time when Laura Z. Hobson's bestselling *Gentleman's Agreement* (1947) conceived the postwar dilemma of American Jews in terms of social anti-Semitism, Jo Sinclair exposed within the context of Jewish family experience the inward roots of Jewish malaise. She represented that malaise in terms of a child's rage at brutal oppression, a child's shame at its inability to rescue the victim, and a child's need of validation and support that cannot come from those subdued by their own suffering. This cluster of feelings writes large the imbalance of power within yet another immigrant family and identifies fragility and need as powerful, negative "gifts" of a weak, silent, immigrant mother.

There may also be a larger context in which this family dynamic should be read. One historian has suggested that "the sight of the death camps had suddenly made [American Jews] very lonely in the world." Their loneliness, moreover, could not be acknowledged: "The murder of Jews in Europe could not be discussed" because of "possible American complicity, by inaction" (Hertzberg 303). Sinclair's *Wasteland* breaks that silence[16] in much the same way as the protagonists' psychiatric analyses penetrate the silences that brood over their own, festering, personal discomforts. Thus, the novel exposes within a family context, through the reactions of two children to their mother's silent pain, the inexpressible impotence, guilt, rage, and shame that made American Jews feel so lonely as survivors. A later novelist, Lynne Sharon Schwartz, names this disturbing cluster of feelings "criminal innocence." In the Braunowitz children's unmet need for response from their silent mother, moreover, the novel may even suggest the unfinished business of post-Holocaust American Jews, who could never experience "parental" recognition from a European Jewry that had been brutally silenced.

Two other postwar writers are similarly sensitive to the power of parental silence and the need for connection rather than separation between daughters and their ethnically identified mothers. Marjorie Duhan Adler's *Sign upon My Hand* (1964) reads a daughter's attempt to pass into gentile culture as a self-destructive but logical outcome of her relationship to her inarticulate mother. This mother is silenced not by suffering but by her inability to speak acceptable English. Emotionally nourished by a gentle, alcoholic father and a kind, non-Jewish nanny, Adler's protagonist locates in her mother all that is vulgar and hateful to her. Like many women's novels during this decade of rising feminist consciousness, this one blames the mother, depicting what one contemporary analyst has called "a defensive separation process" in which the mother's image absorbs negative features that the daughter would deny in herself.[17]

In Adler's novel the daughter's struggle to separate from her mother is also her effort to leave home as a Jew. From the beginning, this mother defines her daughter as superior to other children. But wealthy Jews and non-Jews reject her when she tries to pass into their society. Thus, she feels both threatened and enlarged by her singularity: "Appearing to befriend me, it could, in a breath reshape itself into my enemy" (25). The novel characterizes both parents as similarly ambivalent about their Jewish identity. Here, the daughter's feeling toward her European Jewish mother becomes an analog for a larger social phenomenon in which American Jews, bent on assimilation and ascension into the middle class, feel both proud and ashamed of the features that distinguish them as Jews, and express both envy and contempt for the non-Jews they adopt as models.

Shame is the most prominent feature of this daughter's striving to be unlike her mother, for her mother's ethnic characteristics become this daughter's dreaded inheritance and fuel her determination to pass into gentile society. Disgusted by her mother's Yiddish accent and social ineptness, she winces at the similarities between them: their deep, translucent eyes full of "inherited remembering" (53), their talent (107), and the name they share (31, 51–52). She recoils each time she understands a Yiddishism uttered by her mother or grandmother (29). In this mother, the reader sees clearly the maternal "other" against whom the growing child must define herself. Scarcely described in any detail, the mother is memorable chiefly for her unruliness. Everything about her challenges boundaries: her black hair escapes its tight knot; she mispronounces words and misplaces verbal emphases; her clumsy "helpfulness" actually subverts her daughter's effort to find a husband; her endless criticisms destroy her daughter's confidence in her own choices.

When this disturbing mother is rendered mute and helpless by the mental illness that accounts retrospectively for much of her unruliness, however, her daughter is drawn toward rather than repelled by her. Silent and powerless, her hair cut short, this mother no longer breaks rules or threatens boundaries. Then the daughter moves forward, into the space created by her mother's withdrawal. After her father's death, she assumes his responsibilities toward her mother, visiting and bringing food. She even yearns for the proficiency in Yiddish that would enable her to speak with her mother's friend in the hospital (227). She credits her mother's encouragement as the source of her own "blind confidence" in her ability (138). She likens her mother's creative talents to her own. And she bonds, in the end, with a survivor of the Holocaust whose silent withdrawals have alienated her in the past (133). The story insists on the solace of continuity between mother and daughter in the image that gives the work its title. In the final scene, as she recites in synagogue the mourner's kaddish, the daughter enjoys wearing her mother's diamond ring, a "sign upon her hand" of multiple, though belated, reconnections (313).

American intolerance of minorities after the war may have intensified the desire of many Jews to pass as individuals beyond the ethnic boundaries that confined their less adaptable brethren.[18] But Adler's novel, like Sinclair's *Wasteland*, exposes both the painful self-destructiveness of that desire and its roots in the insecurities of a family. Both novels, moreover, introduce silent, nonconforming mothers who shape by opposition their daughters' development. Both mothers deviate from conventional norms of maternal behavior: Sinclair's silent mother demonstrates the extreme of compliant passivity, and Adler's—for most of the story—the other extreme of transgressive activity. As if emotional development mimicked the laws of physics, both daughters "leave home" by moving away from their mothers toward equal and opposite extremes of behavior. Unlike her weak, helpless mother, Sinclair's Deborah becomes the financial and emotional mainstay of her family long before her strength is adequate to the task. Adler's protagonist, needing to react against her mother's transgressive energy, subordinates herself to social patterns different from her own.

In the silence of these mothers, one discerns its unexpected power to fix and hold a daughter's attention. By their silence these unconventional mothers bind closely the daughters who would leave them. Perhaps the mother who cannot or will not explain herself cannot be easily understood because she provokes by her singularity feelings that can be neither clarified nor dismissed. And perhaps the confusions and uncertainties that gather around her make her irresistible—like a mystery novel without a final chapter. Daughters of silent mothers in both stories grow up determined to be writers—as if they needed to write the stories their mothers could not tell.

The silence of mothers in these stories may also reflect the daughters' own desires. Jane Gallop, for example, observes that an infant, "imagining that the mother demands symbiosis . . . experiences the drive toward separation as a guilty betrayal of the mother" (318). Thus in part, a daughter's guilt, provoked by her rejection of her mother as a positive model, may mute her mother's story. Gallop also suggests that the child within the maturing daughter cannot tolerate her mother's subjectivity because she wishes her mother to be only "a perfect, selfless mirror" of the child herself (326). Such a daughter's drive to command words, then, may be rooted only partly in the self-assertive impulse to tell her own story—but also partly in old childish guilt, in her fear of retaliation, and in her desire to make reparation to the mother she has silenced.

Two final stories of the eighties on this theme by Lynne Sharon Schwartz make explicit the power of the silent mother, the persistent impulse to leave her, and the power of words to fashion the daughter's story—even to reveal the old guilts, fears, and desires that lie within it. These stories demonstrate a shift in perspective on ethnic issues that differentiates the eighties from earlier decades. Concerned neither with the Holocaust nor with the social anti-Semitism that characterized earlier stories, these two stories of the psychologically enlightened eighties take for granted the continuity of mother and daughter.[19] Schwartz's stories consider the ways in which that continuity remains problematic.

In Schwartz's "Melting Pot" (1987), the protagonist's mother is a murderer, a Mexican immigrant who has stabbed her gentle Jewish husband, killing him while their two-year-old child, Rita, slept in the next room. Like an emblem of transgressive behavior that simultaneously affirms and denies the value of transgressing ethnic boundaries, this mother has first loved and then killed what is unlike herself before she disappears from the story. But the grown-up Rita knows her absent, voiceless mother anyway: "In her [own] bones, her blood, the coarseness of her hair. In some essential, inescapable way, she carries her around" (31). Raised by Jewish grandparents, as different from one another as the gentle Jewish father is from the passionate Mexican mother, Rita knows about unmeltable, irreconcilable differences among people who live to-gether. She knows her grandfather "loves rules, constrictions, whatever narrows the broad path of life and disciplines the wandering spirit for its own good. The lust to submit is his ruling passion. It is part of the cov-enant with God: Obey all the rules and you will be safe" (6). She knows also that her grandmother loves freedom, defies rules, and finds "her iden-tity in opposition" (5). Rita "must run between them, pulled now to the safety of rules and traditions, now back to the thrills of defiance and pride" (11). Sensitized to the potentially murderous frictions of marital union, Rita fears to marry the non-Jewish man she loves. She cannot believe in his love or trust her own. Her mother's crime has taught her to believe only in the "transmutations of love" (17), in endless fluctua-tions between one way of feeling and another. She has learned the in-ability of love to embrace difference.

Incorporating the unruly mother, as it were, within the identity of the protagonist, this story refuses to project upon the mother either pathet-ic or contemptible qualities of "otherness." This mother is simply a wom-an who killed a man she once loved. Her motive is mysterious, her sto-ry unknowable. The feelings she engenders are infinite in their variety. She is the most fully silenced of all these postwar mothers, but her voice-less image is powerfully inhibiting. It fuels her daughter's fear of a dichot-omous world. It drains Rita's confidence in her ability to link different visions and ways of being. It sustains her disbelief in love as a reconcil-er of difference.

This negative legacy appears to differentiate this mother from the mothers in earlier stories, whose ethnic identity threatened their daugh-ters or whose gifts of gender and ethnic continuity could comfort daugh-ters who had lost their sense of themselves as women and their sense of the world as homelike. But like those earlier mothers, Rita's mother is a powerful agent, for better or for worse, of continuity between mother and daughter. Her deviance sustains ethnic particularity by subverting the image of society as a "melting pot" that can erase or fuse ethnic dif-ferences. And her silence enhances her power to determine the way her daughter knows herself and the world. Never affirming, she can neither lie nor be contradicted.

Neither separation nor relation is possible for this daughter, whose mother binds her not by exacting compassion or by commanding obedience but simply by withdrawing into silence and invisibility. Rita lives exclusively within the assumptions of her mother's unspoken story. But in a later novel, *Leaving Brooklyn* (1989), Schwartz returns to this theme, creating a mother who speaks endlessly of her own commitments, who makes explicit all the rules that shape her behavior, who clarifies her expectations of her daughter, and whose capacity for articulating the givens of her own story empowers her daughter to leave home without breaking connection. "Home" in this novel "is a state of mind or perception. . . . One can only live in it or flee" (16). Culturally and historically, it is a Jewish home in Brooklyn of the fifties, in which the mother's voice articulates the prevailing values of the period. She always knows "not only what to do in every situation, but what to feel, too. . . . She knew which feelings were proper for the occasion and which must be stamped out like a brushfire or sponged away before they hardened and set" (17). She teaches the conventional fifties' repression and falsification of improper feelings (Breines 1–24). She represents the common parental expectation (wish?) that children will surpass their parents' virtues (*Leaving* 32). She demonstrates the gender distinctions that separate men and women (36). She argues standards (42), communal cohesiveness (37), "settledness" (43), and superficiality: the shallow truth of "slogans" (13). "She was slow to anger, my mother was, even tolerant, but her vision had clear borders that couldn't be crossed. Once you crossed, there was no tolerance" (105).

By articulating her requirements, this mother admits the possibility of her daughter Audrey's nonconformity. Language itself exposes this mother's rules to interpretation. In her favorite slogan, "To thine own self be true," for example, Audrey can hear both her mother's meaning ("Tell me the truth") and her own: "Be yourself." In this way, this daughter learns to play by the rules her mother articulates. But she also learns "to peer beneath the surface of things," for her mother has, inadvertently, bequeathed her daughter a mode of vision that affords a much larger, very different visual field than her own. One eye damaged soon after her birth—a mishap for which she alternately praises and blames her mother—this protagonist sees differing images of the world with her "bad" and her "good" eyes. Her "banal left eye" remains, obediently, "trained on Brooklyn" (79). But her "bad," wandering eye, "hungry for reality" (69), envisions a sexual adventure that transgresses all the norms her mother

represents. Led by her mother to the office of an eye doctor who is supposed to discipline the wandering eye, this fifteen-year-old protagonist
is instead seduced and sodomized by him. She cooperates fully, enthusi-
astically, in these transgressions of her own and her mother's boundaries,
convinced that by doing so, she extends the "Brooklyn" limits of her self-
image.

Here, as in Slesinger's earlier "Mother for Dinner," a male figure helps
a female protagonist to leave her mother. Like Katherine Benjamin's
husband, the eye doctor's sexual aggressiveness in *Leaving Brooklyn* releas-
es Audrey from inhibitions sustained by her mother's image.[20] Although
both stories render questionable, to say the least, the "romantic" value
of the seductive male figure, both draw as a triangle rather than a dyad
the constellation of forces that act upon female individuation. But in
neither work does this sexual male figure loosen the daughter's strong
bond with her mother.[21] Indeed, in order to place in the mother's—rather
than the father's—hands the liberating gift of self-realization through
identificatory love, Schwartz reverses in her novel the distribution of
characteristics she actually knew in her own family. Her father, not her
mother, possessed the gift of language with which Schwartz most fully
identified: "I clearly live as he did, by the word," she writes in an autobiographical memoir. But in *Leaving Brooklyn*, the mother—not the father or his surrogate—is the linguistic "virtuoso" (Schwartz, "Two Portraits" 37, 41).

Socially conventional and rigid, Audrey's mother is linguistically creative and flexible: "She had a number of finely tuned variations: her
unrefined, serviceable idiom for household use, something more sharply
honed for her friends, and more self-conscious for teachers at school. For
the world outside Brooklyn there was this stylish, subjunctive-laden
mode. Her versatility carried over into Yiddish too" (*Leaving* 101). Her
gift of language renders her thoroughly accessible and interpretable to her
daughter—beyond the obscure emotional ambivalences or hereditary
likenesses endured by the daughters of silent mothers. Remembering her
mother's linguistic virtuosity, moreover, the narrator attributes to it her
own writerly competence: "No wonder I had to master all phases of language later on, and wanted to speak other people's words on a stage, to
become promiscuous in every idiom and escape every sort of purity. And
then others' words proved not enough and I had to learn to speak the
languages of both my eyes and invent other I's to speak through, even
this very I speaking now—to be certain no form of vision was denied me,

and by an alchemy of the imagination, to turn vision into speech" (101–2). Nurtured in a world of words by a linguistically gifted mother but visually empowered by a mother with only limited, literal vision, this protagonist uses her own eyes to see beyond her mother's boundaries and then exploits her mother's gift of words to speak what she has seen.

The power of language to both discover and create the self is, in part, the subject of this novel (73). The limits of that power, however, are also sadly apparent; words cannot enlarge this mother's vision or allow her to see through her daughter's eyes (93). Thus, having learned she can transgress her mother's boundaries in order to differentiate herself, the narrator must also accept her inability to share herself fully with her mother, even though she knows that her mother's gift has enabled her to become herself.

She defines, thereby, both the limits and the costs of differentiation, while she celebrates its successful, but incomplete, achievement. The process of leaving home, she discovers, is always incomplete, for ethnic and gender continuities abide, as does this daughter's residual respect for the boundaries they sustain: "I left Brooklyn," the narrator confesses. "I leave still, every moment. For no matter how much I leave, it doesn't leave me" (145). In the end, this protagonist acknowledges also the moral and emotional ambivalences that may have silenced earlier mothers. Indeed, ambivalence appears inseparable from the process that differentiates daughters from their mothers. Audrey formulates this awareness in words, acknowledging "'how completely and / how deeply faithless we are, . . . / which is / to say: how true we are to ourselves'" (145–46). Thus, even the residue of guilt experienced by daughters who leave home is rendered harmless by finding its way, in this novel, into language.

In the course of the twentieth century, American Jewish women's stories expose both the cultural and psychological sources of children's need to leave home—to sever their ethnic and filial connections. But, as Adrienne Rich understood, the family remains the place "from where [one's] strength comes." In these stories, as Rich knew, the family is a "dangerous" place, full of powerful energies that can protect, inhibit, nurture, and/or empower its daughters. According to her daughters, moreover, the mother who transmits those energies can also shape their effects. Mouthing only the conventional truths that devalue her, she encourages guilt and self-suppression in some daughters, defiance or compassion in others. Silenced by suffering and emotionally withdrawn, she simultaneously alienates and binds some of her children and urges others toward extraordinary, sometimes premature strengths. Muted and distorted in her daughter's memory by cultural bias or filial guilt, she encumbers the daughter who would grow beyond her. But daughters who can hear the often unspoken—often unconscious—maternal expectation that they will replicate their mothers can respond, like Hurst's, Ferber's, Sinclair's, Adler's, and Schwartz's protagonists, by becoming, instead, themselves. Empowered in this process by mothers who are emotionally present and linguistically articulate, some of these daughters even accomplish this task without severing the bond between them. Their stories thus reveal the resilience and flexibility of a connection that endures even after they leave home.

Notes

1. On the mother's role in constructing her daughter's gender identity, see Spieler, "The Gendered Self" and A. Schwartz, "Some Notes."

2. In this respect, these stories differ from those by African American women writers that develop the theme of "passing" largely in terms of racial loyalty. But Jewish writers' sensitivity to ethnic issues within the dynamic of separation may help to explain why their stories differ also from writings on this theme by other American women. The protagonists of these Jewish writers often experience conflict but do not simply "oscillate" between the romantic and the career-centered plots often found and recently studied in other American women's writings. See, for example, Baym, *Woman's Fiction*, and DuPlessis, *Writing beyond the Ending.* "Oscillate" is Hirsch's term in *The Mother/Daughter Plot* (96).

More significantly, these stories shift attention focused by other American women writers on maternal inadequacies of the pre-oedipal period. See, for example, Miner, *Insatiable Appetites;* Radway, *Reading the Romance;* and Juhasz, "Texts to Grow On."

3. Among second-generation New York Jews studied by Moore, pressures to assimilate seem to have created equal and opposite pressures to sustain Jewish identity by tailoring the "physical and institutional environment to make possible an ethnic communal alternative to assimilation" (11).

4. According to Horowitz and Landsman, Ferber "was not only widely read in the United States, but her fiction was translated into at least five foreign languages and distributed world-wide" (69). She produced fourteen novels, one of which won a Pulitzer Prize, eleven collections of short stories, and ten plays. Many of her works were made into Hollywood movies.

Hurst published seventeen novels and, according to some sources, more than three hundred stories (Koppelman, "Educations" 503).

5. "All my life I have been inordinately proud of being a Jew," Ferber wrote, "but I have felt that one should definitely not brag about it. . . . As I grew older and became a woman the feeling was intensified" (*Peculiar* 282).

6. This theme surfaces insistently in Ferber's work. In *Show Boat* (1926), for example, even the gentle daughter of a tyrannical mother is revealed, at the end, to have grown into her mother's likeness.

7. Dearborn names this trope "the Pocahontas marriage." According to her, in Ferber's novels intermarriage loses "some of the contradictory emotional connotations it carries in most ethnic fiction" (*Pocahantas's Daughters* 128).

8. Brandimarte argues that Hurst's successful working women offer readers images of both career satisfaction and punishment for deviating from the conventional domestic pattern of women's lives.

9. Slesinger was married for a time to a member of the *Menorah Journal* group of Jewish intellectuals. For details, see Sharistanian, Afterword; and Wald, "Menorah Group."

10. Hirsch points out that such psychoanalytic speculations went public in this period (101). Benjamin updates feminist psychoanalytic speculation on this image: "I think in American theory the omnipotent mother is much less aggressively tinged. It's a less hostile image, it's less anal, it's less about intrusive control and more around the sense of, my mother ought to be the perfect all-giving all-understanding person, my mother ought to be the one that accepts all of my aggression. . . . We start with a problem of fantasy of the perfect mother, as Chodorow calls it, whereas French theory starts with the fantasy of the all-engulfing, dangerous, archaic, and then anal mother" (quoted in Baruch and Serrano 331–32).

11. According to Koppelman, Slesinger's mother, a psychiatrist, never forgave her for writing this story (*Between* 141). This story formulated, years before Chodorow and Dinnerstein worked out the theory to explain it, a powerful image not of a monstrously obstructive mother but of the self-destructive options afforded women by a culture that defines the mother negatively because it conceives maturity in male, rather than female, terms.

12. In *The Hungry Self*, Chernin also analyzes the guilt-induced, self-inflicted suffering of women who grow beyond their mothers.

13. See, for example, Roth, *Portnoy's Complaint*, and Gold, "The Heart of the Artichoke."

14. Her semi-illiteracy is not unusual. Pratt has discovered that parents, particularly mothers, of many Yiddish women writers in America were "almost illiterate" ("Culture" 131).

15. Given the delicacy and power of this mother's ritual presence, it is hard to understand one critic's assertion that Sinclair possesses "a soul-destroying aversion to Jewish identity" (Chyet 35).

16. According to Federman, Sinclair's work belongs to a pattern in this respect, for "the post-war Jewish writer . . . whether or not he had suffered directly from the Holocaust, found himself [sic] forced to assume responsibility, moral responsibility for the entire history and suffering of the Jewish people" (89).

17. Donna Bassin identifies this process not only in the development of the female child but also in the development of the feminist movement: "In the process of separation and differentiation from Mother, in trying to get outside of her, or out from under her, we denied or disavowed her good aspects as well. This defensive separation process was similar to the little boy's defensive repudiation of his mother in his attempt to genderize himself as male. . . . I think . . . we have now begun to forgive Mother and reclaim her" (quoted in Baruch and Serrano 342).

18. On the comparative social comfort of this postwar period for Jews, however, see also Chametzky, "Main Currents": "By the post-war era the condition of American Jews in America had changed, economically, socially, emotionally. Several decades after the shutting off of unrestricted immigration in 1924 they had moved to a position of a more secure American adaptation, beyond the stage of cultural trauma or arriviste defensive-aggressiveness experienced by the earlier generations. . . . Jews became less working-class, began moving into professional and middle-class occupations in great numbers. There was, too, a general growth in tolerance toward Jews . . . awakened probably by the Nuremberg Trials. Revelations of the Holocaust scarred the nation's conscience. It must be remembered that in 1946, according to the Gallup Poll, anti-Semitism was still extremely high in this country. Thus, acceptance of Jews represented a not insignificant reversal of attitudes" (86).

19. The publication of Adrienne Rich's *Of Woman Born* (1976) and Nancy Chodorow's *Reproduction of Mothering* (1978) fostered awareness of the continuing bond between mothers and daughters as a given of female experience.

20. In *Starting with Serge* (1990), Stone also attends closely to the father's role in female differentiation. Like Slesinger's Gerald and the fathers of Schwartz's Audrey and Schwartz herself, the protagonist's father in this novel is a critical man whose anger confuses and emotionally scars his daughter, but whose affection and approval is also dear to her. Like both Gerald and Schwartz's fictional eye doctor, the protagonist's father-surrogate, a psychoanalyst named Serge, also leads the protagonist into the world of heterosexual experience when he attempts to seduce her. Resisting him, the protagonist loses the benefit of his previous professional helpfulness but ultimately experiences both the liberating insight and the enduring anger that lead her into adulthood. Clearly, further work on fiction and autobiography may help

to clarify what American Jewish women "know" about the part that fathers play in their daughters' development.

21. In Wyatt's terms, these stories honor the oedipal pattern that sets women up for heterosexual romance with seductive, powerful men, separating them from their mothers. They honor also the pre-oedipal pattern in which women develop a "shadowy sense of a self continuous with the world . . . sustained by dim memories from a time of global wholeness before boundaries and difference emerged" (2), a sense of self that knows a continuing bond to its mother.

3

Centering the Devalued Mother: Re-vision and Revaluation

> More than the calf wants to suck,
> the cow wants to give suck.
> —Muriel Rukeyser, "Akiba"

If some Jewish women writers either silence the mother or fail to hear her voice, others manage to let mothers speak for themselves. Overcoming various kinds of resistance,[1] these writers adopt a maternal point of view, move the mother from the periphery to the center of their stories, and clarify the drama peculiar to her situation. In that drama they represent the effect upon women of traditional assumptions about mothering. Thus, their stories draw the figure of the American Jewish mother into what Adrienne Rich has called the work of "re-visioning": the effort to see again, from a new perspective, the cultural imperatives that shape her.[2]

The literary work of revisioning motherhood begins in American women's literature before the twentieth century, with stories like Charlotte Perkins Gilman's "Yellow Wallpaper" (1892) and Kate Chopin's *Awakening* (1899). But the earliest twentieth-century American Jewish maternal protagonists resemble neither the mad and suicidal mothers of these works, nor the mothers in later stories of the Progressive era, who reflect the liberation of the "new woman" from the marital plot and maternal destiny that had long dominated women's lives (Ammons 9).[3]

Stories that center American Jewish mothers in the twenties, however, do have something in common with novels by African American women writers of that period, who were also interested in tracing the effects of middle-class imperatives on women's lives. According to Hazel V. Carby, works such as Jessie Fauset's *Chinaberry Tree* (1931) and Nella Larsen's *Quicksand* (1928) embody *either* a conservative *or* a progressive perspective on the cultural imperatives that they revision (168). American Jewish mothers in literary texts between the wars characteristically try to contain the tension between those perspectives, instead of choosing between them. Centered in their own stories, they also center themselves emotionally and ideologically between cultural imperatives that direct them to serve others and impulses that move them to gratify themselves.[4]

Unlike many of their daughters who sought by "leaving home" to resolve the tension between traditional imperatives and American opportunities, the determination of maternal protagonists to sustain this tension links them to the "tradition" created by nineteenth-century American Jewish women writers and recently described by Diane Lichtenstein. These writers sought first to combine the virtues of American and Jewish womanhood. By the turn of the century, their writing struggled to "balance the claims of traditional and progressive" models of womanhood as their protagonists become more "self-conscious" in their "dedication" to their "own complex" selves (Lichtenstein, *Writing* 128–29).

In the twenties, maternal protagonists are still responsive to traditional imperatives, but their stories also begin to note the costs of that responsiveness. Three stories by Rebekah Kohut, Leah Morton (the pseudonym for Elizabeth G. Stern), and Emanie Sachs, for example, reveal the determination of American Jewish mothers to be faithful to traditions that constrain them. Behind this determination are what Kadia Molodowsky, a Yiddish poet, called the "kosher beds" of the "grandmothers": the generations of European Jewish mothers who knew their own value by their faithfulness to their families, whose service at home and in the marketplace sustained Jewish life in a precarious, often hostile, world. As we have seen, the secondary status of Jewish women in European culture, complicated in America by the withdrawal of married women from the marketplace, devalued their service to their families by comparison first with the prayers and scholarship of men and later with the wage-earning power of their husbands and children. Not surprisingly, then, beside the determination to be faithful to the model of the "grandmothers," the effects on women of devaluation by a patriarchal cultural tradition, analyzed in the years between the wars by Karen Horney and developed recently by feminist psychologists, becomes an important issue in stories that center American Jewish mothers.

One early autobiographical mother/persona, for example, neither acknowledges her devaluation nor recognizes its effects. Indeed, her life and its story testify to the public value, resourcefulness, and power of the faithful, traditional, Jewish mother. But the persona created by this autobiographer tells more than she intends about the ideal of service that dominated her personal and public life. In most respects, Rebekah Kohut's autobiography, *My Portion* (1925), celebrates that ideal. A Jewish woman who lived entirely within a traditional culture as both the daughter and the wife of rabbis, Kohut enjoyed unusual advantages and suffered unusual deprivations. She was educated beyond the norm for Jewish women of her time. Nevertheless, she knew even more pointedly than many other women the obligation to nurture, for in many ways she was responsible for her siblings in an otherwise motherless family. A high school teacher reinforced and extended this early training for motherhood by directing the momentarily rebellious girl to serve not only the family but also the Jewish people, who "needed" her: "There was work to be done in their behalf which was more important than the state of my soul," her teacher insisted (66). Responding to this imperative, Kohut devoted her life to the service of her own family, her husband's family, and the Jewish community.

For Kohut, American and traditional Jewish values overlapped in a clear message, common not only among Jews but also among non-Jewish bourgeois women in late nineteenth-century America. From both cultures, a woman learned to look outward—to the needs of others—rather than inward, to the demands of her own "soul."[5] Encouraged to fulfill herself by enabling men to study and worship,[6] the traditional European middle-class Jewish woman thus experienced in America a further opportunity to devote herself to the service of others. As modern Jewish men turned their attention from study to business,[7] Jewish women—like their non-Jewish counterparts—were encouraged to withdraw from the marketplace, "to restrict [their] activities increasingly to the home and homemaking" (Baum et al. 15; Weinberg 196, 227). But to aspiring middle-class women America also offered an opportunity to expand their caregiving beyond their families, because "philanthropic concern, particularly on a personal level, was considered one of the few activities that might legitimately draw a middle-class woman . . . from her home. Charity was considered an extension of the home and family obligations that women bore, and it became another example of her religiosity and purity" (Baum et al. 30; cf. Kuzmack 27). Thus, like many Jewish wives and mothers who reentered the public world in America through voluntary work for the community, Kohut found in the domestic and social nurturer a culturally acceptable model for her own development.

Kohut was faithful always to this ideal of loving service to others. Her ambition and spiritual generosity flowered in the light of tradition's chief imperative for women. She married a scholarly rabbi nearly old enough to be her father; he was a widower with eight children—his eldest daughter only a few years younger than herself.[8] Imagining her life with him before they married, Kohut was "imbued . . . with the thought of spending myself in service, and in leading a life of significance" (118). "I go to New York," she told her disapproving sister, "to be the wife of a great man and to become a mother to the motherless" (119). By her own account, she served them well. And she took great pleasure in her service to both this family and, later, the larger Jewish community.

But she was also aware—and proud of—her "sacrifices." In them, and in the emotional context that surrounds them in the text, appear small but telling cracks in the smiling facade of this busy persona behind which the tension engendered by the traditional ideal becomes visible. In every case, Kohut's "sacrifices" meant giving up her own gratification for the sake of someone else's comfort. "Thrilled," for example, when she was invited to address the first congress of Jewish women in Chicago, she accepted and wrote an essay. On the night she was to leave for Chicago, however, she noticed that her husband looked "unusually pale. . . . Finally he said, almost with tears in his voice: 'How shall we manage without you for a whole week?' . . . My heart gripped me at his absolute dependence, and his sadness," she reports. After she sent her sister off to the conference to read the essay (181), she "went to my room and wept. The disappointment was keen," she confesses. But her consolation was even keener: "In later years I felt it was one of the finest sacrifices I had ever made for Alexander Kohut" (182).

Oddly, the magnitude of her disappointment rather than the gravity of his need appears to have measured the worth of the sacrifice. As her tradition and her teacher had promised her, she fulfilled herself (acquired "a finer soul") when she set aside her own satisfaction to serve her husband. Yet her tendency to take pleasure in self-denial reveals a dimension of the ideal of womanly service that throws a shadow on the face of its virtues.[9] After her husband's death, for example, Kohut gave up for the sake of her adolescent stepchildren—who "felt neglected" (230)—a school she had labored for years to build. Remembering that sacrifice, moreover, she recalls an even earlier one: "Friends have often wondered," she writes, "whether I did not miss having a child of my own. . . . Were I to have a child of my own, beside these stepchildren, mother love would come between me and the others, I should inevitably show the preference, and the family atmosphere would be inharmonious. So I elected undivided stepmotherhood rather than a divided motherhood" (232–33). In keeping with the ideal of womanly self-denial, Kohut sacrificed both the work she longed for and the satisfaction of bearing children because the needs of others were more important to her than her own. In the text she does not even struggle with these decisions, so thoroughly has she internalized her culture's priorities. She takes pride in what she can give up because her culture encourages her to feel proudest of what she does for others.

Beside the professional and communal achievements that distinguished Kohut's career beyond her family, then, her autobiography also identifies a pattern of motive and response that mark the woman who derives pleasure and pride chiefly from serving others. The work of psychologists on such women's devotion to the service of others begins in this period with Horney and continues, as Marcia Westkott and Janet Sayers have pointed out, to animate feminist discourse on the psychology of women. From her clinical practice in another patriarchal culture, Horney learned that the rewards of service could be deeply mixed. In the early decades of the century, Horney observed that her female patients learned to love serving others from cultures that preferred men to women and that devalued women's needs. Although Horney believed that women learned this lesson from "masculine civilization" (Westkott 1, 6–7), later psychologists identified women's first teachers as their mothers, who "convey to their daughters the necessity to hold their needs in check as a way of helping their mothers and gaining love" (Westkott 135). As adults, these daughters continue to hold their own needs in check, for the habit of not needing, or of needing less than others, is hard to break. Moreover, in a culture that expects women to place others' needs before their own, that habit—as Kohut's autobiography suggests—is fixed for life.

While it was a habit that could produce much good work for others, it could also, according to Horney and others, create a set of weaknesses within the daughter that could trouble her development and her relationships. First among these weaknesses was the lowering of self-esteem that attended the habitual restraint or denial of her own unsatisfied needs. Second, she would be angry at those who devalued—and taught her to devalue—her needs. She would condemn herself for that anger and hide it—even from herself. Exposed, such anger might alienate or destroy others. Hidden, it would make her feel yet more unworthy and unsure of her parents' support.

Finally, Horney argued, as a child's fear of losing parental support triumphed "over her anger, she will defensively turn her anger against herself and will admire the devaluing adults, endowing them with idealized virtues and behaving as they demand in order to hide her own feeling of worthlessness. Thus admiring obedience procures safety by destroying the subjective basis of judgment" (Westkott 136). As the devalued woman-child stifled authentic feelings of desire and anger, she lost the power to feel and to judge, which is born of experience and self-trust. Instead, she would try to feel and think only what could protect her from the loss of approval and support that she feared. She paid a high price for her "safety" as she minimized her own value and exaggerated the value of others.

Ultimately, this process also diminished her awareness of what Horney called her "true self": the self in which authentic longings and judgments are at home. In its place, she developed an "ideal" self calculated to please her parents: obedient, nurturant, stoic, highly sensitive, responsive to the needs of others—and self-denying. She became, Westkott reports, "what her parents—and, later, others—wish[ed] her to be, both to protect herself from the loss of their compensatory 'love' and to protect them from her murderous rage" (138). Instead of learning to recognize and satisfy the needs of her own nature as well as the pleasure of serving others, she would learn to please others so as to make them dependent upon her. In this way she would ease her fear of being abandoned and deny that she was really the worthless, angry person she feared herself to be.

Thus, "female altruism" *appeared* to grow out of strength. But, in cultures that devalue women by giving priority to male activities and male needs, Horney and others believed that a woman's need to serve others was partly rooted, paradoxically, in a generosity that masked weakness. Believing they were not worthy of love, female altruists feel "loved only if they are needed; they have a self only as a reflection of and response to someone else's needs" (Westkott 137). Emotional dependency of this sort could exist even when a woman supported a scholarly husband and a whole family of children. In cultures organized to nurture men, Jean

Baker Miller recently observed, daughters grow up unable to "permit themselves to feel that their actions are for themselves, and thus they translate their own intentions into doing for others" (Westkott 125). When they become traditional Jewish mothers, this displacement is rewarded. What they do for others becomes—as it did for Kohut—a source not only of reassurance but also of personal pride and communal respect.

Neither the pride nor the pleasure of self-sacrifice may satisfy the "true self" of the devalued woman who has lost an awareness of her own needs. Traditional culture sustains her "ideal" self by rewarding her self-denial. But once she begins to question tradition, she experiences intense conflict. Stories by two other writers of the twenties who are more distant than Kohut from traditional Jewish belief and observance make explicit the ways in which this conflict surfaces awareness of individual needs in mothers devoted, nevertheless, to the ideals that have shaped them.

The title of Leah Morton's largely fictive "autobiography," *I Am a Woman—and a Jew* (1926),[10] for example, articulates in each half of its neatly balanced formulation two poles of a single conflict that are exposed but never resolved in this narrative. This conflict becomes central to stories in which American Jewish mothers fulfill themselves chiefly by nurturing others. The inward divisions that split Morton's professional and personal life and fragment her narrative persona rise partly out of the ambience of her time and place. In the twenties, as one historian describes it, "the signs of change and the evidence of struggle between the old and the new were everywhere" (D. Brown 2). As the "'new woman' edged in front of the genteel 'true woman,'" new opportunities for education, for social and geographic mobility, and for self-definition in terms of individual needs challenged powerfully the old, ethnic imperatives and exacerbated the differences between some daughters and their immigrant mothers. While Yezierska's Sara Smolinsky left home to go to college, she also appreciated those differences, taking up the task of translating the world of her mother into the American idiom of her own world. Leah Morton also "left home" and went to college, devoting herself afterward to a professional career. By intermarrying, however, Leah effectively silenced the immigrant mother she loved—who could visit only rarely and never mastered enough English to communicate with her grandchildren.

Morton's story reveals that the roots of her inward conflict rose also out of the patriarchal East European dichotomy that empowered men and devalued women. As a child, the protagonist called Leah learned the traditional cultural imperatives modeled by both her mother and father. She attempted to incorporate both male and female models into her adult persona. From her father she learned to be studious and self-asser- tive (55). Her mother modeled the conventional female values of self- denial and the rendering of service to others—socially, domestically, and religiously: "She lit her candles on Friday night, and she felt she served God in their lighting. She cooked the holiday meals and prepared them for honoring Him. She saved, denied herself even things she needed, to send her children to study Hebrew, that they might speak the language of her God. She gave, from her slender purse, to the poor and fed His children" (311). From this mother, Morton learned the virtue of womanly self-sacrifice in the service of others.

Once Morton resolved to forego the approval of her traditional cul- ture in order to satisfy her own needs, however, traditional gendered imperatives not only conflicted but also confused her as she tried to define her goals. For example, she wanted to become a writer. But, silenc- ing this desire because she didn't feel entitled to satisfy it, she chose in- stead to be a social worker, "to do work for the oppressed, the poor, the hunted . . . to learn how to dedicate [myself] to something as beautiful as charity" (34). Twelve years later, her mistake became obvious: "There is nothing, surely, more disastrous than to choose the wrong profession," she realized (39). Her sense of direction confused as she took her first steps away from tradition, Morton tried, but failed, to honor conflicting cultural imperatives. Imitating her father, she achieved a professional life despite his objections. Like her mother, however, she devoted her life not to the work for which she longed but to the service of others.

The impaired sense of entitlement that allowed Morton to struggle toward but not to realize her own goals—unless they served the needs of others—appears again and again in the course of her narrative. Al- though teaching "was my happiness," she allows her husband's objections to turn her away from it (107). Her self-denial earns her—like Kohut— the pleasure of sacrificing her own gratification to serve another: "Not many things in all my life have been to me what that short moment was when I felt his lean hand on my hair, and heard him thank me for giv- ing up what I enjoyed doing most—to please his male pride," she con- fesses (108).

Unlike Kohut, however, whose acceptance of tradition silenced the troublesome voice of her own desire, Morton acknowledges the existence of two strong inner voices, two opposing versions of self, that cannot become congruent. She resolves their incongruity by asserting the priorities she had learned from her traditional mother. What makes her happy must be secondary; what serves her husband's pride is primary. Service and responsibility to others always come "first of all" for her, as for her traditional mother. But her distance from the culture that reinforced these priorities and made them spiritually significant denies her the reward her mother enjoyed. Now she appears simply to prefer subordinating rather than satisfying her own needs.

One large step away from the role tradition ordained for her, this maternal protagonist holds fast with one hand as she lets go with the other. She gives up traditional observances and behavior; she leaves behind family, faith, and culture; she relinquishes communal approval and the spiritual confirmation offered to self-sacrificing Jewish women by their tradition. She achieves considerable success in the world. But, hampered by the traditional devaluation of Jewish daughters, now reinforced by middle-class American ideology, she cannot validate her own needs or pursue without conflict her own goals. She cannot become aware of—much less express—anger at her husband's restrictions and derogations. Instead, she turns her efforts toward service to others. She becomes a powerful administrator of a large social service organization, but she will always have to protect her professional image by keeping it separate from her life at home (268).

Sustaining throughout her life this conflict between two incompatible selves, Morton sustains as well the tension between her determination to reject traditional Judaism and yet remain a Jew. Her father's death reminds her that she is connected to the Jewish people even though she has married a non-Jew and will not "practice [Judaism's] precepts and its faith" (288). Although she has raised her children virtually innocent of any knowledge of their Jewish heritage, she is hurt by her son's denial of his Jewish identity (358). She cannot identify with other Jewish women in New York (347), but she insists on being recognized as a Jewish woman. Resisting to the end the ritual practices that belong to Judaism, she accepts "its history, its psychology" as her own (361). She knows she is a Jew "before everything. Perhaps not in my work or in my daily life. But in that inner self that cannot change, I belong to my people," she declares (362). Thus negation, as always in this memoir, is the companion of affirmation. Neither fully subordinated as a traditional Jewish wife and mother nor fully liberated as a professional American woman, neither pious believer nor rebellious agnostic, Morton manifests as both woman and Jew the deep, inward divisions that attend the Jewish mother's first steps away from the imperatives that shaped her.

Emanie Sachs's *Red Damask* (1927) explores an even more intense conflict created by cultural imperatives that deny its protagonist both work and love. Like Nella Larsen's *Quicksand*, this novel writes large the impossibility of individual self-realization for a woman bound by conventional imperatives. But, like Jessie Fauset's *Chinaberry Tree*, Sachs's novel also validates, to some extent, its protagonist's devotion to the imperatives that bind her. Most important, this novel analyzes both the effects of traditional loyalties upon the Jewish family and the cultural dynamic that defined middle-class women as nurturers and consumers.

In order to clarify the forces that act upon its protagonist, *Red Damask* looks as closely at the world of wealthy German Jewish immigrants as at the quest of its beautiful daughter, Abby Hahl. The image evoked by the title becomes a metaphor for the intricate patterns that not only decorate the walls, curtains, and furniture of this world but also suggest the elaborately interwoven social and familial pressures that create its structure and enrich its texture. Explicitly patriarchal, this world is dominated by Abby's grandfather. He is "majestic, powerful, a human engine fused to fight for the juice it ran on" (373). He controls the destiny of all his offspring and, to some extent, their mates and children. Abby envies him "the thrilling certainty that he was significant to something he considered significant" (373). His devotion to the ideal of "family solidarity" becomes the dominant value of the family.

Sacrifices exacted by this ideal are justified, for Abby, partly by the disappearance of religious ritual and belief from her world. With "no habitual religious responses, smoldering from childhood," Abby is chilled by a rabbi's "abstract holiness" and a synagogue service "not fervent enough to light new fires" (91). But residual religious fervor, "inherited from rabbinical ancestors, made her want to be good for the sake of being good. Denied its mystic outlet, it put emotion into her conduct; it flowed into dreams and ideals. Fighting her energy, fighting her brain, sometimes it betrayed them; sometimes it was betrayed" (2). In this world, then, religious feeling flows into a desire to "do the right thing" (33), and "any need for ritualism was filled by . . . family life" (2).

As family life absorbs the spiritual energies of its devotees, however, it becomes a patriarchal "tyranny" (193). Reckoning the sacrifices exacted of her relatives, Abby realizes that "her family thought they were gods, trying to create children in their own images." Often in the novel, she

retreats guiltily from this insight (60). Several times she grasps the understandings that might liberate her from the pattern imposed by her
family, but duty, gratitude, loyalty, and fear weaken her grip on these
revelations. Although she is capable of conceiving "a world where no
words guided your way . . . a difficult world in which you couldn't stop
thinking" (351), she is unable to enter that world. She moves briefly
toward the dazzling pleasure of work she loves (39–40) but gives it up
when her family belittles it as selfish and unpromising. She falls in love
with an East European Jew but gives him up when his rebelliousness
threatens her idealization of her family. Trained to "obey her teachers"
(38), raised by a childlike mother who follows "every herd formula" (274)
and doesn't "believe in praise" (42), encouraged to doubt that women's
work can succeed in the world (31), and guided always toward her "duty
to others" (32), Abby falters and withdraws from every insight that would
liberate her from the repetitive pattern that decorates, insulates, and
dominates her world.

As she succumbs to that pattern, the novel explores the disappointments and defeats that mark the path of her submission. Her marriage
contaminated by her husband's conventional assumptions about women's
sexual passivity, she renounces desire (262–63), sleeping at last in "a
narrow, nunlike bed, made from an old oak chest, on which carved mer-
maids, forever stranded, wept on chiseled cliffs" (318). Her philanthropic
work subverted by the indifference of those she serves, she retreats to the
nursery. Her efforts to mother frustrated both by her own natural impulses (239, 244) and her inability to "assert her adulthood" (248), she relinquishes her daughter's care to a professional. Her attraction to a married, non-Jewish architect obstructed by her faithfulness to the "kosher
beds" of the "grandmothers," she turns away from adulterous romance as
she has turned away from marital love, philanthropy, study, and training
for a career.

Each new disappointment illuminates the hollowness of the ideals for
which she has sacrificed herself. Disappointments also illuminate her
"real" self beneath the beautiful clothes, social rituals, and dutiful behavior of her "ideal" self. In fact, she is amorphous, unformed, uncertain, full
of incompatible possibilities (68, 159)—all of them unrealized. She turns
the talent that might have made her a successful architect or designer
toward the intricacies of dress and domestic acquisition appropriate to
women of her class. She turns the energy that sought outlet in work toward romantic and maternal fantasies, blaming herself for the intensity

of feeling that then threatens her husband and unnerves her child. She feels the narrowness of the channel into which the pattern set by class and culture has directed her. Eventually she blames "the family for teaching her that 'helping others' was your first high duty, something you could hold to, no matter what failed. . . . Having guideposts recede when you needed them made you doubly lost. If she hadn't counted on them, she might have found her own way" (271).

The novel suggests, however, that beside Abby's belief in her "duty" to others she harbors both a powerful need for activity and a moral code, which transcend her own personal interest.[11] The narrator punctures Abby's credulous illusions about duty to her family, her tendency to mix "moods with morals" (60), and her "need of love" (100). But her love for her child, her persistent longing for "an aspiration to tie to, greater than oneself" (229), and "her amazing energy, her eternal habit of finding future faiths" (294) are validated by the narrator. These traits dignify Abby and set her apart from other women in the novel who amuse themselves in trivial or devious ways to offset the empty repetitions of their lives. When Abby's heart, like theirs, "ached with spring," when her "mind ached with servants' squabbles," she cannot still her pain as other women might—by taking a lover or buying a new hat. She needs spiritual, not sensual or material, gratification.[12] Her inability to satisfy this need within a culture that discourages religious fervor and professional development in its mothers creates the impasse in which her life is deadlocked—like the line that always turns back on itself in the red damask that surrounds her.

These stories of the twenties, which center and revision the experience of American Jewish women after they marry and become mothers, emerge from a historical moment in which the conflict between disparate needs can be seen but not resolved. Irreconcilable cultural, individual, and spiritual imperatives confuse mothers who need to be affirmed as obedient, dutiful, self-sacrificing Jewish women but who crave as well other satisfactions that begin to surface as they leave the framework of traditional Jewish life. In the two decades after World War II, novels by Hana Stein, Jo Sinclair, and Violet Weingarten assess the effects of that departure. One mother begins to see for herself the cost of compliance with tradition. Two others confront the ways in which their defenses against devaluation distort and drain meaning from their lives.

In Hana Stein's *Wedding* (1950), the situation of the maternal protagonist owes as much to the imperatives of postwar America as to the givens of Jewish tradition. During the war, as Susan M. Hartmann has observed, "the new public images of women designed to evoke their contributions to the national effort did not subsume the ageless ideal of woman as wife and mother" (163). In the 1940s, "marriage became the central feature of women's lives," the "key to female happiness," for "psychologists insisted that women could enjoy mental health only through dependence upon a man" (164). Cultural pressures that made marriage imperative, however, also "made wifehood and maternity . . . more psychologically stressful" (166). More exacting models of wifehood "focused responsibility for marital success upon women. That success, moreover, required conformity to such traditional ideals of womanhood as dependence, submissiveness, and self abnegation" (169). Thus, the culture's concern for the comfortable reintegration of men returning from the war reinforced the image of women as powerful—but always subordinate and self-denying—nurturers of others.

Simultaneously exalted and devalued as wives, American women of the late forties also found their maternal roles "more demanding and emotionally taxing" (Hartmann 176). In the twenties, behaviorists had warned that "mother-love" was a "dangerous instrument." Social commentators and psychologists of the forties developed that charge, blaming mothers for the weaknesses of their children and also making it impossible for mothers to avoid blame by correcting their behavior. Experts offered contradictory advice: one extraordinarily popular work warned mothers "against excessive involvement in their children's lives" but also criticized mothers who attended to themselves or cultivated their own interests outside the family (176–77). As theories of permissive childrearing became increasingly popular in the late forties, moreover, mothers' needs were subordinated even more drastically, for "permissiveness required self denial of women," making them secondary not only to the needs of their children but also to the injunctions of the child-care experts. Women were told to "subordinate their own needs for rest, [and] for . . . pursuing nonfamilial interests, and to do so 'with a deep sense of satisfaction and happiness'" (178). Thus, after World War II, American mothers were forbidden not only to have needs but also to mind their denial and devaluation.

Stein's protagonist confronts and reacts against these cultural givens even as she attempts to honor traditional Jewish values that reinforce them. She demonstrates the effects of devaluation. She also manifests a surprising, new capacity for individual choice that develops in American Jewish maternal figures in postwar stories, moving them beyond the deadlock of the twenties. Lacking any identity beyond her function, the protagonist/narrator of this novel is always "Mama" or "*tante* Peppy." A widow entirely enclosed by traditional expectations, enmeshed in the needs of her fatherless family of daughters, Mama will address in the course of the novel the conflict between her "admiring obedience" to the Jewish law that devalues women's needs and her own capacity to satisfy her daughters—and herself.

Like Kohut and Morton, Mama speaks for herself. Unlike them, she allows the anxieties, self-repressions, and guilt that lie beneath the staunch and smiling persona of a devalued, self-sacrificing Jewish mother to dominate her story. Taught by the experts that she is responsible for the well-being of husband and children, this mother blames herself for her husband's death from pneumonia (5), for thinking about the unhappiness of one daughter on the wedding day of another (14), even for the desertion of her older daughter's husband (7). The catalog of her "sins" writes large her readiness to imagine that her unworthiness hurts those who depend upon her. She feels dangerous to them. Fearful always that she will harm rather than help, Mama's perception of the world demonstrates the ways in which anxiety thickens the air around a devalued woman.

In part, this wide-ranging guilt may mirror such a woman's unconscious awareness of her own devaluation and the unacknowledged anger it has provoked. Mama's self-image, however, also reveals her to be a woman devalued by Jewish tradition. Forbidden because she is a widow to give away her daughter-bride (60), taught that because she is a woman her prayers will not ascend to God's ear (7), convinced that her vision of her children's needs cannot equal her husband's (119), this woman has clearly listened well to the devaluing messages of her culture. And she transmits those messages to her younger daughters: she tells them not to ask for the gift they really want, insisting that they content themselves with whatever they are given (4).

Mama habitually stifles not only her daughters but herself, doubting that she can do anything but harm if she acts or speaks freely. Afraid, perhaps, that the negative feelings aroused by her devaluation may turn her most loving impulses against her children, she courts silence. When she wants to scream in panic, "she did not scream after all. Only the heart had screamed inside of her" (168). When a "torrent of words, thoughts, and emotions" rushes "to her mouth," she puts "up her hand to stop them" (22). Thinking one thing, she says another, believing "the truth should be stifled at any price" (119). Although she worries ceaselessly about mishaps that might spoil her daughter's wedding day, she will not speak her feeling.

Believing herself inadequate and rendering herself inarticulate, Mama turns repeatedly to the thought of God. Before God's might, her sense of powerlessness is comforting (25). As a devalued child adopts an attitude of "admiring obedience" toward the parents whose power she depends on, this woman holds fast to the Jewish God who, she believes, has made her a widow and left her deserted daughter an *agunah*—a woman bound to an absent husband. The laws of this God deprive her of power and status but require her compliance and respect, and she obeys.

Even against her daughter's bitterness toward the law of the *agunah* that forbids her to marry again without her husband's consent, Mama argues the wisdom and the goodness of "admiring obedience" to that law. Her daughter Molly wants to marry again without religious sanction, but Mama insists, "An animal does what it likes to do and when it likes to do it, so we tie it with rope and put it in a cage; but people have to be controlled for their own and the next one's happiness. You think the rabbis made the Law to hurt? They meant to save the home" (62–63). In such a way, as Horney understood, the devalued woman transforms— and tries to teach her daughter to transform—anger into admiration of the authority that opposes her.

But this mother is capable of insight and change as well. As she argues, her sensitivity to Molly's despair conflicts more and more urgently with the advice she presses on her daughter. In the end, as she watches Molly withdraw from argument and slip numbly into a "sudden denial of living" (235), Mama subordinates Jewish law to her daughter's need: "'If you marry, I will stand by you,'" she says (246). At first, Mama is terrified of the consequences: "She had never felt so forsaken in all her life. She seemed to be a heap of ruins and memories" (247). Ultimately, she rationalizes her decision, discovering in herself not only the pleasure of serving her daughter but also the sudden, joyful expectation of satisfying herself. When the novel ends, Mama is thinking of the suitor who wants to marry her. She discovers that her "longing was stronger than anything else. She needed him more than she had ever needed anyone in her life" (250). Responding to her daughter's need has validated her own—beneath the old habits of self-denial, silence, and admiring obedience to traditional imperatives.

A woman who insists that she and her daughter both "need" male mates conforms to both traditional Jewish thinking and the prevailing American female image of the 1940s. From the rabbinical period[13] onward, Jews assumed that women were more eager than men to marry (Gafni 15). But in asserting Molly's and her own needs as priorities beyond the strictures of the Law and the disapproval of the Jewish community, Stein's Mama reverses the traditional bias of her judgment and changes her pattern of behavior.

This mother's capacity for decisive self-assertion appears particularly refreshing after the irresolutions of the twenties and thirties. But in another postwar novel, maternal strength and self-assertiveness appear to be stigmatized by anxieties very common in the fifties. *Anna Teller*, by Jo Sinclair (the pseudonym for Ruth Seid), critiques to some extent cultural imperatives of the fifties that drove women into traditional nurturing roles to keep them from competing with men in the workplace and to insure their service in the family as guardians of traditional values (Kaledin, preface). Against the threat of communist infiltration and the erosion of cultural norms, the family appeared as a kind of fortress. While some women, as Eugenia Kaledin argues, "found strength" in the "separate but equal" sphere of home and family (Kaledin, preface), that strength became problematic because Americans worried also in this decade about the growing "convergence" of gender roles. In a time when veterans were being transformed into organization men and becoming less autonomous and more dependent on the approval of others, Americans felt a "deep anxiety about masculinity" that became "closely linked with fears of female strength" (Breines 33). Despite the insistent fears of male social scientists of the fifties (e.g., David Reisman) that men were becoming more like women, however, gender roles in this period were not actually converging. Although girls, like boys, were "prepared in school for a career," a girl earned the "full stamp of cultural approval only if she later achieves [sic] husband and children" (quoted in Breines 35). But the fear of women's strength persisted.

Even in the sixties, such fear surfaces in social scientists' anxieties about the figure of the strong, black "matriarch" who headed, like Stein's Mama, her own household. Daniel Patrick Moynihan described her in his 1965 report as "all-powerful, domineering, sexually permissive, and aggressive." In what historians have called the "flawed and even racist social theory" of the sixties, such women were believed to deprive men of their "self-respect," creating what Moynihan labeled a "'tightening tangle of pathology'" (quoted in Linden-Ward and Green 404). In 1971, Maya Angelou argued that the "formidable" adult "American negro female" was "an inevitable outcome of the struggle won by survivors and deserves respect if not enthusiastic acceptance" (quoted in Linden-Ward and Green 405). Sinclair's *Anna Teller* (1960), published a decade earlier, anticipates Angelou's argument by creating a formidable European Jewish mother who heads her own family and survives the Holocaust. But Sinclair's image is also contaminated by the fear of pathology such a figure excited.

Like her earlier story, *The Wasteland,* Sinclair's novel defers to reigning psychological pieties, like the persistent Freudian assumption that healthy women should be gentle and sensitive and should accept behavioral norms rather than rebel against them (*Anna* 384–85). The novel also scrutinizes the ways in which Anna's "formidable" strengths react not only against the murderous hostility she attracts as a Jew but also against the devaluation she has suffered as a woman.

Anna continues the European model of the strong, practical Jewish woman who sustains her family even though she has lost any sense that her actions serve God or a believing community. Fully secular in her behavior and ambitions, Anna betrays only once the felt emptiness of a life without God. When, for one moment in a European refugee camp, she yearns to pray, "her queer behavior made her flush. That is enough, old woman, she thought. Busy yourself at once. The old patterns were still the safest. She had always been able to find answers for herself" (468). Work and self-sufficiency substitute for religious belief in a reactive pattern that characterizes her throughout the novel.

Yet she will ultimately discover the "wordless choke of inferiority" (282) behind the "old patterns" that feel safer to her than religious belief. Like other devalued women who cultivate others' need for their services, Anna literally binds others to herself by nurturing them. A widowed Hungarian peasant and mother of four small children, she builds a farm and mill to grow the food and grind the grain that will sustain her dependents and neighbors. Later, she runs a bakery. And later still, a refugee in America, her passionate giving and growing of food reveal themselves as "old weapons long outdated" (282) in her battle to secure the regard she is never sure she deserves.

Maternal nurture used as a defense against devaluation is peculiarly contaminated in this novel by the pathology it provokes. Anna has spoiled the lives of two children—now dead in the Holocaust—and

alienated a third, the eldest son, who has emigrated to America. Anna
names the sources of this pathology in herself. First, acquisitiveness: "the
insistence about money and frugality" that led one son to his death during the Nazi occupation. Second, control: "the opportunistic clutch on
anyone and anything usable" that arranged the marriage of her daughter to a man who fatally betrays her (282). She even discovers the source
in herself of a quality that has preserved her but poisoned her relationships: her tendency to withhold emotional response. Strong and beautiful as a young woman, she learned to excite love without satisfying it,
"to use love without paying much for it" (17). She does not see until the
end how this strategy corrupted her relationship with her children even
as it helped her to feed and control them.

Proud, much admired, apparently triumphant in her strength, Anna
becomes a paradigm of the woman who chooses what Horney called "the
quest for power, prestige, and possession" as a way of "obtaining reassurance against anxiety" (162). Like many of her predecessors in this literature, Anna has learned as a woman and a Jew to doubt her own worth.
Unlike the mothers who respond to self-doubt by pursuing what Horney
called "the quest for affection," Anna has striven instead to possess others
by dominating them. Her strategies sustain her and many others during
the Nazi and Soviet occupations. But the anger and anxiety that lie beneath Anna's powerful facade declare themselves when she is reunited
in America with her surviving son. Now, when she attempts to ingrati-
ate herself with others, she discovers she has "lost her gift of talking to
people. Uncontrollable tones leaped into her voice. So abruptly that she
felt sick at heart, she was saying something derogatory, making someone
small; she, who had always selected words that drew people close, made
their eyes shine, impelled them to ask her advice" (281). Her defenses
weakened by the stresses of age and dislocation, Anna begins in America to question her old strategies of survival. Through Anna's increasing
malaise and through the bitter alienation of her American son, Sinclair
explores the dangers inherent in the quest for power, possessions, and
control that would compensate for what Horney called a devalued woman's "crushed self-esteem."

Like the other side of a pair of brackets, Violet Weingarten's *Mrs.
Beneker* (1967) demonstrates the futility of what Horney called the compensatory "quest for affection." This protagonist manifests a curious, trou-
bling combination of devaluing influences left over from the fifties and
spiritual longing that would not find political expression among Jewish

women until the seventies. Mrs. Beneker is stranded, as it were, on a watershed between a culture that insisted women must be "submissive, dependent, emotional, and subjective" (Kaledin 184), that bound and secured women in "domesticity in its most extreme forms" (Kaledin 185), and a culture in which feminists were reconceptualizing and revaluing women and Jewish feminists were demanding equal access to the study of texts and the performance of communal worship that had long offered spiritual validation to Jewish men. Mrs. Beneker is a relic of the fifties in that she values herself chiefly as a wife and mother. But she also presages the seventies by taking courses in comparative religion to satisfy her spiritual hunger. Devalued both by cultural pressure to efface herself in her roles as wife and mother and by parental criticism (203), this protagonist bears no name but her husband's. Without a voice of her own, she depends on a narrator both to overhear the words she thinks but never speaks and to tell her story.

As the novel revisions the forces that shaped Mrs. Beneker and her futile defenses against them, it also reflects the shift in the sixties toward acceptance of "sexual pleasure as a legitimate, necessary component" of a man's life, "unbound by older ideals of marital fidelity and permanence" (Linden-Ward and Green 377). As the divorce rate "climbed significantly in the sixties" (Linden-Ward and Green 401), women like Mrs. Beneker, who had proved their healthiness by conforming entirely to the marital and maternal roles they played, confronted the possibility of their husbands' faithlessness and the reality of their own dependence upon them.

> She could not leave. To begin with, she had nowhere to go. . . . What would she do with herself? Baby-sit for Norah? Move up to Cambridge and keep house for Tommy? Take care of her mother and father? (How could she possibly explain to her parents? It would break their hearts.) She could get a job, she supposed, but alas, any job that would have her, after all these years, she wouldn't want. . . . Marry again? Who? It was unlikely that she could do better than Mr. Beneker, most probable that she would do a lot worse—*if* she did at all. (70)

Entirely dependent on a marriage that gives both her and the novel a name, Mrs. Beneker learns—like Anna Teller—that "an unmarried woman stood for nothing" (*Anna* 12). Fidelity to the "kosher beds" of the "grandmothers," however, cannot now secure a husband, whose loss threatens a woman's own identity.

Feeling, like Stein's Mama, inexplicably and pervasively guilty (115, 132, 141) though she is innocent of offense against her husband and children, Mrs. Beneker becomes religious. Alienated from Jewish prayer and practice (132), she prays to strange gods and studies comparative religion at Columbia University. But there she learns to see her need of God as "a panic reaction. It comes when a man [*sic*] with nothing to believe in finds himself helpless" (193). Mrs. Beneker's "helplessness" is also partly self-determined. Unlike Anna Teller, who earns the nickname "General" because she fights Nazis, Mrs. Beneker uses her energies primarily to stifle herself both verbally and emotionally (10, 11, 143). "The deeper her feelings," the narrator observes, "the more her words became all thumbs" (52).

Having raised her children in the "permissive forties" (27), she has learned to efface herself so as to leave them free to feel. When her daughter asks what childbirth is like, Mrs. Beneker remembers, "in the midst of a tidal wave of pain," a sudden "great joy, the exhilaration of realizing that every single being ever born had come to life this same way, that she was sister to every woman who had ever lived and was yet to live." But only the narrator overhears this recollection. Mrs. Beneker merely says, "It's really terribly interesting, at least the first time" (53–54). "It was Norah's baby, not hers," she silently reminds herself; "she was going to keep out of it. As was proper" (51). Fearful of influencing her daughter, she silences her own powerful insight, taking "comfort in the hope that her children were free to seek out their own feelings" (53), uninfluenced by their mother.

This mode of mothering by self-effacement not only stifles her voice but also confuses her messages to her children. For example, although she has always affirmed her daughter's needs, she withholds both sympathy and support when Norah, a woman of the sixties, refuses to subordinate her own professional ambition to the needs of her child and husband. Such maternal complicity in the circumstantial frustration of daughters is a long-standing feminist grievance.[14] In part, as Stein's Mama demonstrates, that compliance reflects a devalued mother's "admiring obedience" toward the forces that dismiss women's needs. Weingarten's novel complicates that insight, however, by suggesting that even a mother who does not devalue her daughter may ally herself, nevertheless, with the forces that shape women into devalued mothers. Ambivalent about her own entitlement to satisfactions deeply desired but denied her by conceptions of gender and role prevalent in the fifties, Mrs. Beneker experiences an inner conflict that prevents her from speaking with a single voice. Wanting her daughter to satisfy herself but believing also that—as a mother—her daughter will have to consider first the needs of others, Mrs. Beneker knows incompatible truths. She has developed what Marianne Hirsch has called the "double or multiplied [maternal] consciousness" (165) that accounts for the mixed messages and several voices in which mothers speak to—and confuse and alienate—their daughters.

Mrs. Beneker alienates not only her daughter but also her son's angry girlfriend, who pierces the mask of submissive maternal affection by verbalizing its effects: "'You make yourself into a doormat and force people to step on you, and then when they do, you make them feel so guilty they're paralyzed. Everyone is always terrified they'll hurt your feelings,'" she complains. As Mrs. Beneker acknowledges that she has never learned to "get angry" (155), she discovers, like Anna Teller, the futility of her defenses against devaluation. The novel thus demonstrates that what Horney called the "quest for affection" is as ineffective against devaluation as the "quest for control." A devalued woman cannot secure, even by fidelity, endless patience, or generosity, the love that her self-esteem depends upon.

· · ·

Like needles that probe for the splinter in the flesh, these stories that center the mother become for Jewish women instruments of discovery. They expose the condition of mothering women, laying bare the assumptions that disable their self-esteem. Maternal narrators before World War II reveal the givens of their own devaluation as effectively as the silences of Anna Teller and Mrs. Beneker, after the war, reveal maternal failures to overcome it. Their silences also testify powerfully to the pain and rage that complicate a mother's care of others and demonstrate her faithfulness to imperatives that obscure her own needs. In the hands of other postwar writers, moreover, stories move beyond the work of exposure, as Tillie Olsen and Grace Paley attempt not only to revision the devalued mother but also to revalue her and to develop her voice.

Historians often identify the sixties as the decade of the women's movement because of the 1963 publication of Betty Friedan's *Feminine Mystique*, which formulated the malaise of middle-class mothering women for the first time as a social, rather than psychological, problem. But Beauvoir's *Second Sex* had appeared in English translation in 1952, and stories by Tillie Olsen and Grace Paley, in which mothers found their own voices and spoke their own malaise, also began to appear at the end of the fifties. Beauvoir, Olsen, and Paley figure as harbingers of the reawakening of masses of American women to their own needs and their own situations—a reawakening of energy as well as consciousness that surged through the next two decades.

According to Leila Rupp and Verta Taylor, the period "from 1945 to the mid-1960s" was "a particular stage of the women's rights movement that survived from the suffrage struggle of the early decades of the century to connect with the resurgent movement of the 1960s" (vii). Olsen and Paley are clearly indebted to this movement—if only because it made their early stories visible and buoyant: "It was a wave that came and carried us upwards," Paley says, "and gave us a chance to be seen and heard" (quoted in Isaacs 114). But as Paley acknowledges, "the *influences* on me happened long ago" (Isaacs 117). For both Paley and Olsen, those "long ago" influences can be traced to what Bonnie Lyons called the "radical Jewish background" in which both writers grew up (89).

According to Erika Duncan, there was never a time when Olsen "didn't have a first hand knowledge of oppression and revolutionary tradition." Her parents had fought against the Russian czar; in America her father became state secretary of the Socialist party ("Coming" 209). In the thirties, at age eighteen, Olsen joined the Young Communist League (211). By the time she encountered the work of her "literary foremother," Rebecca Harding Davis, she was already long familiar with "working class hardship" and the frustrations peculiar to women (Kamel 57). Most important, from her early experience of socialist oratory, as well as her later experience with literary texts like Davis's *Life in the Iron Mills,* Olsen knew the power of the human voice and the terrible pain of its stifling. She knew that some voices moved the great economic and political wheels that made the world go round, but she also knew that "literary history and the present are dark with silences" (*Silences* 6). Her first stories draw out of one of those dark silences the voice of the working-class mother. In "Tell Me a Riddle" (1956), Olsen enables one such mother to hear her own voice. In this story, *her* need and anger appear to reflect Olsen's long acquaintance with oppression, rebellion, and the frustration of working-class women.

Many voices complicate Olsen's "Tell Me a Riddle," for the mother's voice is not single or unified. In order to clarify it, Olsen needed to listen also to her husband, her children, and her past. Thus, listening becomes one theme of the story, as its maternal protagonist, grown hard of hearing, tunes in and out the sounds of her life, exercising a new power to choose among the claimants for her attention. Having lived for others since her revolutionary girlhood in Russia, this working-class, immigrant mother knows well "the long drunkenness; the drowning into needing and being needed" (*Tell* 93). "Immolated" for most of her life in the "passion of tending," she struggles in this story to hear beyond others' needs the voice of her own past that can unriddle the meaning of her life.

Her effort to hear herself within the hum and buzz of other needy voices reflects Olsen's preoccupation with the circumstantial silencing of women's voices and creates the conflict that directs the story. As Eva turns down her hearing aid to ignore her husband's demands, she also withdraws from traditionally imperative interactions with her children and grandchildren. After surgery for cancer, she will neither tend, feed, nor touch her daughter's new baby. She rejects the noises of superficial talk and television, wanting only to hear music and listen to the past.

The energy that enables her to reject others' claims on her attention is generated partly by anger. The voice of maternal anger, long silenced in the narratives of devalued mothers, becomes clear for the first time in this story. When her husband refuses to stay with her in the evening, she rages wonderfully: "After him she sobbed curses he had not heard in years, old-country curses from their childhood: Grow, oh shall you grow like an onion, with your head in the ground. Like the hide of a drum shall you be, beaten in life, beaten in death. Oh shall you be like a chandelier, to hang, and to burn" (83). When he would send her to die in the hospital, she fights him: "'Weakling,' she taunted, 'to leave me there and run. Betrayer. All your life you have run'" (115). Remembering in the course of the story his long indifference to her needs, noting also his "old habit . . . of parading the queerness of her for laughter" (104), she speaks, for the first time in this literature, the anger of the devalued woman.[15]

Anger and the determination that her own needs be considered give color and resonance to this maternal voice as Olsen's protagonist moves beyond denial and futile defenses against devaluation. Her withdrawal from those who betray her or obstruct her final quest isolates her so that she may "journey to her self." That withdrawal allows her to recall the child, the revolutionary girl, the neglected wife, the devoted mother she has been. It also guides her anger toward targets other than herself and unifies her voice, drawing love and pain, memory and song into a mode of discourse as powerful as a poem. Deliberately self-centered in this last phase of her life, yet devoted still, like all her predecessors, to the ideal of nurturing, Eva defies devaluation with this voice and uses it to resist— rather than admire or obey—those who would move her, again, to a subordinate role in the family story.

Her voice, actually a composite of the different voices she has needed to sing, weep, instruct, and rage, achieves dignity and coherence as her recovery of past selves discloses the logic of her life. She has rejected the religious tradition in which the ideal of caring for others was rooted. But her commitment to that ideal has dominated her entire life.[16] Imprisoned and exiled in her Russian girlhood for revolutionary activity on behalf of the poor and the powerless, devoted in her immigrant motherhood to the needs of seven children, contemptuous still of the indulgences of the rich, with her only remaining "social duty" (77) the sorting of old clothes for the poor, she has never betrayed the ideal of service. It is an ideal that renders coherent a life lived in different cultures, different circumstances, value systems, and languages. Unlike older people in California who sing simply to express the "unused life" within them, she sings at the end of her life the same revolutionary songs that have inspired her since her youth. Even as she lies dying, her songs help her husband to realize that he has betrayed the ideal of service they once shared. But she has been faithful. Her commitment, moreover, transforms and revalues that ideal by denying its gender specificity and by making it an imperative for humankind.

As the disparate voices and personae associated with different phases of her life are drawn together by this narrative, so the disparate images of this woman are gathered—at the very end—in a moment of sudden vision by her husband. He has neglected, betrayed, and also loved her. As he hears her recalling the songs of her childhood, the suffering of her youth, the trials of her mothering years, he sees her manifold self as one:

> As if to rebuke him, as if her voice had no relationship with her flailing body, she sang clearly, beautifully, a school song the children had taught her when they were little; begged: "Not look my hair where they cut. . . ." (The crown of braids shorn.) And instantly he left the mute old woman poring over the Book of the Martyrs; went past the mother treading at the sewing machine, singing with the children; past the girl in her wrinkled prison dress, hiding her hair with scarred hands, lifting to him her awkward,

shamed, imploring eyes of love; and took her in his arms, dear, personal, fleshed, in all the heavy passion he had loved to rouse from her. (123–24)

As music, to which her spirit returns at the end, gathers separate tones that remain distinct even though, together, they create harmonious sound, as shining bits of silicone and mica are compressed without losing their separate identities into single stones like the ones her grandson collects, so this immigrant woman reveals herself to him in that moment as manifold, yet single. Thus, she solves the riddle that names the story as her husband names her for the first time, for the mother of all women: "Eva."

The magnitude of Olsen's achievement in this story, like the image and voice of her protagonist, is manifold. By allowing this mother to sense and to gratify her own need, the story addresses itself to the problem of devaluation that constrains all the maternal protagonists in this literature. By validating this mother's anger, the story also makes visible the circumstances that provoke it. By centering this mother's withdrawal from her family as she struggles to become aware of herself, and by listening to her as she makes that effort, moreover, the story introduces a new maternal voice into the literature of American Jewish women.

The comic voice of Grace Paley develops even further Olsen's representation of the mother's need to "journey to herself" and Olsen's revaluation of the ideal of nurturing. As Judith Arcana has noted, Paley's stories expand "mothering into a mode, a metaphor, a way of being in the world that . . . is radically opposed to the patriarchal militarism and rapacious domineering that dominate our planet" ("Truth" 199). This expansion of motherhood into a mode of being addresses the social, economic, political, and historical dilemmas of the world. But Paley understands that an expansion of such magnitude cannot happen without change in the individual. She makes such change visible in her most persistent maternal protagonist, Faith Darwin, who recapitulates Eva's quest for self-awareness. In the course of three collections of short stories, Faith identifies the sources of her devaluation, surfaces and transforms her rage against it, and reveals the powerful pleasures of nurturing as she moves between the "sexy playground" of family life and the wider world of friends, work, and social responsibility.[17] As Faith develops, the American Jewish mother's voice comes into its own—no longer muted by devaluation or fragmented by suppressed rage and self-denial.

Paley believes she owes the resonance of her own voice to the new liberties of mind and spirit conferred upon her by her historical and social circumstances. Among those circumstances are her relative economic comfort, her descent from Russian Jewish immigrants who were socialists and multilingual, and her gender in a time of women's liberation (Isaacs 116, 142–44, 147, 113–14). She identifies her richly languaged childhood as a source of special gifts: "For the eventual making of literature," Paley suggests, "my early life was probably healthy—lots of women in the kitchen talking, two strong languages, English and Russian in my ear at home, and the language of my grandmother and the grownups in the street—Yiddish—to remind me of the person I really was, the middle-class child of working people, the comfortable daughter of hounded wanderers, resting for a generation between languages" (quoted in Taylor 3). An American Jewish woman who matured as a writer during the feminist movement, Paley knows—like her maternal protagonist Faith Darwin—not only that "feminism and Judaism . . . have to be looked at together once in a while" (*Later* 81) but also, as Jacqueline Taylor has pointed out, that both feminists and Jews use language as a "crucial means of resistance" to oppressors (58–59).

One virtue of Paley's voice is its power to exploit the real intimacy that exists between mothering women and the men and children for whom they care—an intimacy obscured by more conventional, androcentric modes of discourse. According to Mikhail Bakhtin, laughter destroys distance, for it

> has the remarkable power of making an object come up close . . . where one can finger it familiarly on all sides, turn it upside down, inside out, peer at it from above and below, break open its external shell, look into its center, doubt it, take it apart, dismember it, lay it bare and expose it, examine it freely and experiment with it. Laughter demolishes fear and piety before an object . . . making of it an object of familiar contact and thus clearing the ground for an absolutely free investigation of it. (23)

Olsen's Eva achieves self-awareness by permitting her anger to distance and isolate her so that she can focus attention on herself, but Faith's anger forges from her intimate connections a laughing voice that destroys the hierarchical distance between a powerful man and the woman who "lies down to adore him" (*Little* 143).[18] It exposes also the power given by caretaking women to the children whose lives depend upon them.

Free of fear and piety before the hallowed imperatives that have mandated maternal self-subordination, Faith Darwin—whose name suggests
two powerful ways of looking at experience—revisions those imperatives
from "up close." In the process, she becomes herself.

In several stories of the late fifties and sixties, Faith sees through false
comforts and supports. Thus, her embroidery needle "pierces" the conventional stereotype of a "happy home" (*Little* 128), while her comic
voice penetrates the illusion that mothers are supported and protected
by parents, husbands, and lovers. In "Two Short Sad Stories from a Long
and Happy Life" (1959), Paley exposes the subversive effects of three
lovers and husbands. Angered by male foolishness, irresponsibility, and
aggression, Faith argues, judges, and finally sends about their business two
disappointing husbands and fathers. She later attacks, injures, and expels
from the family nest the lover whose violent "play" has hurt her children
and whose arrogance blames *her* for disturbing the family peace.

Learning from her reactions her own vulnerability to blame, she identifies the rising and falling of her self-esteem as she moves between "success at work" (*Little* 139), the uncertainties of raising children "all alone,"
and the devaluing attacks of men who "warn" her she is growing old
(129), complain about her cooking, or criticize her for doing "a rotten
job" (138) with her sons. Self-awareness and self-righteousness arm her;
laughter diminishes her attackers and reconciles her to the loss of their
carnal companionship. When she can perceive the disparity between her
own and her children's vulnerability, she can laugh ironically at the difference between her need for sex or solitude and their need for protec-
tion and comfort.

In "Faith in the Afternoon" (1960), like Olsen's Eva remembering her
youth in Russia, Faith explores an even earlier period of her life to identify the sources of her own unsteady self-esteem. Recalling first her husband Ricardo's habit of naming his women by their defects, Faith discovers that her self-love depends entirely on his attentions to her (*Little* 35).
When he leaves, her confidence goes with him. When her family blames
her for his desertion and her unhappiness, she identifies an even earlier
source of the devaluation that has subverted her self-esteem (33, 36).
Like this critical family, some readers also blame Faith in this story for
her "egotistical . . . 'indifference'" to the sufferings of former neighborhood friends (41).[19] But, like Olsen's Eva, Faith must move away from
sympathetic engagement, momentarily, to see "up close" the sources of
her fluctuating, uncertain self-regard. She will not weep here for those

whose needs marginalize her own and distract her from her "investigation." But she bows "her head in sorrow" for a friend, also abandoned by her husband, whose story—like a mirror—shows Faith to herself (44).

Like "Tell Me a Riddle," these stories ironically link the occasional self-centeredness of mothering women to both their deprivations and their belated quests for awareness of what Horney called their "true" selves. In these stories, this quest also performs a necessary cultural task, for as mothering women work to understand the vectors of their own malaise, they revision the cultural imperatives that encourage parents and lovers to blame and husbands to abandon them. "Faith in a Tree" (1967) traces the next phase of this "free investigation," chronicling the step beyond self-absorption of a single mother "forced" by the needs of her children to deny or postpone her own gratification. Elevating Faith's point of view as she looks down from the branch of a tree, Paley's comic perspective allows Faith to perceive without pretension or self-pity the dignity of mother-work. Familiar now with the difficulties of single mothering, knowing both her handicaps and her strength, she no longer weeps for herself or for others like her. Instead, she sees a friend as a "a coworker in the mother trade—a topnotch craftsman" (*Enormous* 78). Knowing also the unreliability of men and their power to support her, she makes jokes about her unmet financial and carnal needs but neither devalues nor denies them. Descending from her tree to acknowledge these needs, she can turn away from them, looking beyond the "sexy playground of the family" toward the needs of others in the world.

The attractiveness and untrustworthiness of men's love and support persists as a theme in this and other stories by Paley of the seventies and eighties (see especially "Dreamer in a Dead Language" in *Later*). But in the later decades Faith moves beyond the effort simply to identify needs and sources of disappointment and devaluation. Instead, stories like "The Long Distance Runner" (1974, in *Enormous*), "Friends" (1979), and "The Expensive Moment" (1983, both in *Later*) trace the movement of this maternal protagonist outward from the family that she sustains by her solitary devotion and that nourishes her, in turn, through the loving wisdom of her sons and the intermittent attention of lovers and husbands.

Deliberately self-liberated from the small, stiffening movements imposed on mothers by the nature of their work (*Enormous* 196), Faith trains herself to "run," to withdraw from her nearly grown children and current spouse—like Olsen's Eva from the demands of *her* family. Faith "runs" to recover her past, to feel again her mother's benign presence in the significant places of her life (180–81, 187), and to grasp both the connecting similarities and the urgent differences between the lives of mothering women of different classes, races, times. Faith's work in the world beyond the family, like the brave, socially sensitive, and unpretentious testimony of her women friends, testifies, like Olsen's "Riddle," to the ethical legacy of their ethnic tradition. The work and words of these women also link that wider consciousness of human need to the power of mother-love for the vulnerable, the powerless. Thus, Paley revalues the mother by allowing her to choose her own commitments to others without idealizing them and without silencing the voice of her own needs. Indeed, Faith is responsive at the end even to the neediness of undependable men. Although she notices that "in time you love the children more and the man less," she hastens to reassure her current husband that, nevertheless, she loves "his pink ears and his 243 last hairs" (*Later* 194). In all of Paley's stories, this comic voice emphasizes the power of another's need to stir—and to imprison, like the "short, fat fingers" (*Little* 145) of her small son—the deepest movement of her own heart.

As Olsen's and Paley's stories revalue the nurturing mother, three other writers of the seventies show that she needed to reclaim not only the ethical but also the physical and emotional experience of pregnancy, childbirth, and infant care from silence and patriarchal institutionalization. That these writers identify themselves as Jews is particularly interesting given the traditional anxiety, "fear and repugnance" toward women's sexuality and biological functions as well as the rabbinic restrictions those feelings provoked. By "imposing strict standards of modesty" (Baum et al. 9), the rabbis rendered virtually unseeable the givens of women's bodies. By calling "impure" the discharges associated with menstruation and the aftermath of childbirth, moreover, rabbinic tradition not only rendered the birthing woman untouchable to men but also, one suspects, powerfully inhibited the impulse to share openly, publicly, the experiences that came only to women and that transformed them into mothers.

In the seventies, three American Jewish women writers broke that long silence. Until the eighties Adrienne Rich would not develop publicly her identification with the Jews through the father who had concealed that connection. But a decade earlier, through memories of her non-Jewish mother and herself in *Of Woman Born* (1976), she retrieved awareness of the historical and political processes that had devalued and disempowered mothering women. Thus, her work exposes imperatives that are not particular to rabbinic Judaism but that work nevertheless to

silence and obscure maternal experience. Rich looked first into the dark
places of that experience to unveil there the impulse toward violence.
She identified as provocations a mother's inevitable, repeated failure to
love "continuously, unconditionally" (4) as all the mother-myths demanded, as well as "the solitary confinement of a life at home enclosed
with young children, or . . . the struggle to mother them while providing for them single-handedly, or . . . the conflict of weighing her own
personhood against the dogma that says she is a mother, first, last, and
always" (285). Her work counted the ways in which "institutionalized
motherhood" alienated women from their bodies, diminished their power, and subverted their primacy as givers and sustainers of new life.

Despite this clear-eyed revisioning of maternal experience under patriarchal control, Rich believed that women could reclaim motherhood.
She asked women to "try new ways of living" (288)—and to respect their
experiments even when they failed. She suggested that women "reckon
fully with the ambiguities of our being, and with the continuum of our
consciousness, the potentialities for both creative and destructive energy in each of us" (290). She insisted that women must begin, "at last, to
think though the body" (290), to recognize "the full complexity and
political significance of the woman's body, the full spectrum of power and
powerlessness it represents" (289).

Like new imperatives capable of restoring maternal control of maternal experience, Rich's recommendations echoed in two important
memoirs of the decade: Jane Lazarre's *Mother Knot* (1976)[20] and Phyllis Chesler's *With Child* (1979). Both women experiment with "new"
ways of living by mothering their children and sustaining their marriages—without sacrificing their work as writers. The struggle to maintain
their work becomes a metaphor for the larger task of gaining control
of the experience of motherhood. Essential to that task is the transforming of sensation and feeling, long silenced, into language. The
"child of Jewish Communists" (17), not traditionalists, Lazarre breaks
that silence. The process itself calls for description: "While I was writing," she recalls, "the thoughts kept coming, getting all tangled, unrec-
ognizable, oppressive. I could not grasp them for long enough to hear
them. But if I continued to write, a process began, a sort of translation
of the tension into words; and the words created the possibility for clarity to develop. Just keep writing, I had learned. Soon punctuation
would appear, sentences became shorter. Things would clear away"
(12). In the welter of sensations, feelings, and thoughts that threaten

to overwhelm the mothering person, the act of writing restores control by achieving form and clarity.

Equally important, Lazarre and Chesler—whose faithfulness to Jewish rituals like circumcision and the Passover seder testify to her continuing identification as a Jew—defy the cultural imperatives that have long kept women's bodies and biological functions out of sight and out of mind. They try to "think through the body," to deliberately record the roots of mental and emotional states in bodily experience. For example, the physical effects of labor and delivery distance both narrators from their bodies: "I had cried, vomited, tried to convince my miserable body to give forth the child. Nothing worked. All sense of unity with my body seemed to be broken. We were separated by a cement wall," Lazarre recalls (28). Chesler too realizes, many months after the event, that she has accepted "the fact of my out-of-body experience during labor. . . . I wonder how many women in labor have experienced this without naming it," she asks (161), thus emphasizing—like Rich—the need to think and then to say what the body experiences. In such a way, these writers suggest, women reclaim motherhood by naming it instead of allowing it simply to "mark" them.[21]

The pregnant body is reclaimed similarly in these memoirs by mothering women who can name physical sensations and discern their effects on thought, feeling, and behavior. Inability to control the shape of her body during pregnancy, for example, subverts Lazarre's sexual responses to her husband: "When I looked into that mirror at the foot of our bed and saw my naked body next to James," she remembers, "my vaginal canal suddenly felt as dry as an old sponge forgotten under the sink for months. I couldn't believe the sight of myself, belly protruding and breasts huger than they had ever been with nipples which had suddenly doubled their size. No one had ever told me to expect such things. I was outraged. . . . It was months before I could make love gaily, enjoyably again" (20–21). Her outrage is provoked partly by loss of bodily control but also by anger at other women for having kept such knowledge from her.

Chesler also loses control of her body shape during pregnancy: "I lumber, like an astronaut on the moon. My feet are one shoe size larger than before. . . . My breasts are huge. . . . My calves have nearly doubled in width" (45). But these bodily changes augment, rather than diminish, her sexuality: "I want to have orgasms without foreplay three or four times every day," she writes. "I am without shame. Never have I been in such sexual heat. Is this natural in pregnancy?" (50). Her question, like Lazarre's outrage, articulates the need of mothers to hear one another's voices, a need that spurs Lazarre's quest for a women's group and Chesler's frequent consultations with other mothers. Her question also makes visible both the darkness in which bodily states of being have been shrouded for modern women and the range of options that come to light when emotional and sexual reactions to physical experience make their way into language. Culture may program women like Lazarre to distance their bodies when they no longer conform to gendered ideals. But the recalling of specific bodily changes, linked to fantasies, visions, intuitions, insights, and reactions, weakens the grip of cultural programming by drawing it into the light of collective consciousness. As these writers speak the mother's body, it ceases to be what Peter Brooks has called a "place of inscription" (1). As Rich predicted, the act of thinking and speaking through the body converts maternal "physicality into both knowledge and power" (*Of Woman* 290).

Lactation, as well as pregnancy and delivery, is also renamed and thus reclaimed in these memoirs. At a women's meeting, Lazarre folds her "arms gracelessly over my bosom, which was bursting with milk, dampening the blouse which an hour before I had thought made me appear slim and unmaternally attractive." As she looks at the women who are not mothers and compares herself with them, she feels "about as liberated as a caged lion" in her spotted blouse (52). Chesler's lactating body takes her to a different, less humiliating awareness. Through it she discovers the hostility of restaurant owners (149) and the indifference of physicians toward the special needs of nursing mothers (162)—political insights into the condition of women that rise out of immediate bodily experience. From the ache in her breasts when she must leave her infant to promote her book, she also learns the depth of her connection to her baby: "It's as if I'm in love," she thinks (148). Both memoirists thus "deromanticize the symbolics of milk" (Davies, "Mother Right" 51), problematizing it as a signifier for motherhood by extending the range of associations, thoughts, and feelings with which it is linked—not for the nursing infant but for the mother who nurses.

That shift in point of view is crucial to the work of writing mothers, for it not only centers her experience in the family but redeems her right to the position of subject in her own life. Lazarre and Chesler claim that position not only by thinking and speaking through the maternal body but also by recording the astonishing fluidity of their emotions. They marvel at the nearness of extremes of feeling to one another—as if to respond to Rich's request that women acknowledge the "ambiguities" of their being, their potential for "both creative and destructive energy." Lazarre confesses that her emotional life has always been too intense (11); she is always troubled by the readiness with which she moves be-tween rage and love toward her infant son (36). Chesler also records her ambivalence toward her child (189), but she notes as well deep chang-es in her emotional being as a result of her mothering. Because she is a mother, she becomes capable of forgiving and loving her own, imperfect mother (206); she sees herself as both "doubled" and "halved" when she is without her baby (190); she learns to see and accept her own limita-tions and her "relation to human vulnerability and nakedness" (191). She grows "wise," "provincial, tribal with child" (192, 194); she learns to listen instead of arguing and to "disarm by being as personal as possi-ble" (247). "Tempered" and "deepened" by maternal experience, Chesler begins to trust life even when she cannot control it (183), for she has acquired the power that comes from acknowledging powerlessness: "I am Atlas, holding up an entire world: you. Something holds me up too" (183). As they describe these emotional changes, or fluctuations between extremes of feeling in themselves, these new mothers puncture the myth of what Rich called "continuous, unconditional" mother-love that has stoked into despair the self-doubts of generations of mothering women.

What Rich called "the continuum of consciousness" is also vividly invoked by these memoirs, for fantasy and dream here become compan-ions to deliberate, conscious, waking thought. From dreams and fanta-sies recollected and recorded, both new mothers learn to perceive a con-tinuum not only of consciousness but of time and individual identity. Confused sometimes about the boundaries of their own identities, they wonder whether they are mother or child; they hear their mothers speak-ing through their own voices; they feel, as Lazarre does when she bathes her child, their mother's hands upon their own bodies. Or they discov-er, through their dreams, the fears that make them seem strangers to themselves (Chesler 96).

Despite the indignities and discomforts that both memoirs record, the memoirists find themselves strangely empowered by maternal experience. Lazarre begins to understand "a part of [her]self which was always frus-trating me by remaining hidden despite my conscious attempts to express it. It kept hidden because it was frightened, frightened of its own pow-er. . . . Pregnancy and childbirth had exposed that power, made it impos-

sible for me ever to deny it again. There it was: I had created a child"
(55). Chesler senses in herself a similar kind of maternal power, for she
has learned that "to become a mother is to open the gates of your womb
to admit life—and death into the world." But she, like Rich, links the
silence surrounding and obscuring such power to patriarchal forces that
have always resented and diminished it. Birthing a child, she writes, is
"so significant an act it is *devalued*":

> Under patriarchy, pregnancy and childbirth are savage "tests" of
> your ability to survive in the wilderness alone. And to keep quiet
> about what you've seen. Whether you're *accepted* back depends on
> your ability, your willingness to live without any confirmation that
> you've undergone a rite of passage. You, who have undergone an
> experience of total aloneness in the universe. You, who are totally
> responsible for another life. *You* must keep silent, pretend to return
> to life as usual.
>   Is it too dangerous to treat motherhood as so existentially grand
> an event—*when most men don't become mothers?* (133–34)

For Rich, personal power had once lain in the writing of poetry, and
"poetry," she remembers, "was where I lived as no-one's mother, where
I existed as myself" (*Of Woman* 12). As these memoirists break the silence that patriarchal culture imposes on them as mothers, they find, as
Rich found in the seventies, that power rises out of mothering itself.

On the whole, the traditional imperative to nurture persists in stories
that center American Jewish mothers throughout the century, even
among protagonists who no longer notice its roots in traditional Jewish
culture. In the enduring effects of that imperative, the stories allow one
to see the dignity of lives given to the service of others, the weaknesses
born of devotion to an ideal that devalues the devotee, and the courage,
fidelity, kindness, and resilience forged by the constraints of motherhood.
The devalued mothers who are given to silence and self-suppression
speak confusingly, with several voices. But the maternal protagonists who
move beyond denial hear and transmit new imperatives capable of transforming maternal experience and redeeming it—as well as the mothers
who live it—from devaluation. First, they identify those who have failed
to value and support them. Second, they clarify their needs and trans-
mute their anger—into the harsh, accusing poetry of Olsen's Eva and
into the dazzling comic utterance of Paley's Faith. They validate their
own commitments by choosing them. In some cases, they even manage

to write the physical, mental, and emotional givens of motherhood so that it can be reclaimed in its wholeness by the women who live it. Ultimately, they find in mothering itself a source of empowerment for themselves and one another and a model for human behavior nearly sufficient to the need of a precarious world.

Notes

1. Hirsch has identified "four areas of avoidance and discomfort with the maternal": (1) the "perception that motherhood remains a patriarchal construction," (2) discomfort with mothers' "vulnerability and lack of control," (3) "fear of and discomfort with the body," and (4) a "complicated ambivalence about power, authority, and . . . anger" (165–66).

2. In "When We Dead Awaken," Rich called revision "the act of looking back, of seeing with fresh eyes, of entering an old text from a new critical direction." She believed this act was, for women, "an act of survival" (*On Lies* 35). In one of the first and still one of the most useful scholarly works on American Jewish women, the writers asked, "Why were there no Jewish women novelists recording [Jewish women's experiences]? . . . Had the daughters of these women been so psychologically damaged that they were incapable of generating a voice of their own?" (Baum et al. xi). This chapter responds, in part, to those questions.

3. Donovan describes these writers' attempts to address, from the daughter's perspective, the problem of female existence in a world that devalues the mother.

4. In "Transitions," Pratt describes the developments within Judaism that both alienated women and involved them more fully in the work of the community.

5. A Jewish woman traditionally cultivated her soul by acts of self-sacrificing service to others. Weinberg describes the ways in which the religious piety of shtetl women "intertwined with their daily functions" to create a "domestic religion" tied to homely rituals surrounding the family's life support system at home (17–19).

6. Braude suggests that traditional Jewish women—"excluded from male religious activities"—developed a "parallel religion with its own set of rituals and standards of piety" (152). But their practices were oriented largely toward "help[ing] men fulfill their religious obligations" (151). Women's acts of piety were directed, for the most part, toward what Rachel Adler has called "some physical goal or object" (15). A traditional woman's "major mitzvot," acts she is obliged by law to perform, "aid and reinforce the lifestyle of the community and the family, but they do not cultivate the relationship between the individual and God," according to Adler (14). Barred

from the religious activities accorded primary status by her community, a Jewish woman's "greatest pleasure," Weinberg observes, was supposed to come "from encouraging a learned husband or seeing a son become a scholar," not from pursuing such activity herself (16).

7. Hyman reports that "with their emancipation and acculturation, Jewish men achieved status virtually exclusively through their success in the world of business or the professions. Only in limited circles did the alternate path of mobility through Torah study remain a viable option" ("Modern" 182).

8. N. Anderson highlights the oedipal dimension of such a decision.

9. Kohut's "covert resentment" is noted by Baum et al. in their biographical summary of her career (35); see also Lichtenstein, *Writing* (129).

10. Umansky brought Morton's ethnic identity into question in an essay delivered at the Association for Jewish Studies in December 1991. This essay appeared later in print ("Representations").

11. Spacks argues that women's autobiographies reveal their writers' need for public commitments to both extend and escape from personal feelings (112–32).

12. This need continues to appear and be valorized in Jewish women's writing. See, for example, J. Greenberg, *Season of Delight* (1981), and Rapoport, *Preparing for Sabbath* (1981), two novels whose maternal protagonists find satisfaction of this need in Jewish ritual and service to their communities and families.

13. According to Wegner, the rabbinical period is roughly between 200 and 600 B.C.E., the period during which the classical rabbinic texts were edited (68–69).

14. For example, according to Hirsch, one feminist has argued recently that "mothers in our culture . . . deny the truth about their own experience of bondage and frustration and lie to their daughters whose growth then is constrained by the perpetuation of mutual deception." Hirsch hears in this argument "the feminist daughter's anger at the mother who has accepted her powerlessness, who is unable to protect her [daughter] from a submission to society's gender arrangements." She concludes that "this anger may well be justified in many cases" (165).

15. Despite the differing circumstances of the speakers, Eva's responses to her husband recall what Braxton describes as the "sass" of the outraged mother in slave women's narratives (30–31).

16. Lester described long ago the ethical overlap for Jews like Eva and her husband, "whose geographical move out of the shtetl was accompanied with a philosophical journey from passionate belief in God to a religious belief in an international socialist Utopia. For them, coming out of a terror-ridden world, freedom, knowledge and the brotherhood of mankind were palpable holy words, not rhetoric" (78).

17. For a different reading of Faith's development, see Baba, "Faith Darwin."

18. Paley has said, "I think what happens is humor sometimes takes the place of anger, and it may even subvert it. You know, in a way, sometimes there should be more anger, and there's humor instead" (Isaacs 129). There is "more anger" in the maternal narrator of A. Roiphe's *Lovingkindness* (1987), whose development diverges from the trajectory traced in this chapter.

19. Baba, for example, calls Faith "egocentric" because her sympathy here "is merely another form of self-pity" (44).

20. According to Reddy, Lazarre thinks of this text not as a memoir but as an "autobiographical novel" (225). For the purposes of this study, which considers memoirs as "stories," that distinction is valuable but beside the point.

21. Davies discusses the distinction between "marking" and "naming": "Marking is the product of abuse and is linked to societal inscriptions on the body of the Other"; thus, the "mark of motherhood inscribes the domination of men into women's bodies. . . . [but] naming or remarking has to do with redefinition" ("Mother Right" 46–47).

4

⚭

Mirroring the Mother:
The Ordeal of Narcissism

My mother is my mirror and I am hers.
—Marge Piercy, "My Mother's Body"

As the women's movement gathered force in the sixties and seventies, American women's fiction recorded the changes that feminism provoked in women's lives. Some novels allowed to female protagonists the "uninhibited" quests for sexual satisfaction previously reserved for men. Some took a "bitter, cynical" look at "instrumental bonds" between the sexes. Some traced women's efforts to "change the stories written for them by the patriarchy" (Wandersee 70–71). As chapter 5 will demonstrate, these turbulent decades also stirred many Jewish women to seek change within their own community: they articulated "anger and frustration with patriarchal traditions" (Linden-Ward and Green 181); they protested their exclusion from the prayer minyan and the study house; and they demanded larger leadership roles within the community.[1] But beneath the churning mainstream of social, sexual, and institutional change, some American Jewish women's stories in this period identified the pull of a deeper emotional current that moved, persistently, in another direction.

These stories located resistance to change in the relationships of mothers and daughters who could not grow because they were narcissistically absorbed in themselves and one another. Mothers, in short, became an issue for Jewish women writers in these decades.[2] No longer constrained by the imperatives of traditional Judaism or the insecurities of immigrant experience, a protagonist often defined herself *against* her mother: she reflected her mother negatively. But while she magnified her mother's defects, she revealed at the same time her own inability to look away.

Daughters were also mirrored by their mothers, confronting their own images in their mothers' eyes. Like white, middle-class American women in general, as Wini Breines has pointed out, Jewish protagonists in the late sixties and seventies knew enough about their mothers' lives in the family-centered fifties to know they wanted something different for themselves (x, 77–83). They were aware of new options for personal growth that had been clarified by the feminist movement. However, as they sought to achieve sexual autonomy and to expand social, sexual, educational, and professional opportunities, they were still susceptible to the gendered cultural imperatives that had drawn their mothers into domesticity and parenthood. Indeed, their mothers' voices often reinforced those imperatives. Thus, daughters confronted two very different agendas for their own lives.

From the disjunction between these agendas, many American Jewish women writers[3] in the late sixties and seventies wrote stories about protagonists who found themselves trapped between two ways of being: between the choices their mothers had made and the alternatives offered by their own time. They stood, as it were, between mirrors that offered incompatible images of the world and themselves.

As they peered into the mirrors held up to them by feminism on the one hand and their mothers on the other, they belonged to what Christopher Lasch calls "the age of narcissism." Lasch's work elicited considerable criticism from contemporary feminists.[4] But American Jewish women novelists of the period confirmed his image of the narcissist—even though they differed significantly with his reading of both the causes and consequences of her condition. Sensitive to the ways in which individualism seemed to be running amok, Lasch worried mostly about the future of a culture in which "self-gratification was the norm, and a larger moral or political meaning in social life had been lost" (Breines 81). He traced this loss, in part, to its psychological roots, for he recognized that narcissism in this period was "an important element in the so-called character disorders that have absorbed much of the clinical attention once given to hysteria and obsessional neuroses" (35). From clinicians he learned that narcissists experience "'pervasive feelings of emptiness and depression'"; they suffer "'violent oscillations of self-esteem'"; and they attach themselves, usually romantically, to "'strong, admired figures whose acceptance [they] crave[d] and by whom [they] need[ed] to feel supported'" (37). Such attachments, he believed, were rarely successful.

American Jewish women novelists of the period created characters with many of these symptoms. Like the patients whose failed relationships had become the object of clinical attention, protagonists' attempts to find satisfaction in love often appear as futile as Narcissus's courtship of his own image in a still pool. The failures of romantic love in novels of the seventies owe something, of course, to the burgeoning feminist suspicion that marriage was a patriarchal institution. But these failures also seem rooted in the inability of protagonists to love—or to find in love the satisfaction of their most pressing needs.

Experts of the period attributed these and other inabilities to poor mothering. From the twenties to the sixties, as Barbara Ehrenreich and Deirdre English have observed, experts had become pivotal figures "in the new mid-twentieth century drama of the Mother, the Child, and the Expert" (212). Lifting up the banner of permissiveness under which all children were supposed to be raised, experts directed mothers to love instinctually, to sense and respond to their children's needs, putting aside whatever desires they might feel for lives and work outside the family nest: "Only the wholly domestic, nonworking mother . . . could hope to release the libidinal unself-consciousness, the blissful ignorance, that was now the *sine qua non* of good mothering" (224). Mothers in whom such exemplary attributes failed to appear were believed to be harmful to the welfare of their children.

Thus, the clinicians Lasch had studied in order to understand narcissism reflected a more general cultural tendency to exaggerate the doleful effects on children of parental (read "maternal," according to Ehrenreich and English [219]) deprivation. A rejecting mother, they reasoned, would provoke by her rejection the pain, rage, and self-doubt that would disfigure her child's later relationships (Lasch 35). The child, believing herself undeserving of love, would try again and again "to 'recreate a wished-for love relationship . . . and simultaneously to annul the anxiety and guilt aroused by aggressive drives directed against the frustrating and disappointing'" parent (Lasch 36).[5] In this light, narcissism appeared not as an elevated form of self-love but rather "a psychic formation in which 'love rejected turns back to the self as hatred'" (35). Driven to "reestablish" or "recreate" as an adult the "wished-for" relationships that had failed and enraged her as a child, the narcissist, psychologists believed, was all but doomed to reexperience her initial disappointment in each new love affair. Each disappointment would renew her rage—at both herself and the parent she blamed for initially rejecting her.[6]

The dominant mythology of the period thus doomed the narcissistic children of rejecting, preoccupied mothers to endlessly disappointing love stories. To some extent, American Jewish women's fiction of the seventies confirms the cultural myth by telling stories of women trapped between mirrors that foreclose the possibility of love. But the romantic drama that Lasch and other experts conceived as central to the plight of the narcissist is actually marginal to the drama of self-realization—whose plot was complicated by the fascination of daughters with their own and their mothers' images. In those images, mothers outgrow their mythic limitations and begin to reveal to the daughters who cannot look away from them the sources of their mutual imprisonment. Some fictional mothers even furnish the insights that release daughters from the stasis of endless reflection into the uncertainties of their own, very different lives.

For example, although the novel is anomalous in several ways, Cynthia Ozick's *Trust* (1966) anticipates the next decade's cultural and fictional preoccupation with narcissism by describing the travail of a protagonist who breaks the spell of her mother's reflection to become herself. Through the non-Jewish characters in this novel, Ozick studied elements of family interactions that have not reappeared in her later work. Allegra Vand, the non-Jewish mother of a nameless narrator/daughter is incapable of attending to anything other than herself. She has nothing in common with Ozick's later maternal figures. She owns neither the social conscience of Ruth Puttermesser (in "Puttermesser and Xanthippe"), the maternal pride and confidence of Hester Lilt (in *The Cannibal Galaxy*), nor the maternal despair of Rosa (in "The Shawl" and "Rosa").

Like other characters in *Trust* who are first identified with and then differentiated from mythical prototypes, Allegra initially appears to be a Demeter figure, a source of nurturance for everyone in the novel. Allegra's vast inheritance, like Demeter's bounty, is "all around us," her husband says, pervasive—like God (224–25). But unlike the treasures of earth that Demeter provides, Allegra's money is actually controlled by a male trustee, not by Allegra herself. Even after her father's death, his will makes her dependent on another man for her sustenance. And her lavish expenditures are not nurturant. She funds nothing vital, only tissue-of-gold party dresses for a daughter who hates parties, a literary magazine that neither enlightens nor entertains, and a museum that preserves nothing. Moreover, her self-indulgence in clothes and travel speak of vanity and rootlessness, not fruitfulness. Even her thinning hair proclaims her difference from the goddess, who personifies abundance in all respects.

Allegra is, nevertheless, a powerful figure in the novel. She fascinates several men, marrying two and taking another as lover. She also commands, almost to the end, her daughter's attention. Her criticisms, her scoldings, her advice are recorded in considerable detail—for the landscape of her daughter's emotional universe is determined by the vagaries of this quicksilver mother who is never still, who plays out her feelings in a drama that keeps her always at the center of attention. For example, as her daughter watches, Allegra is suddenly transformed by a momentary enthusiasm: she throws off her dressing gown, leaps naked into the rain, stands "barefoot . . . with her long thighs apart, wetly skeined, and her face welcoming the deluge, like a nereid in a pre-Raphaelite painting"—and catches cold (35). Her enthusiasms invariably dampened in the long run, she manages nevertheless to amuse even the soberest of husbands and to captivate her always attentive daughter.

Allegra's narcissistic needs are evident from the beginning. She keeps trying to snare what the narrator calls "the bird of the world," for she is hungry for distinction, longing to be more than wife and mother, "more than the best heating plant in the world" (624). She drives her current, Jewish husband, Enoch, toward career goals attractive to her own ambition. She believes that, like Medea and Lady Macbeth (her examples), a woman can achieve distinction only through marriage to a promising man. The child of a sickly mother who died young, unmothered and grudgingly fathered, Allegra knows nothing of nurture or family love.[7] She desires only to be reunited with the romantic, but elusive, partner of her early youth, the narrator's father. Abandoned by him, she strategizes feverishly to satisfy in other ways the vanity and ambition that work to strengthen her uneasy sense of self, revealing the matrix that engenders the narcissistic daughter.

Unnourished by this dazzling, scheming, self-absorbed, needy mother,[8] the narrator/daughter rarely looks away from Allegra. Always in motion, like a gleaming water snake, this mother yields few and contradictory clues to the daughter who needs her love. Thus the daughter neglects her own emotional life to concentrate on her mother. The daughter is nameless, colorless, featureless, for she becomes visible to herself only in the mirror of her mother's criticisms. She appears to the reader and to other characters as what she believes herself to be: less beautiful, less interesting, less vivid, less emotionally spontaneous than her mother. Knowing, moreover, that she cannot command her mother's attention, remembering the doors her mother locked between them, the marital intimacies that excluded her, the maternal absences that condemned her to the care of irresponsible nannies, the narrator/daughter lacks a sense of herself as lovable. Rejected, her love has turned back on herself as doubt, if not hatred—as Lasch's experts had predicted.

This novel deviates in an important way from others that take up this theme by its faithfulness to Freudian expectations that only fathers could liberate daughters from bondage to their mothers (Chodorow 115–23). As Jessica Benjamin has recently observed, for Freudians "the admired and powerful phallic father actually saves the child from helplessness at the hands of the mother. The 'natural scorn' for women that Freud often noted and the transfer of power to the father actually conceal and assuage terror of the omnipotent mother." Many psychoanalytic thinkers since Freud accept "the transfer of power to the father as the only means by which the child can free herself from the helpless subjection to the omnipotent mother and enter the reality of the wider world" (Benjamin, "Omnipotent" 130). Benjamin questions the dichotomous thinking that accounts for this long-standing imbalance in roles assigned to mother and father. But Ozick, apparently susceptible to this reading of child development, provides her narrator with two effective father figures. One makes of her a heterosexually enlightened and competitive woman and a storyteller. The other helps her to become a Jewish writer.

Her biological father, Nick, first reveals to his daughter her youthful superiority to her aging mother (532) and touches her into erotic self-awareness. He leads her to a moonlit beach where she will see "the gleaming membrane" of her own young mouth in Circe's mirror and receive her father's kiss (534–35).[9] He will later initiate her into the mysteries of sex by performing the sexual act—with another young woman—before his daughter's eyes. Although he thus performs two significant functions for his daughter, his value to the narrator is more deeply qualified than other readers have understood. According to one critic, he "becomes the role model his daughter has longed for . . . a man of spontaneous passion, of faunlike immersion in the moment, of Greek/pagan heresies suggesting the 'spontaneous gods of nature'" that Ozick admired (Strandberg, "Art" 274). But Ozick's Nick actually has little affinity with the godlike, the natural, or the spontaneous. His hair is dyed, his beach strewn with broken, rusting machinery, his sexuality exploitive and un-loving, his body—at the end—covered with vomit. Like Allegra, Nick is diminished by comparison with the god he resembles. Like Allegra in another way, this father is vain, self-centered, and self-indulgent. After his death by drowning, Allegra's husband Enoch identifies him as Nar-cissus, who "always vanishes by way of water" (633). Enoch exposes in Nick's adulterous irresponsibilities the radical self-doubt that plagues all "solipsists": "He didn't believe in himself," Enoch says (634).

Despite his seductive irresponsibility, Nick bestows upon his daugh-ter not only the questionable blessings of sexual knowledge and compet-itive advantage over her mother but also the gift of language. He func-tions as muse to several women in the novel. He has inspired Allegra to write a trivial novel (389) and given to another young woman the power to tell the story of his death (613). His kiss also unlocks in the narra-tor's mouth the "skill" (535) of the storyteller. But this gift, like others from this source, is rendered dubious by the novel. On Nick's island, people play with language as they play at sex—valuing words "not for their uses—rather, as magic in themselves" (551). The narrator accepts all of Nick's gifts but makes them her own by transforming them.[10] As she performs the journey by water to the island of her feckless father, the narrator resembles maidens in myths and fairy tales who must also go to the seductive "beasts" that summon them. But this narrator distinguishes herself from maidens in fairy tales by returning home again to become herself. Confirmed as a sexual being by Nick's kiss and erotic demonstra-tion, she will "go to weddings," but she will not languish—like her moth-er—without a lover. Rendered competitive with Allegra by Nick's admi-ration, she will be able to look away from—but she will not leave her mother. Endowed with her father's narrative skill, she will tell not his "tawdry" stories but her own.

Mirroring both mother and father in her own way, she mirrors also, in one respect, her creator, for Ozick too values words not "as magic in themselves" but as a medium through which one can attend to moral and historical matters undreamed of in stories by other writers. The muses, Ozick was to write years later, "are not Jewish but Greek" (*Bloodshed* 10). Thus the narrator, like Ozick herself, who began this novel for "the Gentiles" but finished it for "the Jews" (*Art* 158), will be touched into creativity on the island of her father/muse with his dyed hair, winy breath, and unnaturally youthful eroticism. But she will return to the influence of her mother's current, Jewish husband.[11] Attentive, like Ozick herself, to the world beyond ambition and sexual self-indulgence that captivates Nick and Allegra, this second father makes lists of Holocaust victims and studies Talmud.

Thus, the narrator grows beyond both narcissistic parents: the father who "doubted his existence by declaring it" and the mother who must listen "to the hairs of her head grow and prosper, to assure herself of life" (634–35). The daughter escapes the trivial romance plot they have set for her as she, like her creator, assumes the responsibilities of a Jewish writer—mindful not only of romance and ambition as appropriate subjects for the storyteller but also of the often tragic, morally significant dimensions of human experience that enlarge the field of this narrator's vision.

While Ozick's *Trust* announces the theme of narcissism for the seventies, it deviates in several respects from other stories of the decade by American Jewish women writers. Its non-Jewish characters and its Freudian bias, which insists on a daughter's need for a father—or two—to release her from absorption in her mother's image, differentiate this novel from most stories of the seventies. But like those stories, *Trust* insists on several points consistent with the feminist perspective that flourishes in later works. The novel demonstrates and critiques the worldly arrangements that endow fathers—not mothers—with financial, social, intellectual, and moral power. Thus, the bond that imprisons mother and daughter as they gaze upon one another is partly forged by a patriarchal world that denies women power—and places it in the hands of men who are either irresponsible, like Nick, dominating, like Allegra's father, or cold, like her first husband. Despite her other deprivations, moreover, this emotionally gifted mother manifests—even though she does not know and cannot tell—the failure of what Carolyn Heilbrun has called "the marriage plot" to bestow such power on women (*Writing* 48). The clarity of Allegra's demonstration becomes as precious a gift to this daughter as those she receives from her fathers. As Allegra plays out her repeated failures to satisfy herself, her social defeats, her trivial acquisitions and accomplishments, her restlessness and hunger for recognition, she enlightens her daughter. The daughter will emphasize in her own life the work of writing that her mother's life subordinated to the marriage plot. The novel itself demonstrates her successful empowerment as a writer who can tell both her mother's and her own stories. The narrator of *Trust*, unlike many later protagonists, reverses her mother's priorities. Allegra discovers and confirms herself only through her interactions with male lovers, admirers, and husbands. Discerning the narcissistic wounds her mother manifests, the narrator becomes herself by telling the story her mother cannot tell.

Later protagonists struggle less successfully to satisfy themselves within the romantic/domestic labyrinths that seemed to their mothers the only proper scene in which a woman's drama of self-realization could be enacted. Their struggles, however, develop the inadequacies of the "marriage plot" itself as they expose the forces that confine women to it. Like images of mothers, images of romance and domesticity in these stories outgrow the limited stereotypes in which cultural experts confined and expected to understand them. Lasch, for example, believed that heterosexual relationships were contaminated by the feminist movement, which had taught women "to make new demands on men and to hate men when they fail to meet those demands" (196). But, like Ozick's *Trust*, several novels of the seventies offered instead images of narcissistic women so uncertain of themselves, so dependent on their reflections in the eyes of others, that their romantic attachments faltered beneath the weight of their own needs.

The protagonist/narrator of Anne Roiphe's *Up the Sandbox!* (1970), for example, focuses on her own, not her husband's, inadequacies by punctuating the story of her ordinary, domestic experience with adventures that display the courage, the brilliance, the readiness to take risks of several imaginary surrogates for herself. These adventures win for her surrogate selves the recognition she craves but cannot command. Alternate chapters tell the story of her own life as wife and mother, revealing her uncertainties about her own ability and her dependence on others to confirm her sense of self. She loves "to be loved," for she needs the "reasonable reassurance" that loving attention offers her (63). "I wonder if I'm good enough," she confesses. Unlike one of her adventurous surrogates, however, who seeks attention from one man after another, the protagonist is faithful to the fifties' code exemplified by her mother: she courts only the affection of her children and husband. Although she had planned to be "as unlike" her mother "as possible," she knows she has reproduced her mother's life of "feeding and caring" (85). She finally reduces even her imagination to conventionally acceptable limits. Instead of doing research in jungles or blowing up bridges like her earlier surrogates, her last imaginary self simply conceives another child. Transforming all the people she loves into reflectors who give back images of herself, she welcomes the "fierce combat of mother-child love . . . joyfully" because she depends on it to "give me a self" (156). This novel explores, then, not only the ways in which marriage and motherhood limit this protagonist's growth but also her own tendency to diminish herself to fit within those limits.

Alix Kates Shulman's *Memoirs of an Ex-Prom Queen* (1972) also clarifies the inner forces that subvert her narcissistic protagonist's ability to satisfy herself through love and marriage. This narrator, too, depends upon mirroring, self-validating relationships because she is radically uncertain of her own value. Shulman links this uncertainty to gender-specific cultural programming in which the narrator's mother plays an important part. Schooled by her beautiful mother to believe she can "be somebody" only if she attaches herself to the right man (72), programmed by her culture to believe that winning a man is every woman's highest calling (273), and convinced by the media that only beauty will attract men, the ex-prom queen distrusts mirrors unless their message is confirmed by the eyes of others who reflect her. But she studies herself obsessively in reflections, and she turns all interactions into reflections of herself. In a fluorescent-lit beauty parlor mirror (261), she examines facial flaws concealed by her earlier reflection in the dirty window of a bus. Beauty magazines reinforce her preoccupation with her own image. Daydreaming over them, she fantasizes a panel of judges who first approve her "shiksa nose" (268) and then dismiss her, contemptuously, because she has a pimple on her chin (270). She is disturbed by her children's indifference and her husband's anger at her new haircut. Feeling "his eyes on me still" (274), she seeks by phone, from a woman friend, a more affirmative reflection of herself. Like Roiphe's protagonist, she needs what no one can give her: a sense that she is valuable apart from her appearance and the admiration it evokes from others.

Protagonists in both Roiphe's and Shulman's works match the image of the self-absorbed, never satisfied female narcissist described by Lasch and others. But the novels link these attributes to neither the inadequacy of men, nor the new demands of feminists, nor rejecting mothers. Instead, these protagonists of the seventies suffer from the gendered cultural messages and imperatives that postwar American culture, as Betty Friedan and others pointed out, had broadcast to women of the fifties. Forgetful, like their fifties mothers, of the practical strength and assertiveness they might have inherited from the immigrant women who came before them (Breines 137), indifferent to the spiritual rewards of communal work,[12] these protagonists seek only social confirmation of their status and desirability.

Ironically, now that Jewish women were finally at home in postwar, middle-class America, their stories reflected its most characteristic malaise: a double agenda that programmed women, on the one hand, to seek eternally the lovers who would, like mirrors, affirm their value and, on the other, to find every lover incapable of that affirmation. Thus, Erica Jong's progatonist in *Fear of Flying* (1973) keeps trying to find "a man to complete me," until she learns that "if we haven't the power to complete ourselves, the search for love becomes a search for self-annihilation" (299–300).

Even more explicitly than Roiphe's and Shulman's protagonists, Jong's Isadora Wing connects her own dilemma with the mixed messages broadcast by her culture and transmitted by her mother. Isadora's red-haired mother is actually two mothers: a "good" one who praises, comforts, and encourages her daughter's talent and a "bad" one whose eccentric, ambitious demands alienate her daughter and reveal her own failure to "complete" herself. Vivid and energetic but frustrated in her own artistic career, this mother teaches what life has taught her: in this culture one cannot be both an artist and a woman. Her message is reinforced by male cultural authorities who teach Isadora the constraints of gender: "women never can be artists"; "they have no religious feeling"; they "can never be quite rational"; "they are earth mothers"; and "they have deficient superegos and are ever 'incomplete' because they lack the one thing in this world worth having: a penis" (154). While Isadora is pushed by her mother to succeed artistically, she is also restrained both by the gendered messages broadcast by male writers and by the mother who models and transmits those messages.

At first, Isadora refuses to become a "blurred carbon copy" of her mother (153). She chooses instead to "complete" herself through analysts and lovers. But after a long series of comically unsuccessful analyses and love affairs, she consults the only mirror likely to give her a usable image of herself. In the self-reflective journal she has kept for four years, she finds the wisdom and the courage to re-envision her life—as a writer who can contradict both her mother and the cultural authorities who subverted women's confidence in themselves.

Even popular novels—whose protagonists are testing, on one level, the viability of marriage as a social institution or pursuing their own sexual or social satisfactions—are also analyzing, at another level, the cultural dilemma of daughters subverted and misdirected by mothers who reflect restrictive, dated cultural imperatives. In some stories of the seventies, daughters reject their mothers, blaming them for giving bad advice,[13] for being weak, submissive, and ineffective,[14] for lacking self-confidence and subverting it in their daughters,[15] or for punishing imagination and audacity in their daughters while rewarding obedience and passivity.[16] Again and again in novels of this period, mothers are blamed for offering inadequate models and misleading images of reality to their daughters: in other words, for mirroring badly the image of woman their daughters admire and wish to emulate.[17]

Stories that feature rejecting mothers, however, move beyond blame—like Ozick's *Trust*—to locate the roots of maternal rejection in maternal deprivation. Shelley Steinmann List and Rosellen Brown account, in part, for these deprivations by identifying their maternal figures as Jewish immigrants. Thus, their novels summon into the post-sixties' struggle of relatively pampered young women—used to the securities and comforts of postwar, middle-class America—the memory of the dislocations and compensations that haunted the lives of earlier generations. By refracting the image of the immigrant daughter through the experience of her American-born offspring, their novels clarify the cost to both generations of Jewish women's adaptation to the new world. In the eyes of these American Jewish daughters of the late sixties and seventies, the immigrant woman who found her way into the world failed either to secure there her own self-image or to affirm her daughter as a subject capable of loving others and becoming herself.

List's *Did You Love Daddy When I Was Born* (1972), for example, records the petulant demands and pathetic vanities that entrap three generations of narcissistically deprived American Jewish women, revealing the neediness that confines them to the images they reflect of one another. Obsessively attentive to their mirrors, these women blame one another for their own faults and disappointments but continue to seek in one another's eyes the positive regard that might confirm their self-respect.

Rachel, the narrator, recalls the lack of maternal affection that afflicted both her mother and herself. "She never loved me," Rachel's mother laments, "I don't know if she ever loved any of us. . . . She never kissed me." To her mother's litany of deprivation, Rachel adds her own: "And

you, Mother . . . you never kissed me yourself" (80). Mother and grandmother, Rachel knows, have been "elusive . . . not really listening, caring yes, maybe caring, but not really touching, breathing, for you the
child . . . not really there" (6, ellipses in original). Scarred by her own
childhood deprivations, Rachel reenacts them, marrying a man as emotionally withholding, as "elusive," as her mother and grandmother. Even
Rachel's lover disappoints her, for he can "give her only so much, never
quite enough" (105).

Like narcissistic women in the clinical descriptions Lasch relied upon,
these women keep trying—and failing—to satisfy in their adult lives the
unmet needs of their childhoods. List's novel foregrounds the generation-
al dynamic that traps these women in an endless spiral of blaming their
mothers and trying—but failing—to do better with their daughters. They
cannot help themselves because, like princesses ensnared by an evil sorcerer in a fairy tale, they are held captive by their reflections in mirrors.
The vanity of Grandmother Sadie, eighty-five years old and only days
away from death, increases her suffering; she won't "take any pain
killers. . . . It's bad for the skin, it makes wrinkles, I'd rather suffer" (62).
Her daughter, Manya, assembles herself daily in a room "where you could
see yourself twenty, maybe thirty, times at once if you opened up the
mirrored closet doors" (5). Rachel also consults mirrors obsessively. Every time she arrives in New York to see her grandmother, she visits first
the ladies' room, to "redo the face, look in the mirror, another mirror.
Another Rachel" (56). Needing to be mirrored by an approving man so
that she can believe in her own attractiveness (137), worrying that
Sadie's death will destroy a part of herself that only Sadie can reflect,
Rachel cannot even realize her own grief when Sadie dies until she
catches the reflection of her own face "flattened and stretched in the
rounded mirror of the coffee urn" (144).

Even when her mirror reflects a face other than her own, Rachel sees
in it only her own malaise. Consulting, as usual, the washroom mirror
in the railway terminal, Rachel sees another woman whose image "stayed
in her mind a long time." Thin, black, pretty, she seems to Rachel to be
talking to herself in the mirror because she has no one else in the world
to talk to (107–8). This woman doesn't divert Rachel from her own self-
absorption, for she is, almost literally, blind to the racial issues likely to
differentiate this woman from herself. Instead of seeing her, Rachel uses
her as a mirror, making of this "other" only an ominous, monitory image of her own condition inside the closed circle of her narcissistic pre-

occupations. Rachel can never turn the mirror of her narrative attention away from herself: she wants mostly to be alone, "to sit at her typewriter and see what comes out"; she doesn't want to "feel sorry for anyone and worry about anyone" but only "to think about Rachel" because "she did not know who she was" (85).

Instead of blaming any of these mothers for their daughter's malaise, List's novel focuses on the failure of narcissistic women to win from one another the gift of self-assurance they cannot bestow because they do not possess it. Each is unsure of herself, uncertain of her appeal to others, "feeling not quite daughter but mother herself, sometimes, and woefully not quite enough as a person" (55). Although they have all found their way into the world through their work, worldly experience fails to satisfy their need for confirmation. Neither lovers nor work can distract mothers and daughters in this novel from their mirrors or satisfy the need that keeps them turned always toward one another.

Clearly, American Jewish women novelists of the seventies were not insensitive to the effects upon children of unloving parents, but they had also discovered that mothers were as uncertain as their daughters of their own value and as dependent on mirrors of all kinds to confirm their sense of themselves. Theorists had long understood that people learned something important from their mirrors, but theoretical understanding of *what* was learned changed considerably in the seventies.[18] Jacques Lacan had argued as early as 1936 that a six-month-old infant recognized in a mirror both "the persons and things around him [*sic*]" and "his" own "specular image." "This Gestalt," Lacan reasoned, "symbolizes the mental permanence of the 'I' long before the child becomes socially determined (1–2).[19] In 1972, however, D. W. Winnicott argued that a child's sense of self depended upon even earlier reflections and recognitions in the mirror of its mother's face. When a baby looks at its mother, Winnicott believed, "what the baby sees is himself or herself." In time, the child would learn that the mother's face was not a mirror. But throughout life, "when the average girl studies her face in the mirror she is reassuring herself that the mother-image is there and that the mother can see her and that the mother is *en rapport* with her" (27–28). For Winnicott, therefore, "the actual mirror has significance mainly in its figurative sense": women continue to consult their mirrors for reassurance, needing to know that their mothers see and approve of them.

This theoretical emphasis in the seventies on the mirroring function of mothers developed further in the late eighties, when Benjamin argued that mothers, too, depended upon the mirror held up to them by their children. Benjamin described the "recognition" that a new mother experienced when her baby responded to her: "In this early interaction, the mother can already identify the first signs of mutual recognition: 'I recognize *you* as my baby who recognizes *me*'" (*Bonds* 15). Thus, Benjamin's work in the eighties theorized the element of mutual dependence on mirroring that had emerged in novels written by Jewish American women more than a decade earlier.

Rosellen Brown and Camille Baum not only developed the theme of narcissistic mirroring of mothers and daughters but also linked the tragic consequences of their mutual fascination with their need to see likeness—not difference—in the mirrors they become for one another. Baum's novel highlights both the failure of the romantic/domestic myth so pervasive in the fifties and the painful alienation of mothers and daughters who cannot affirm the differences between them. Baum's work attributes this failure of mutual mirroring to the disparate cultural imperatives of different generations by portraying a mother who cherishes her talented daughter but who misleads her by transmitting the fifties' promise of womanly fulfillment in the "marriage plot." The title of her 1971 novel, *A Member of the Tribe*, foregrounds the ethnic implications of her protagonist's experience. But the novel focuses instead on the gender-specific suffering of Jewish women who hear the voices of their own time break against the litany of ethnic and gendered imperatives intoned by their mothers. The protagonist's mother, Mrs. Kramer, believes in marriage and motherhood as she believes in God. For her daughter, Selene, this mother's voice carries nearly divine authority, for Selene identifies the law of God with the law of her mother as "calculated, defined, and made inexorable by the world" (229). Mrs. Kramer is also affectionately close to her daughter, who knows that "the feel of this closeness is a thing forever unto itself" (18). But their intimacy is problematic, for Mrs. Kramer can always see what Selene wishes to conceal. She inspires in her daughter not only affection but also the guilt associated with disobedience, moral deviation, and sexual play. She wishes to deliver her daughter, still pure, into her domestic future.

Mrs. Kramer knows but does not teach the limits of married domesticity. Her husband, Aaron, beautiful and sweet, does not possess the emotional, intellectual, or practical strengths of his wife: "He was utterly lacking in ambition and strength of purpose. His intelligence was as uncomplicated as the poetry he composed, his needs as primitive as a

child's, his pleasures few and unvaried. He had no flame for life, no calling that burned. He had no dream" (77). Romanticized by his wife and
idealized by his daughter, this man exists at the margin of the family,
never seen closely enough to render visible the cost of his inadequacies.
Mrs. Kramer is aware of that cost; she knows that her passionate, talented, ambitious daughter "will not truly find the end of [her] search in a
marriage" (124). But she believes marriage will provide the essential,
compensatory satisfaction of family life.

Secure in this belief, Mrs. Kramer romanticizes heterosexual love, fash-
ioning the story of Selene's conception into a romantic tale—a myth that
conflicts rudely with both the facts of life detailed by Selene's adolescent
friends and Selene's own sexual initiation. After her wedding night, Selene blames her mother for her own "frigidity," believing that the inhibitions set in place by her mother to keep her virgin until marriage now keep
her from enjoying her husband. But the novel suggests that the physical
reality of the sexual act disturbs Selene because it doesn't conform to her
mother's romantic myth. She sees her husband's nakedness; she experiences his desire; and she wonders, "Where was the sacredness of love? Where
dwelt the beauty and the promised fulfillment?" (135).

The disjunction between the mother's romantic myth and the daughter's realistically portrayed first experience of sexual intercourse painfully
foreshadows the deepening estrangement between mother and daughter,
for Selene turns to other men to satisfy expectations awakened by a
mother who is now outraged by her daughter's attempts to satisfy them.
Ironically, both women continue to share the same value system. Like
her mother, Selene blames herself for bringing moral "horror" into her
mother's life, for wanting what she "can't ever hope to have . . . without
hurting everyone around me." In the end, she begs her mother to forgive
her, insisting that "we're not the same, you and I. . . . We want different
things out of this life" (180). Mrs. Kramer, longing to forgive, possesses
neither the strength nor the courage to embrace a daughter different
from herself: "There would be neither forgiveness nor forgiving, not
when shameless and defiant sin promised the destruction of so many others" (211). Their similarity accentuates the differences that estrange
them. They both judge adultery sinful. But the daughter cannot, like her
mother, content herself within a marriage that constricts her growth and
denies her opportunity for self-realization. Her expectations complicated and intensified by her mother's romantic stories, by her own early
success as a musician, and by the encouragement of her friends, Selene

cannot achieve the compromise that would resolve for her, as it has for her mother, the conflict between domestic reality and romantic desire that they both experience.

Mrs. Kramer's failure to acknowledge this conflict, a failure common to women of the fifties,[20] transforms her best and most loving maternal advice into a recipe for her daughter's undoing. Faithful to the maternal agenda, Selene allows her earliest sexual impulses to propel her into marriage; at age eighteen she gives up the musical career that might have satisfied her ambition. Confronting her mistake too late to correct it, she takes full responsibility for it: "In her own hands had been the power to create, and in her own heart were the visions which she lacked the courage and decisiveness to pursue. No, the blame was not in her husband or their marriage. She had simply given up the struggle for truth" (148). Like Isadora Wing, Selene discovers that only she can "complete" herself. But this novel insists also on the mother's destructive confidence in romance and domesticity and exposes the mutual inability of mother and daughter to accept the differences that lie beneath their likeness to one another.

Rosellen Brown's *Autobiography of My Mother* (1976) looks even more deeply into the tragic dilemma of a mother and daughter who can neither look away from one another nor affirm the differences they see.[21] Like many protagonists in stories of the seventies, both Gerda and her daughter, Renata, have been scantily nurtured by hardworking mothers who bore entire responsibility for their families. Although Gerda rejects her stoic, immigrant mother's religious piety and vulnerability to the patriarchal imperatives of Jewish tradition (Seligman 116–17), she has assumed the burden of mourning her mother's deprivations (*Autobiography* 98). She has also learned from her father's failures to "become all that he was not": she acquires the legal skills he lacked, and she uses them to help others. Turning the weapons of a patriarchal society against itself, Gerda wins freedom for the weak, the deviant, the powerless, the oppressed. Thus, she becomes "the mother who has won permission from the father" (197). For herself, however, she wins only two moments of freedom from the discipline that ensures her success in a male-dominated world. Momentarily liberated from that iron discipline, once by sex and once by rage, she experiences freedom as "the same phenomenon that would overtake your hand if you kept a clenched fist too long, so that when you opened the grip your fingers would tremble, they would drop things" (172).

Intellectually and emotionally clenched to wrest from the world the power her immigrant parents lacked, Gerda is also imprisoned by the very qualities that empower her. "Impatient with the obsessions of others," she believes passionately in "order" (160) and "restraint" (113). Linking always the individual to the general case, she respects "repetition as the true and only movement of history, both public and private" (84). These principles carry Gerda beyond her father's failures and her mother's stony despair. But her daughter, Renata, defies the logic of "repetition," values neither "order" nor "self-restraint," and recognizes only the needs of individuals, never the general demands of history or "civilization." Gerda's rejection of her own mother's values are thus replicated by the daughter who defies every imperative that structures Gerda's life.

In this mother-daughter pair, Brown juxtaposes two strikingly different women who reflect one another like concave and convex mirrors in an amusement park. The logic of each one's development and heredity is clear: neither can be other than she is. Both carry forward and react against elements of their own childhood families and cultural circumstances. But neither can accept the other or affirm herself without the other's acceptance and affirmation. Gerda sees Renata only as her husband's child: "Ethereally blond, her father's pale hair . . . unfamiliar in my eyes. . . . Even her eyelashes are negative, wholly unrelated to anything of mine" (44). Thus, she dissociates herself from her child, "accidentally conceived, genetically and spiritually . . . her father's only, and he a phantom who passed meaninglessly into and out of my life with the speed of sound" (82). Renata, in turn, rejects the mother who loves "through a window, you know, glass in between. No touching" (225). Knowing only "the tradition of American mothers tethered to the kitchen door within hearing of their beloved children's every cry" (83), Renata is unable to value a mother who works in the world. She blames Gerda for the work that is the cornerstone of her self-respect and the guarantor of their financial security. Gerda blames Renata for weeping instead of working and for seeking "comfort" in the arms of men she does not love. Both women find intolerable the characteristics that differentiate them from one another.

Their differences obstruct and endanger the passage of feelings between them—like sharp rocks curtained by the waterfall in which Renata's child, Gerda's grandchild, ultimately drowns. When Gerda looks at Renata, she thinks, "She bore me not sufficient resemblance to involve my flesh in hers" (82). When Renata looks at her mother, she thinks:

"The sight of her face . . . is still and forever a finger down my throat" (32). But both discover they cannot look away from one another. Listening to Gerda's criticisms, Renata realizes that "her look is a mirror of mine. . . . We are appalled by one another" (135). Made fearful by Renata's hostile silence, Gerda learns that "if she looks through me long enough soon I will not be there. . . . Why must she answer me to make me feel I am truly here?" (216–17). The novel carries both women toward deeper awareness of their need to be reflected by one another but denies them the affirmative reflections that would satisfy that need.

Like Camille Baum, Brown identifies another important facet of mother/daughter mirroring that Benjamin would later theorize in the early eighties. Winnicott had thought that the child seeks the mirror of its mother's face to assure itself of her approval and its likeness to her. But Benjamin argued that recognition, not reflection, is the function of child/parent mirroring. Moreover, in her view, recognition includes not just likeness and approval as Winnicott had thought but also identification and acceptance of differences.

The goal of mutual recognition, Benjamin believes, is not to merge with a being like oneself but to share experience with someone who is both like and unlike: the same in some ways and different in others. Indeed, Benjamin insists that "one of the most important insights of intersubjective theory is that sameness and difference exist simultaneously in mutual recognition" (*Bonds* 47). The importance of this insight lies in its power to de-pathologize the sensation of love, describing it no longer as what Freud had called an "oceanic feeling" of merging, of union and lost boundaries, but imaging it rather as a process of coming together and parting, of affirming and being affirmed, of being separate and together, of being both like and unlike the "other" whom one sees as a mirror of oneself.

Able to recognize but unable to affirm the differences they perceive in each other's reflections, Renata and Gerda can neither love nor look away from one another. Like Selene Kramer and her mother, Renata and Gerda are connected by a narcissistic bond that never matures into mutual recognition but becomes destructive: as mother and daughter look at one another, they cannot see the small grandchild who needs their attention and who drowns in the rocky waters that rush beside their common path. Unable to see themselves in one another or in the child who is, audaciously, herself, mother and daughter in this novel can neither nurture, nor affirm, nor love, nor sustain in life one another or the child who depends on them.

Beneath the image of the rejecting mother who had been demonized by experts in midcentury, these American Jewish writers of the seventies perceived not only the narcissistic deprivations that scarred maternal images but also the inability to tolerate difference that distanced mothers from their daughters—and vice versa. Thus, the perspective of the seventies magnifies in retrospect the power of immigrant mothers and American daughters to respect the differences between them, by comparison with the inability of many postwar women to achieve mutual, reciprocal recognition. Unlike the daughters who affirmed their mothers even when they believed they needed to leave them, many protagonists of the seventies blamed mothers—as Renata does—not only for rejecting them but for being different, or for denying the differences between them. Writers of the seventies see that the mutual rejection of mother and daughter is partly a reflex of unavoidable cultural differences and partly a consequence of their inability to love what is different from themselves.

These novels of the seventies, as Lasch assumed, are indeed preoccupied with the failures of romantic love and domesticity. But they look beneath these unsatisfactory social arrangements—to the malaise of women and their mothers who belong to different cultural moments and therefore conceive differently the interface between self-realization and the love of others. Unlike the liberated women Lasch described, the "narcissistic" protagonists of these novels blame themselves and their mothers, not just their patriarchal husbands or lovers, for the failure of the marriage plot to satisfy their needs. Some protagonists see in their mothers' inability to love them maternal deprivations equal to the deprivations they inflict on their own daughters. Other protagonists charge their mothers not with coldness or failure of love but with the sins of conventionality and compliance that subvert a daughter's sense of herself and deny her the satisfactions she seeks in a changing world. Still other protagonists expose—even when they do not fully accept into their own consciousness—their likeness to mothers who cannot acknowledge in some cases and affirm in others the differences between them.

Daphne Merkin's *Enchantment* (1984) carries the theme of narcissism into the eighties, finding in it the salient insight that mother/daughter relationships cannot thrive unless and until daughters become aware of their mothers as subjects. In some respects, this novel critiques a peculiarly virulent form of midcentury maternal demonization. Confirming the wisdom of the experts, male writers like Philip Roth enshrined in fiction of the sixties the overprotective mother as the mirror opposite of the rejecting mother. The narrator of *Portnoy's Complaint* exposes to his analyst his "history of disenchantment" with his mother (9) in order to free himself of her exaggerated expectations, her intrusive, aggressive anxieties and control. But the narrator of Merkin's *Enchantment* (1984) tells Portnoy's sister's side of the family story. Bearing the same first name as Portnoy's older sister, Merkin's Hannah Lehmann blames her mother for expecting too little of her, for caring too little, for giving too little. Her grievances owe something to both culture and gender. The child of wealthy German, rather than lower-middle-class East European immigrants like the Portnoys, Hannah knows the culture of deliberate restraint—of orange juice rationed by a servant in tiny glasses rather than forced feedings supervised by Sophie Portnoy with a bread knife. Like Portnoy's sister, moreover, Hannah Lehmann is not the star of her family. She feels keenly her secondariness, making her mother guess her identity through a closed door to assure herself that she is recognizable among her siblings.

Doubting her value, uncertain about her identity (like virtually all the protagonists in stories of this period), Hannah looks to mirrors, lovers, and friends, to clothes and makeup, and to images of women in film, books, and television to tell her who she is and ought to be. Her narrative persistently questions not only her own self-worth but also the reliability of her own point of view. She critiques her memories by comparing them with those of her siblings and with photographs; she questions the value of her interpretations and the accuracy of her perceptions; she analyzes her reactions by considering the difference between them and the reactions of others in her family. Like Hannah, all her siblings visit the family home regularly for what one analyst calls "more orange juice." But unlike Hannah, her brothers and sisters marry, have children, leave home, and pursue careers and relationships, while Hannah continues to tell everything to her mother and her analysts and is drawn only to withholding men who like to punish her.

Like the narcissists studied by Lasch and his experts, Hannah appears to be bound by her deprivations to the mother who deprived her and to the men who repeat that early pattern. But Merkin emphasizes two elements of Hannah's attitude that redistribute responsibility for her continuing enchantment. In part, she shares Renata Stein's inability to accept the difference between her own mother and the mother image purveyed by her culture. "What I wanted," Hannah confesses, "was for her to stand over a hot stove, like all the immigrant mothers I had ever read about, and stir soup: I yearned for the stereotype instead of the unpredictable, powerful person I had been born to" (20). Thus, this daughter's energies are always spent on producing "a miraculous transformation" in her mother (35), on bending her "to my concept of how things—she—ought to be" (20). Although her mother tells her early and often that "your tears don't move me," Hannah continues to weep and rage and weep again. She is imprisoned—like Renata—by her own refusal to accept the discrepancy between the mother she has and the mother her culture has taught her to want.

Both protagonists are also limited by their inability to see into their mothers, beyond the surface of the image mirrored by their memories. Like Renata and even Portnoy, who both see their mothers only as reflexes of their own needs, Hannah knows her mother is both the wicked witch and an object of desire. But as her narrative progresses, she begins to wonder, "Who is my mother when she is not being my mother?" Eventually she realizes that "I never think of her this way, as a daughter in her own right" (186). Thus, Merkin's Hannah stumbles at the end of her story upon the self-reflective, self-validating power of mutual recognition.

Theoretically, the child who learns to see her mother as a subject in her own right, responsive to her child's needs but also moved by forces other than her child, achieves in that moment of complex recognition an awareness of itself as a subject, too. But the ability to see a mother in this way is usually obstructed by images contaminated partly by the peremptoriness of everyone's childhood needs, partly by the cultural tendency to undervalue on the one hand and exploit on the other the services of mothers, and partly, as Benjamin has recently observed, by the persistent bias of psychology. "We have only just begun to think about the mother as a subject in her own right," Benjamin notes, thus acknowledging that psychological literature has historically allied itself exclusively with the child's point of view. "No psychological theory," she points out,

> has adequately articulated the mother's independent existence. Thus even the accounts of the mother-infant relationship which do consider parental responsiveness always revert to a view of the mother as the baby's vehicle for growth, an object of the baby's needs. The mother is the baby's first object of attachment, and later, the object of desire. She is provider, interlocutor, caregiver, contin-

gent reinforcer, significant other, empathic understander, mirror. She is also a secure presence to walk away from, a setter of limits, an optimal frustrator, a shockingly real outside otherness. She is external reality—but she is rarely regarded as another subject with a purpose apart from her existence for her child. . . . Yet the real mother is not simply an object for her child's demands; she is, in fact, another subject whose independent center must be outside her child if she is to grant him [sic] the recognition he seeks.[22] (*Bonds* 23–24)

The inability of fictional protagonists to perceive mothers as subjects, independent of their own needs as children, then, reflects a given of our culture—not a neurotic symptom of a narcissistic personality. But stories on the theme of narcissism in the seventies develop in their protagonists an awareness of the mother that facilitates perception of her as a separate being—with unmet needs, perceptual limitations, and inadequacies very like her daughter's. In Merkin's story of the eighties, one protagonist finally moves through the looking glass toward a "recognition of the mother as a person in her own right" (*Bonds* 24).

Hannah Lehmann gradually grows into that complex awareness, achieving it when she affirms her mother and herself as both different and alike: "We are all daughters of yet other daughters," Hannah says, "and everywhere are strewn the mothers with broken hearts. . . . The half of my mother that is not me is like the dark side of the moon, unknowable" (178–79). Grasping in one moment both the likeness and the unknowable otherness of mothers to their daughters, Hannah can then dream her own rebirth: in this dream she discovers that the female images drawn by a loving father resemble her; and then she runs forward into her own life, "freer than can be," waved on by her mother.

By developing in her protagonist the power to imagine a facet of her mother that can never be seen, and to hear what her mother cannot (will not?) say, Merkin's Hannah foreshadows protagonists of the eighties who enter into a fuller dialogue between mother and daughter. But her movement toward that insight is the characteristic story of the seventies. In that decade, protagonists, who rejected the norms of female behavior mandated for women of the fifties, begin to penetrate the mysterious, hidden needs and deprivations of their mothers—whose lives had been determined by those norms. Denied by postwar culture the honor that tradition had given to maternal sacrifices, and prevented from developing the formidable strengths that had distinguished the immigrant mother, postwar mothers were domesticated by experts who neither honored their sacrifices, nor dignified their work, nor understood their dilemma. When their stories of self lost clarity and integrity, their daughters in the seventies fell under the spell of their mothers' images. Indeed, the fascination of so many protagonists with the mother as mirror testifies richly to the power always possessed by images before words come to clarify, interpret, or explain them. More important, the apparently narcissistic absorption of daughters in their mothers also performs the cultural work of probing for stories that cannot yet be told.

Notes

1. Hertzberg notes that "the question of self-definition was being posed in the mid-sixties, but most Jews paid no attention" (353). In these novels, self-definition is very much the issue but not, for the most part, within a Jewish framework.

2. In this respect, these stories differ markedly from films and TV programs of the same period from which images of mothers and daughters had almost entirely disappeared, according to Walters (108–11).

3. This chapter considers the following novels: Ozick, *Trust* (1966); Roiphe, *Up the Sandbox!* (1970); Baum, *Member of the Tribe* (1971); Shulman, *Memoirs of an Ex-Prom Queen* (1972); List, *Did You Love Daddy When I Was Born?* (1972); Jong, *Fear of Flying* (1973); R. Brown, *Autobiography of My Mother* (1976); and Merkin, *Enchantment* (1984).

4. Barrett and McIntosh review some of the critical responses by feminists.

5. Lasch has recently been criticized by one feminist biographer for "profound misogyny" (Rudnick 120–21). With many theorists of his time Lasch shares a readiness to blame mothers for the malaise and misbehavior of their children. One contemporary feminist psychologist has also linked narcissistic mother-blaming to the resurgent women's movement of the sixties. Donna Bassin suspects that, as the women's movement raised women's consciousness of their social situations, it also encouraged antagonism between daughters and their mothers. Feminists who needed both to blame someone for and to liberate themselves from gendered social restrictions, Bassin suggests, were caught in a "defensive separation process" (quoted in Baruch and Serrano 342). Needing to strike out at limits that oppressed them, they targeted their mothers, who were both the most obvious "victims of patriarchal society" and also the earliest and most familiar limit-setters their daughters had known.

6. Experts thus reproduced the mother-blaming child in their own image. Ehrenreich and English cite several clinicians of the forties, fifties, and

sixties who developed a "pathology of motherhood" that held mothers responsible for both overprotecting and rejecting their young and that located in maternal mistreatment virtually all the ills to which humankind is heir.

7. Though not a Jew, she is as famished as the Jewish mother who feeds others to secure their love (cf. Duncan, "Hungry" 232).

8. One critic, however, reads Allegra as "more like a hallucinated projection of the heroine's resentment than a credible mother or wife or woman" (Goodheart 14).

9. This crucial reunion links two apparently contradictory paternal behavior patterns that contemporary feminist scholarship has recently identified as "mirrors" of one another. When the narrator's father, who abandoned her in her infancy and ignored her until she was grown, summons her to his island and turns his seductive charm fully upon her, he demonstrates that—as Boose has argued, "avoidance, abandonment, and discarding of the daughter" often function in literature as "inverted mirrors that reflect the father's flight from incest" (31).

10. Theorists have long believed that only fathers can help daughters separate from their mothers. Indeed, according to one analyst, women desire "to confer power on men or on fathers to liberate themselves from maternal dominance" (Baruch and Serrano 112).

11. In this context, one wonders how seriously one ought to take the possibility that Nick's portrayal reflects the early influence of Henry James on Ozick as a young writer.

12. Umansky argues that "participation even in seemingly nonreligious organizations like Hadassah" offers a way "in which many Jewish women throughout the twentieth century have sought to give their own understanding of Jewish self-identity greater public expression" ("Spiritual" 274).

13. Parent, *Sheila Levine*; Lukas, *Fat Emily*.

14. Reich, *Mara*.

15. Piercy, *Small Changes*.

16. Schaeffer, *Falling*.

17. Theorists have speculated on the psychological origins of mother-blaming. Freudians, for example, believe that "primitive archaic conflicts with the mother" account for her daughter's "negative relation" to her (Baruch and Serrano 111–12). Melanie Klein, on the other hand, theorizes that children project onto images of their mothers their own envy and possessiveness (Baruch and Serrano 254). More recently, Luce Irigaray has suggested that the mother, rendered powerless and excluded from "social and creative activity," seems oppressive because she "reproduces the oppression to which she is subject" (Baruch and Serrano 156). Julia Kristeva suspects that daughters' anger against their mothers demonstrates their "rejection of the maternal function—a fascinated rejection" (Baruch and Serrano 138).

18. On these changes, see Garner, "Constructing the Mother."

19. Lacan saw "the mirror stage as formative of the function of the 'I' as revealed in psychoanalytic experience" (1–2).

20. Breines suggests that "postwar culture was a culture of containment," composed of people who were anxious enough to want to control or exclude difference rather than to acknowledge or understand it (10).

21. Wolk shows how the novel demonstrates the loss of boundaries between a mother and a daughter who are estranged and yet unable to look away from one another.

22. All the essays in the recent publication *Representations of Motherhood* (Bassin, Honey, and Kaplan 1994) attempt in various ways to surface maternal subjectivity.

5

Re-storying Jewish Women:
Hearing the Mothers,
Speaking the Feminist Self

> Mother, Queen of the roses,
> wearer of forks and petals,
> when may I be free of you?
> When will I be done
> with the force of your magic?
>
> —Maxine Kumin,
> "A Voice from the Roses"

> Like those old pear-shaped Russian dolls that open
> at the middle to reveal another and another, down
> to the pea-sized minim,
> may we carry our mothers forth in our bellies.
> May we, borne onward by our daughters, ride
> in the Envelope of Almost-Infinity,
> that chain letter good for the next twenty-five
> thousand days of their lives.
>
> —Maxine Kumin, "The Envelope"

Stories by American Jewish women writers have developed a cluster of
common themes around issues related to ethnicity and the family. But
their course seems to run directly into the American mainstream. They
trace the trajectory of their protagonists away from ethnic and religious
particularity, toward a larger commonality with non-Jewish, middle-class
American women who are also becoming consumers, awakening as feminists, centering themselves in their own maternal narratives, or simply
reacting as individuals against the ethnic and religious imperatives of

their families and communities. Absent from most of these stories are the ingredients many readers expect to find in "Jewish" stories: the "Jewish sense that we are all responsible for each other and for the survival of our culture"; the "deep sense of community, even of family, which enables members of a group to see themselves as part of a larger whole with the continuity of tradition and history" (S. Smith 62). The stories seem to have lost the collective Jewish consciousness of an urgent connection between human beings and God, of specific rituals that order human behavior, of a world to be repaired, and of strangers to be cared for by Jews who remember that they, too, have been strangers in a strange land.

In the seventies, however, this trajectory returns upon itself. Anticipated in some respects by the bold parochialism of Cynthia Ozick[1] and the social sensitivity of Tillie Olsen and Grace Paley, many American Jewish women writers of the eighties and nineties turn in their stories to the wellsprings of Jewish belief, practice, and collective experience. From these sources, recent writers draw the energy that motivates protagonists, that renders their lives meaningful, and that rekindles in narrative the light of Jewish ethnicity and spirituality.[2] Many protagonists now "carry forth," in Maxine Kumin's phrase, the visions of women who came before them. They deliver them, however, enriched—modified/augmented—by their own experience. Thus, in an important sense, writers of the late seventies, eighties, and nineties are re-storying Jewish women. Their protagonists speak themselves through narratives that both recall and transform the stories of their collective and individual mothers.

No one in these decades writes larger than Vivian Gornick the emotional intensity of this process. She restories the *Fierce Attachments* (1987) that bind daughter to mother, recalling the plot of her mother's narrative and uncovering the legacy it conceals. This autobiographical memoir is the story of a quest for the contemporary equivalent of the immigrant mother's embroidered tablecloth: the gift that can transform the mother's into the daughter's story—without severing them from one another. As the narrator recalls the emotional landscape they share, she recognizes domestic romance as the plot she inherits from her mother. Like many middle-class American women in her generation, Gornick's mother believes in the romance of domestic love. Defining herself as a happily married woman, "not just happily married. Magically married. Definitively married" (22), Mama worships "the goodness of her married life" (23). After her husband's death, when she can no longer believe in herself as a wife, widowhood provides her "with a higher form of being": "Mourning Papa became her profession, her identity, her persona" (76). Mama's life has been narrowed—one might say impoverished—by this nearly religious devotion to the romance of domesticity. She has been, briefly, a talented political organizer and communist fellow traveler (17). But when her husband insists that she "'stop this work' to stay home with the baby," she obeys (17). She has also known the pleasure of paid work in the world (195). But when her husband asks her, again, to stay home because "no other wife in the neighborhood works" (196), she quits. Her daughter cannot overlook the negative effects of these sacrifices on her mother's life: "Mama worships at the shrine of Love," Gornick realizes, "but that lifelong boredom of hers is a dead giveaway" (175).

The ideal of romantic love in this memoir is also tarnished by the absence of sexual vitality from Mama's marriage—an absence made visible by the steamy sexual rages and couplings of neighbors in the tenement. One neighbor in particular, a promiscuous, non-Jewish woman, kindles and tries to sophisticate Gornick's appetite for a more purely erotic kind of loving. Nettie, a beautiful, red-haired widow "trained to attract, not to domesticate" (49), cannot perform any of the tasks that have traditionally defined and evaluated the Jewish woman. Because she is inept and disorganized, her home and child receive meager care. She feels only contempt for the men she attracts, and her bruises illustrate the power struggle implicit in her erotic liaisons. But her beauty "radiated a kind of promise" that the adolescent Gornick cannot "stay away from" (37). Even as an adult, she feels the power of Nettie's image to stir her own deepest erotic response. Nettie's image remains "quick to the touch, warm and alive," the protagonist discovers as she analyzes the sexual failure of her own marriage: "I could imagine her. She was real to me, he was not" (154).

"Mothered," thus, by two women who believe in romantic love, this daughter hears the same message twice in different registers: from Mama, "Life without a man is unlivable"; from Nettie, "Men are scum but you gotta have one" (113). The conflict between domestic and erotic love, as well as Gornick's insight into the deficiencies of *both* modes of heterosexual attachment, make the love story an unacceptable plot for the narrative of this daughter's life. "I don't think I can learn to do that one," she tells her therapist, a third maternal figure who joins Mama and Nettie in insisting that Gornick needs a man to love.

Instead, her narrative finds in her mother's story a current that runs deeper than romantic love. From its source at the kitchen window where the listening child first hears her mother turning into stories the calls and cries of neighbor women, this current carries both mother and daughter toward the work that draws meaning from the confusing incoherence of experience. Their window opens onto an alley in the Bronx where "there were no trees, or bushes, or grasses of any kind." But Gornick remembers it as a "place of clear light and sweet air, suffused, somehow, with a perpetual smell of summery green" (137). Here, she suggests, not in the bedroom or the nursery, not at the stove or the sewing machine, is the Jewish mother's garden. Here the child learns to appreciate the interest of women's voices, to feel contempt for the work of cooking and cleaning, and to prize above all things the narrative skill that distinguishes her mother from other women. Mama's "running commentary on the life outside the window was my first taste of the fruits of intelligence," her daughter remembers. Like the fairy-tale sorcerer who can spin straw into gold, this mother does not fabricate; she transforms: she "knew how to convert gossip into knowledge" (15).

Women's voices in this novel are never limited to the presymbolic murmur and babble of pre-oedipal mother and child. For Gornick, Mama's voice is associated from the outset with the power to read experience as though every nuance of tone and diction were symbolically suggestive, meaningful. Mama herself takes pride in her extraordinary interpretive skills: her certainty, for example, that a dark shape lying on a country road is the passionate Kornfeld—a woman who, longing for love, has run away from their communal summer cottage. Gornick, too, feels both pride and love when Mama speaks out of the thoughtful, analytical, interpretive part of herself that can seize from the muddle of sense and feeling the jewel of meaning. "I feel pleasure when she says a true or clever thing," Gornick confesses. "Her faded brown eyes, dark and brilliant in my childhood, brighten as the meaning of her words and mine penetrates her thought. Her cheeks flush and her pudding soft face hardens wonderfully with new definition. She looks beautiful to me" (32).

Even Mama's withdrawal as she turns inward to seek the meaning of an experience creates pleasure, not pain, for her daughter. Ordinarily, when Mama withdraws into herself Gornick discovers how powerfully she needs the "live, warm presence of my mother," needs "her to respond, to be there with me" (135); "it's death to me, her not knowing I'm there" (104). But when Mama turns inward to think, Gornick celebrates her mother's power rather than mourning the loss of her mother's attention. She watches as Mama "stares off into the middle distance. . . . She's alone inside that faraway look on her face, but this alone . . . is . . . full of interest, not a trace of self pity in it. Now when her eyes narrow it is to take in more clearly what she knows, concentrate on what she has lived" (61). As Gornick celebrates the thinking person within the maternal persona, she restories the traditional mother whose role was limited to nurturing and sustaining others. She transforms also the imprisoning, narcissistic love of a daughter dependent on her mother's mirroring attention and recognition. Instead, she develops what Jessica Benjamin would call an identificatory love that prizes her mother's particular gift even when it diverts her mother's attention—because that gift is hers as well.

The preciousness of this shared gift becomes evident particularly in the moments of illumination that Gornick celebrates in herself as well as in her mother (102). She knows in herself the process that appeared so beautiful in her mother. In that process, she reports, "the space inside me enlarges. That rectangle of light and air inside, where thought clarifies, and language grows, and response is made intelligent . . . opens wide." Like the alley beyond the kitchen window with its inexplicable scent of summer green, the mind within opens outward to the world, admitting light and producing utterance.

This finding of voice in concentrated, clarified thought makes Mama, the married lady, a storyteller and interpreter whose place is still "woman's place," the kitchen window. But it makes her daughter a professional writer. Whatever she is paid for her work, whether she travels or works at home, Gornick realizes that the joy of clear thought and meaningful utterance is unsurpassable: "Not an 'I love you' in the world could touch it" (152). Lovers repeatedly disappoint her, but she never doubts that "the desk—not the satisfactory resolution of love—was the potential lifesaver" (189).

Possession of this lifesaving power will make Gornick her mother's successor, for the stories she tells will identify her beyond question as her mother's daughter. Unlike Nettie, whose fantasies are always romances (52–54), the adolescent Gornick is drawn, like her mother, to "'stories of large meaning.' . . . To be saved from meaninglessness, I knew, was everything. Largeness of meaning was redemption" (55–56). In her search for meaning she will turn away from stories that still speak to her mother of a Jewish past, that "remind and persuade . . . heal and connect . . . let people make sense of themselves" by providing an ethnic context for their uncertainties (47). Mama responds to them, but Gornick declares that "being Jewish can't help me any more" (48).

Her own earliest stories reflect, nevertheless, the heroic implications of her mother's early political commitments, the strong, morally vital, social consciousness that other American descendants of Jewish activist women in Europe brought to socialism, progressivism, the labor movement, and communal work. "I always daydreamed," she recalls, "I was making eloquent speeches that stirred ten thousand people to feel their lives, and to *act*" (54). When she sees a worn and tattered streetwalker, her compassion for the woman's need—like Mama's for Nettie—provokes yet another kind of heroic fantasy: "I had begun to imagine myself healing her" (57). Ultimately, the streetwalker's image will blend, in her mind, with images of Nettie, her mother, and herself. Thus, the impulse to identify with the outcast survives in this daughter's stories—severed though it may be from the specific historical Jewish memories that are still powerful for her mother.

Inheritance of her mother's narrative gift makes Gornick a threat as well as a successor to her mother, for Mama's distinctive style is incorrigibly adversarial. Whether she responds to panhandlers on the street, to neighbors, or to her daughter, she labels "ridiculous" whatever she disapproves of, disagrees with, or doesn't understand. Gornick recognizes the adversarial quality of her mother's style as the "idiom of her being": "That dismissiveness of hers; it will be the last thing to go. In fact, it will never go. It is the emblem of her speech, the idiom of her being, that which establishes her in her own eyes. The dismissal of others is to her the struggle to rise from the beasts, to make distinctions, to know the right or wrong of a thing, to not think it unimportant, ever, that the point be made" (198).

When Gornick learns to think, when the study of literature sharpens her own critical intelligence, when she reinterprets her mother's stories, Mama angrily ridicules her daughter's pretensions. For example, when Gornick questions Mama's self-protective reading of an old family story, Mama defends her own narrative authority by belittling her daughter's motives and intelligence (6–9). The issues they fight over vary through the memoir, but the provocation is always the same. "What drove her, and divided us, was me thinking," Gornick realizes. Thus, when Mama's control of their collaborative story is threatened by her daughter's developing powers of language and critical thought, both women fall into the pattern of "accusation and retaliation" that always makes "fierce" their attachment to one another. The flashes of belligerence that punctuate their interactions only illuminate the likeness of style and the mutual need of narrative control that both bind and set them against one another.

At the end, Mama will acknowledge in two ways her awareness that Gornick now possesses the power not only to shape the plot of her own narrative but also to restory her mother's life. In Yiddish, "the language of irony and defiance," Mama first concedes her daughter's interpretive control: "'So . . . you'll write down here on my tombstone,' she says bitterly, 'From the very beginning it was all water under the bridge'" (204). Laying down a dishtowel as though it were Prospero's wand, she asks a final question that goes to the heart of their joint story and acknowledges her daughter's power to both write and interpret it. In a voice "remarkably free of emotion—a voice detached, curious, only wanting information—she says to me, 'Why don't you go already? Why don't you walk away from my life? I'm not stopping you.'" Mama wants to know the plot of the next chapter. But Gornick, still "half in and half out" of her mother's house, cannot yet say—much less explain—what will happen next.[3]

With true writerly instinct, Mama Gornick seizes the central problem of American Jewish women's stories of the eighties and nineties: When heterosexual romance no longer dominates the imagination, what *is* the plot of women's lives?[4] At the end of her memoir, Gornick's position offers its own response to that question. She has written elsewhere that women must leave their mothers, must "detach without withdrawing," to put childhood behind them and enter the world. "The writer knows," she points out, "what really goes on between a mother and a daughter when the daughter wants to live not the given life but a free one, one that won't repeat the mother's life. That's *true* separation" ("World" 53).

The power to achieve such a separation is within this narrator's grasp, for the tools she needs come to her still warm from her mother's hand. The energy, ferocity, and narrative skill, the analytic and interpretive keenness that allow her, as "writer," to "know" the task she must perform, are the likenesses that keep her from withdrawing from her mother's house—as well as the abilities that enable her detachment.

Thus, like the passionate Kornfeld of her mother's generation, lying on a country road longing for love, Gornick becomes what Bonnie Zimmerman has called a "metaphor of position" ("Lesbians" 3). She stands between her mother's life, her own childhood, and her adult future, and also between the private world of the family home and the public world outside it. Not prostrated, like Kornfeld, by the quest for romance but standing firmly on "the borders between mutiple cultures and identities," she suggests a new plot for women of the eighties. As she restories the effort of mother and daughter to make sense of their joint and separate lives, she takes up what Zimmerman recognizes as the task of the eighties: "the hard and often unsettling reconceptualisation of the nature of identity and the subject" ("Lesbians" 3).

As Gornick's daydreams of speechmaking before vast crowds suggest, that task becomes political as well as personal, for American Jewish women who undertook it after the seventies understood that the two contexts were actually inseparable. This awareness reinvigorated a tradition of Jewish women's activism that had begun to transform the nature of their identity in the shtetls of late nineteenth-century Eastern Europe. Jewish women's activism has long been part of American culture. But several features of its European genesis both contextualize its American embodiment and clarify important elements of feminist stories after the sixties. For the purposes of this study, Jewish women's prominence in revolutionary European politics was notable primarily because, in order to become politically active, they needed first to sever ties that bound them to their families, their communities, and the traditions that would have denied them public voice and agency. Multiply alienated, they sought "self-esteem through political involvement," taking "strength from Old World traditions of women's work . . . while rejecting Jewish notions of female inferiority" (Glenn 6). As socialist and Zionist women studied together and worked to change society, they also began to "transform" the social identity of the Jewish woman (Glenn 6). In the process, Naomi Shepherd reports, they lost awareness of themselves as Jews.

This nineteenth-century European reconfiguration of Jewish women's identity demonstrated the tight connection between the personal and political. The readiness of these early Jewish women activists to perceive at the intersection of politics and psychology an opportunity to "create a new identity for themselves as women, in defiance of the norms of their own society," made them, in Shepherd's eyes, "pioneers of women's liberation" (290). But the new identity lacked the ethnic and spiritual elements that belonged to earlier versions of Jewish women's sense of themselves. It also diminished activist women's sense of likeness to their mothers. Indeed, in Shepherd's view, "Jewish women's breach with the past, the refusal to be one more link in the golden chain and to follow their female ancestors into 'kosher beds' is most dramatically obvious in the change in mother-daughter relationships, and not in the rebellion against patriarchal standards alone" (290). Unwilling to enter traditional marriages and to assume the traditional burdens of family life, activist Jewish women sought instead "to appropriate the world of ideas—hitherto, in their communal tradition, the world of men alone—and to build a new and egalitarian relationship with men" (294). Many activist Jewish women enjoyed "complex and often intimate relationship[s] with their fathers, against whom they rebelled but whom they also wished to emulate" (7). Respectful toward "their fathers' intellectual interests" (292), they sought to share *them* rather than the domestic and economic concerns of their mothers. Instead of marriage and family, they desired "an emotional and intellectual partnership of equality with a man—a totally new concept in Jewish mores, and one which often proved hard to achieve" (66). Thus, these activist women introduced into the historical experience and self-awareness of Jewish women not only a new way of conceiving female identity but also a new way of conceiving heterosexual relationships.

On the way to America, some elements of European Jewish women's activism underwent a sea change, but others crossed the ocean intact. Jewish women's concern for the improvement of working conditions and for the cause of social justice remained unchanged. Like their European predecessors, Jewish immigrant daughters were also drawn into various forms of social and political activism because it offered them "compelling new opportunities for public recognition, dignity, and respectability" (Glenn 5).[5] Thus, in America, Jewish women remembered the stories of their European "mothers" who had learned the power of activism to construct identity—and to break the silence tradition had imposed upon them. In activist work they discovered the "power of their public voice and political agency" (Glenn 169). It was a distinctive and powerful voice.[6] In union meetings, women's voices not only achieved clarity of ideas but also evoked "sympathy" because they avoided generalities.[7] Attention to the specifics of human experience, as Gornick's mother demonstrates at her kitchen window, remained the characteristic mark of the Jewish woman storyteller. But Jewish working women, as one letter-writer to *Life and Labor* indicated, also preferred stories like the heroic daydreams of the young Gornick that always reached out for large meanings: stories "that tell of struggle, and that tell of people who want justice passionately" (Glenn 191).

In general, the activist American Jewish women who worked for the labor movement or women's suffrage, or who fought prostitution and white slavery, resembled in many ways their European counterparts. But there were important differences between them as well. American women who became activists no longer needed to rebel against ethnic, religious, and family ties; they were most often supported and encouraged—rather than condemned—by their families (Glenn 205).[8] Thus, they enjoyed not only the power to become themselves by speaking and acting publicly but also the comfort of knowing they belonged to a "tradition" of activist Jewish women.

As they moved into various forms of social and political activism, moreover, they also carried with them the more problematic expectations of European activists that heterosexual relationships would change into "something rich and strange." There was a public as well as a private dimension to those expectations. "Jewish women had always known," Susan Glenn points out,

> that the struggle for daily bread took place in partnership with fathers, brothers, and husbands. But [they were] changing the terms of the discourse, redefining and renegotiating the meaning of that partnership. No longer would young women be content to struggle as the silent half; now they wanted the voice, the recognition, the respect that as working partners they had long been denied. This was a revolution in immigrant women's thinking . . . a new definition of womanhood being constructed on the foundations of the old. (208)

Activism transformed—in a way that marketplace activity had not—the Jewish woman's sense of herself and her relationship to men.

In several important respects, however, the old ways continued to exert a restraining influence on the development of activist American Jewish women. They were, for example, reluctant to press to the limit their demand for equal status within their organizations. Although women made "little headway" into the top echelons of the labor movement (Glenn 222), they accepted "junior" status rather than withdraw to form their own groups. Remembering the traditional Jewish women who came before them, they were determined not to move backward "to the gender separation that had limited their access to public life and underscored their cultural inferiority in the shtetl. . . . To return to a world that isolated the sexes would have been to take a step backward to the world of their mothers and grandmothers, a world defined by the exclusionary, misogynist traditions of Old World culture" (Glenn 237). In Jewish communal organizations as well, at least until the seventies women were notably underrepresented in "honorific roles and positions of influence" (Cohen, Dessel, and Pelavin 193). But they continued to serve as volunteers in organizations that included both men and women—accepting their secondary status as my mother accepted her silence and impotence in the synagogue. Thus, for these women as for their European predecessors, the memory of traditional restrictions made gender equality secondary to inclusion in the previously all male world of social and political activism.

In personal terms, ethnic and gendered memories also continued to shape the decisions of activist American Jewish women and their sense of themselves. Because they remembered *both* the domestic priorities of their traditional mothers *and* the romantic expectations of radical Jewish women in Europe, they were peculiarly susceptible to the "romance plot" that ultimately dominated the lives of American women like Mama Gornick. Even women like Rebekah Kohut, who organized and led separate communal organizations for Jewish women, modeled in their private lives conventional domestic arrangements. Union women, Glenn reports, wanted not only to enjoy "a greater regard than misogynist traditions of shtetl culture had bestowed" on women (214) but also to marry—romantically, if possible (157–59, 239). Recalling and transforming both the values of their domestic mothers and the romantic, egalitarian ambitions of European radicals, they complicated further the identity of Jewish women by refusing either to critique institutions and conventions that limited them or to edit out apparently incompatible goals.

Instead, they developed a mode of life and a sense of self remarkable for what one historian calls its "fluidity." Though they remained politically aware after marriage, they moved, like Mama Gornick, "in and out of political life as easily as they dropped in and out of breadwinning," Glenn observes. For them, "work, activism, and domesticity were never clearly demarcated stages in the life cycle" (240–42).[9] Thus, they embraced alternatives without choosing among them. In the new circumstances of America, they would be *both* activists *and* Jews. They would seek respect, romance, *and* domestic respectability. By moving into and out of public and private life, they would restory the more limited choices of both European radicals and immigrant daughters.

After the war, *their* daughters would withdraw from this fluctuation between private and public worlds into the private world of family as they began "to feel more at home with the cult of domesticity" (Glenn 242). But in homes devoted to that cult—as we have seen—mothers would also nurture daughters like Vivian Gornick and other writers of the late seventies, eighties, and nineties who would reject domesticity and the romance plot. In search of other plots, these women would become activists. But they would be feminists and Jews as well: less tolerant of "junior status" in relationships and organizations, more willing to separate themselves from men when gender equality was withheld, more intentional as Jews than the Europeans, and more critical of both Jewish tradition and romantic domesticity than the American women who had been activists before them.

The narratives of these Jewish feminist daughters "reconceptualize" female identity in ways that both recall and transform—that restory—European and American Jewish activists of earlier decades. Like the European women who were radicalized as much by traditional repressions and exclusions as by revolutionary socialist ideas, American Jewish women of the sixties came to the feminist movement out of their confinement in the cult of domesticity. In consciousness-raising groups they discovered anew the formative link between "the personal and the political." But that rediscovery bore different fruit for them than for their activist "mothers."[10]

Encouraged by the feminist movement to affirm their gender as well as their ethnic identity, they were quick to recognize the disjunctions between them. As Jews, they inherited a religious tradition that rigidly dichotomized gender, that validated sexuality only in marriage, and that honored only "domesticated women as value-keepers, family preservers, and queens of the home" (Frymer-Kensky 214). But as feminists, they sensed possibilities of self-realization that could not be contained within the domestic and gendered boundaries established by tradition. Thus, when Jewish women began in the seventies to think about the forces that had shaped them and the ideologies that still commanded their respect, they stumbled immediately on the conflicts between secular feminism and Judaism: two apparently incompatible sources that nourished their sense of themselves.

Some writers, as Sara Horowitz has recently argued, continue to conceive that conflict in terms of the dichotomous choices it presents to Jewish women.[11] Others, like true daughters of the patriarch Jacob, wrestle with the mutually exclusive polarities ordained by tradition. They recognize the tendency of Orthodoxy to dichotomize options by making distinctions between them—calling some kosher and others *treyf*.[12] But they resist that tendency. Their tenacity, moreover, like Jacob's refusal to let go of the angel, achieves for them a new sense of identity. Instead of choosing or alternating between secular feminism and Judaism, they confront and adopt—without resolving—the apparent dichotomy between them. Reconnecting themselves as feminists to the secular tradition of Jewish activist women, they continue to define themselves as Jews—without silencing, like my mother's generation—their critique of traditional Judaism. Thus, they orient themselves in a new way to a very old Jewish woman's problem. Within a decade this new orientation transforms the stranglehold of conflict into a strenuous tension that can be embraced.

Judith Plaskow's work demonstrates the effect of this shift in orientation toward the reconceptualization of Jewish women's identity. In 1973, Plaskow described the conflict within herself as a "conflict between communities . . . the first level on which I experience the conflict between being a woman and a Jew." At that time, she could see only the need to choose between her feminist and her Jewish commitments. It seemed to her that although "we can belong to many communities, only one can be our organizing center. Only one community can be the 'Rosetta Stone' through which we view and interpret and give room to others" ("Jewish" 3–4). Between the Scylla of her patriarchal tradition and the Charybdis of her feminism there seemed at first to be only one choice.

The conflict Plaskow identified remained stressful for many Jewish women throughout the eighties, for the feminist critique of Judaism continued in that decade to clarify, in Paula E. Hyman's words, the ways in which a patriarchal tradition had "excluded women from entire spheres of Jewish experience and . . . considered them intellectually and spiritually inferior to men" ("Other" 111). But the need to choose between Judaism and feminism as "organizing centers" of a Jewish woman's identity yielded eventually to a new and more generous way of conceptualizing the female self. Plaskow described her own sense of this change as a gradual process of refusing the split between a Jewish and a feminist self: "When Jewish feminists allow Judaism and feminism to be defined by others in oppositional ways, then we are stuck with two 'givens' confronting each other," she wrote, "and we are fundamentally divided. When, however, we refuse to sever or choose between different aspects of our identity, we create a new situation. . . . This change, moreover, may lead to a new life for us and for the tradition" (*Standing* ix–x). This refusal "to sever or choose between different aspects of our identity" became the touchstone of efforts by Jewish feminists to redefine themselves.

The deliberate inclusiveness of this reconceptualization of identity, its determination to reconfigure "Jewish woman" generously enough to honor diverse and even incompatible impulses, characterizes stories by many Jewish feminists since the seventies. This new sense of self emerges most clearly in the work of Adrienne Rich, whose autobiographical memoir, "Split at the Root" (1982), describes her long struggle to reclaim the Jewish part of herself from her assimilated father's deliberate silence and her southern gentile upbringing. The struggle produces an image of self richly endowed by its multiple sensitivities and commitments, looking backward in order to move forward

> into accountability, enlarging the range of accountability. I know that in the rest of my life, the next half-century or so, every aspect of my identity will have to be engaged. The middle-class white girl taught to trade obedience for privilege. The Jewish lesbian raised to be a heterosexual gentile. The woman who first heard oppression named and analyzed in the Black civil rights struggle. The woman with three sons, the feminist who hates male violence. The woman limping with a cane, the woman who has stopped bleeding, are also accountable. The poet who knows that beautiful language can lie, that the oppressor's language sometimes sounds beautiful. The woman trying, as part of her resistance, to clean up her act. ("Split" 90)

Rich acknowledges that her narrative perspective contains "too many disconnected angles: white, Jewish, anti-Semite, racist, anti-racist, once-married, lesbian, middle-class, feminist, exmatriate Southerner, *split at the root.*" She knows she will "never bring them whole." But she can name them separately and thus introduce them, unreconciled and unintegrated, into the forward, activist movement of her life.

As a Jew, Rich does not identify herself with the religious tradition of Orthodoxy; she sees it as "yet another strand of patriarchy." Instead, she draws from the larger fabric of Jewish history and culture other threads that can reconnect her to it. As a woman and a lesbian, she is particularly responsive to historic Jewish suffering: "The Jews I've felt rooted among," she writes, "are those who were turned to smoke" (*Sources* xvi). Beyond victimization, she identifies with Jewish women who fought against that which oppressed them—by "believing in a new life" as Zionists, "socialists, anarchists . . . excitable, sharp of tongue" (*Sources* xix). Through them, she knows herself to be

> . . . a connective link
> in a long, continuous way
> of ordering hunger, weather, death, desire
> and the nearness of chaos. (*Sources* xv)

Reimagining what "tradition" means, Rich restories the European activists whose alienation from "Jewish sorrows" she will not recapitulate. From those radical "mothers" she draws the style, form, and moral energy that inspire her sense of self as a Jewish woman. But she sustains, as they did not, both compassion for "Jewish sorrows" and a profound respect for the ethnic traditions from which she believes her strength comes.

Among those who, in Rich's words, "without a faith are faithful," other Jewish feminists who are lesbians share Rich's identification with the activist women who came before them. Knowing, like her, that sexual orientation is not "the exclusive ground of . . . identity" (Martin 94), they are particularly sensitive to what Teresa de Lauretis has called the "contradictory, multiple construction of subjectivity" (quoted in Martin 82). Marginalized by a culture that assumes heterosexuality as the norm,[13] they are also keenly aware of the political value of speaking themselves. For them, the very act of speaking as lesbians and Jews becomes a political act because they have been rendered silent and invisible by a culture that would forget/deny their existence. Thus, their narratives become political gestures, acts "of empowerment"; they have learned that power, as Zimmerman points out, "traditionally is the essence of politics, [and] is connected with the ability to name, to speak, to come out of silence" ("Politics" 671). Knowing their need to name themselves, Jewish lesbian writers write large the power of the story to create as it declares the feminist self.

Their personal narratives also restory earlier Jewish women who redefined *them*selves by acting and speaking publicly. For example, Irena Klepfisz identifies herself by recalling earlier Jewish women whom she reclaims from silence: "Women need to know of the powerful, brave, creative women from my culture," she says. "The political activists, the Bundist women in Poland and Russia, *di yidishe froyen*, the Jewish women who fought for workers' rights and human conditions, for Jewish respect in hostile environments; *di yidishe froyen* who led and participated in strikes, self-defense groups, workers' educational circles; *di yidishe froyen* who took endless risks for justice, for Jewish survival, for socialism, and who died for them" (47). For Klepfisz, restorying these women means speaking and writing again in Yiddish because it is the mother tongue she shares with them. Yiddish provided her "with a sense of peoplehood," shaped her "consciousness and helped [her] formulate [her] relationship to other Jews." Her "entire intellectual growth was bound up" in the world that Yiddish articulated; most of her "political ethical thinking was done" in Yiddish—not in English. Thus, she struggles to recover the language of her mothers, knowing that she can no longer speak it like a native but that the effort to speak and write it at all is reconstructive (35).

From one point of view, that task binds her to the historical task of her Jewish ancestors. Because Yiddish is composed of fragments from other languages learned by Jews in their long diaspora, her efforts to re-learn and speak it link her to them: "As my tongue, mouth, lips, throat, lungs, physically pushed Yiddish into the world—as I, a Jew, spoke a Jew-ish language to other Jews, Yiddish was very much alive. Not unlike a *lebn-geblibene*, a survivor, of an overwhelming catastrophe, it seemed to be saying '*khibn nisht vos ikh bin amol geven.*' I am not what I once was. '*Ober khbin nisht geshtorbn, ikh leb.*' But I did not die. I live" (48–49). Identifying herself, like this language, as both a survivor of the Holocaust and a fighter against cultural extinction, Klepfisz demonstrates the recon-nective as well as the self-declarative and self-creative power of the word.

Like Plaskow and Rich, Klepfisz also identifies the "refusal to sever or choose" as vital to the reconceptualization and reclamation of Jewish women's identity. She knows the destructive capacity of intolerance born of respect for dichotomies. She sacrificed Yiddish to such intolerance in the fifties—when American culture did not tolerate "bi-culturalism and bi-lingualism" and when Yiddish culture did not tolerate English, the language she needed to make herself at home in America (40). She put Yiddish aside a second time in the seventies when she discovered that her lesbian identity "remained virtually unspoken in the Jewish world," and her Yiddish identity was virtually invisible to "feminist and lesbian friends." Twice, then, she submitted to dichotomous cultural imperatives by severing her connection to the Yiddish world and its language.

But she has learned that she cannot "afford the luxury of an 'all or nothing' attitude" (45). Neither, she points out—making the personal point thoroughly political—can the Jews. Among Yiddishists, she says, she has "found provincialism, exclusivity, isolationism, a refusal to honor Jewish difference, a stubborn insistence that our *yidishe kultur* is *di gantse velt*, the whole Jewish world: a narrowness that has frequently looked down upon and denied the richness of Sephardic culture. . . . A narrowness that dismisses the hard, sincere struggle of many American Jews to make up for what history and previous generations withheld from them." She concludes, "We are all *goyim* [non-Jews] to each other." Until that tendency to polarize and dichotomize is corrected within both self and community, Klepfisz suggests, Jewish culture—like individuals within it—will tend toward loss and division. Like Plaskow and Rich, she believes that cultural and personal creativity are born of the refusal to "sever or choose." And now she speaks that refusal in her own, recovered mother tongue.

Even in English, the stories of Jewish lesbian women link their recovery and affirmation of Jewish identity to the refusal of dichotomous choices. Often alienated from a Jewish community that "'does not want homosexual or lesbian . . . orientation openly declared'" (quoted in Fishman 113), these women sustain nevertheless "strong ties to Jewish culture" (Fishman 113) by restorying in their own lives the European and American secularists and activists who came before them. The nature of that process, which recalls and transforms earlier women as it reconstructs the female self, becomes particularly clear in the autobiographical narratives of Evelyn Torton Beck. She describes her growth as a moving forward by turning backward—a restorying of the self from a perspective once abandoned but gradually recovered.

In two autobiographical essays, Jewish, lesbian, and activist elements of herself are woven through the fabric of her interactions as a child with her mother and as an adult with her daughter: "It was my mother who taught me to love women," the narrator recalls, despite her mother's homophobia and commitment to the romance of heterosexual domesticity.[14] Only after twenty years of marriage can the closeted daughter who names herself "Evi B" come out to herself—readied for that new awareness by her own lesbian daughter. "Her example paved the way for me," she confesses ("Daughters" 9).

Evi B recovers her ethnic identity in a similarly proactive and retroactive way. Exposed as a child in Vienna to Nazi anti-Semitism, she grew up frightened of exposure as a Jew. But coming out as a lesbian when she is more than forty years old enables her to "face the unsafety of being Jewish" ("Mother" 22). Speaking herself is empowering: "Becoming visible as a lesbian" makes her "less safe in the world but more secure in myself." Thus for her, the process of "coming-to-myself" ("Daughters" 10) as both a sexual and an ethnic being is many directioned, capable of re-calling into the present earlier portions of life as well as moving coura-geously forward into the future.

This restorying of identity makes growth a matter of influences that also move back and forth across generations.[15] For example, Evi B can now tell the daughter whose coming out she once opposed, "You were a role model for me when I was coming out. Once I got to know you bet-ter and came to believe in your strength and courage, that gave me the strength to become the lesbian I always was" ("Mother" 27). Becoming what one always was by the interaction of three generations of women—this construction of identity looks like a gathering in of awarenesses that sometimes double back on themselves, never fit neatly together, and culminate in a sense of self that is still, perhaps always, in process.

Beck's sense of what "Jewish" means is similarly processual. She and her daughter continue to struggle both to understand the tradition and to make it meaningful in their lives. The assumption that underlies that struggle is common to many activist Jewish women writers. They believe in their own faithfulness to "tradition" because they construe it largely in terms of social and political activism.[16] They believe their activist commitments identify them as Jews. Thus, unlike the European Jewish women radicals who severed the ties that would have bound them to their communities, families, and tradition, Jewish feminists' political activism has become a powerful mode of reconnection to Jewish identi-ty as well as a strong bond with their activist Jewish parents. Recalling the European socialists, American Jewish feminists conceive their con-cern for repair of the world and the comfort of the "stranger" as deeply consonant with the spirit of Judaism. Recalling those earlier Jewish wom-en radicals and the American activist women who followed them, they also conceive the activist work of world repair as consonant with their identity as women.

These ingredients of Jewish feminist identity are particularly clear in the work of Melanie Kaye/Kantrowitz. She explains that, "for Jews, de-bate about the origin and meaning of evil is less important than the com-mitment to oppose it. Once you are of an age to know what is going on in the world, you are responsible for every injustice committed" (*Issue* 90). Like radical Jews who came before her, Kantrowitz substitutes so-cial activism for ritual observance. Unlike her radical forbears, she shares these priorities with her parents. She remembers that for her mother and father "breaking religious observance was progressive" ("To Be" 298); thus, she was never taught to pray, to perform traditional rituals, or to study Jewish texts. Instead, her parents raised her to conceive the "capacity for resistance, [the] longing for freedom" as "the holiest thing I know, in myself and others" (*Issue* 90).[17] Recalling their political and social activism, she sees them and herself as faithful to one facet of a complex tradition.

Years of absence from Flatbush, of absorption in feminist work, and of unconcern with Jewish issues pass before she reconnects with being Jewish the moral and political commitments that drove her parents and that continue to motivate her. Thus, like Rich, Klepfisz, and Evi B, Kaye/Kantrowitz moves toward a sense of herself as a Jew by reaching backward to reclaim the ethnic context that she abandoned many years before. Within that context she can "hear" her parents' stories and write her own.

A similar drama of reconnection furnishes the plot line of many autobiographical stories in the seventies, eighties, and nineties. But, for both lesbian and heterosexual Jewish feminists, its conventional culmination has been transformed. Whereas marriage to a nice Jewish boy once signified the return of an alienated protagonist to the Jewish fold, feminist writers now find in other women the mentoring, enabling presences in which personal growth and reconnection with both the community and religious tradition become possible.

For example, a young Jewish woman enables Kaye/Kantrowitz to reclaim ethnic markings long contaminated for her by the anti-Semitism of the fifties and sixties. She remembers that looking and sounding like a Jew or bearing a Jewish name once felt shameful to her. In postwar America she felt, as a Jewish girl, "blamed" for her strength and exposed to contempt by her name, nose, eyebrows, and the Yiddish words and accent that colored her speech ("Some" 38–41). One evening, however, she hears a younger woman singing a Yiddish song, and the woman's "pleasure in the words, the sound and lilt" of them suddenly seem "pretty." "She seemed like a daughter I might raise, braver and less scarred— the sounds she speaks, her inflections are the very sounds I grew up trying not to make," Kaye/Kantrowitz recalls. In the voice of this symbolic daughter, the sounds that Kaye/Kantrowitz had learned from an anti-Semitic culture to despise are transformed: no longer "'uneducated English,'" they become Yiddish, simply another language ("Some" 41). Like

Evi B who is mentored by her daughter's courage in the process of coming out, Kaye/Kantrowitz is able to hear and value in the voice of a younger, daughter-like woman, who is "less scarred" by anti-Semitic contempt, the "mother tongue" of her own Jewish forbears.

For Grace Paley, too, other women become not only "friends" and "coworkers in the mother trade," as they do in her stories, but also enablers who restore to her the option of reconnecting with Jewish communal worship. Like her secular, activist parents, Paley has always identified herself as a Jew through political activism.[18] For her, being Jewish meant primarily feeling a "sense of outrage when others were treated badly" and recognizing "common history" with other Jews (quoted in Kaye/Kantrowitz and Klepfisz 323). Recently, however, she has begun to attend synagogue on Jewish holidays. She feels comfortable there now because Jewish feminists have modified the religious tradition against which her parents rebelled. "It's very possible," she says, "that I'm able to come back to this, to go to the *shul*, to do it whole heartedly, to feel I have a natural place in that community—it's possible I'm able to do all of this because of the women's movement and its influence. Because of the way a lot of Jewish women took hold, women much more religious than I. Without their courage and what they did, I might not have begun to go to this temple" (329). Among these secular Jewish feminist writers, the tendency to identify—as Jews and as women—with those who suffer and with those who work to end suffering is still very strong. Equally strong—and more surprising—is the desire to reenter, sometimes in nontraditional ways, a spiritual tradition that was unacceptable to their mothers.

For some writers, however, that desire is obstructed by dichotomous and exclusionary tendencies within tradition and among Jews who remain, as Klepfisz discovered, goyim to each other. The most critical and separatist response to these tendencies appears in Judith Katz's recent novel, *Running Fiercely toward a High Thin Sound* (1992).

Of three sisters in Katz's novel, one, Electa, adopts the priorities of the conventional Jewish community, studying to become a lawyer and marrying a nice Jewish boy. The other two are lesbians and feminists, profoundly alienated by the rigid gender expectations, sexism, and homophobia of their family and community. Nadine sets herself on fire in response to her mother's animosity and bears—like Cain—the visible scar of her alienation. For most of the novel, the other sister, Jane, is torn between her desire to belong to her family and her love for her outcast sister, Nadine.

In its portrayals of conventional and unconventional rituals, Katz's story of these sisters develops the failure of family and tradition to meet the needs of Jewish feminists and lesbians. Two weddings, for example, suggest the parameters within which this critique takes place. Electa's wedding demands of Jane that she mask and costume herself to conceal her lesbian identity. The experience of self-denial splits Jane into two personae. When she looks into the mirror, corseted, dressed, and coiffed to satisfy the expectations of the bourgeois community, she sees "the ghost of a woman I knew well. A woman with a sprayed helmet of hair and raccoon markings around her eyes. A freaked-out, lesbian Barbie doll" (89). Only after she scrapes off the makeup can she see "real skin, my own face, me, Jane Morningstar, lesbian activist, upstart and sister. The Zombie Jane was gone for the rest of the evening, exactly where she belonged" (90). Divided between the demands of a conventional wedding and the givens of her own nature, Jane becomes an image of the dichotomy Plaskow described, which forces Jewish feminists to choose between self-limiting, incompatible opposites.

The effect of this conventional ritual on Nadine is even more painfully limiting. Uninvited by a family that can neither understand nor accept her, Nadine can attend her sister's wedding only by hiding herself in the Ark among the Torah scrolls. There, she wishes that "the rabbi would open the Ark, take me out and cradle me in his rabbinical arms, walk with me among the congregants to be kissed and blessed, blessed and kissed, how I wish someone would hold me up on the *bima*, untie me, unravel me, read my wisdom and stories out loud, bring blessings one to the other from inside of me, the holy teachings of Nadine, my own code of ethical love" (81). Rendered invisible and silent, Nadine becomes dangerously explosive. Leaping out of the Ark, she breaks up the ceremony.

The novel gives Nadine and her would-be lover, Rose, the opportunity to participate in another wedding in which all the women get Nadine's wish; they become Torahs, "dancing and praying and kissing and marrying" (151). This wedding unites a whole community of women rather than one heterosexual couple. It recalls the harmonious implications of sanctified coupling but transforms them into the more inclusive promise of "union between us all" (152). At this wedding, sexual union is beside the point. Even the romantic Rose, who narrates this event, learns from it that "there was a lot more to life than my romantic problems" (150). She abandons her erotic pursuit of Nadine once she discovers that "*all* those women were really beautiful to me, and dancing and eating and telling jokes with them was really as much fun as having sex, and a lot less scary" (152). Thus, the novel not only dismisses—like so many stories by Jewish feminists—the conventional romance plot but also restories the ritual of marriage, substituting agape for eros, community for couple.

Recalling traditional speculation about the female gender of the Torah,[19] the novel literalizes and transforms that notion within the context of an all-female world. But that world exists only "underground," "beyond the looking glass," where it recalls into life the historical female victims and resisters of social repression and exclusion: orphans, widows, whores, ghetto fighters, seamstresses who dove from the windows of the burning Triangle Shirtwaist Factory, even women who "broke windows up and down the Lower East Side of Manhattan because [their] children were starving" (149). These women transform the image of mothering contaminated by the sisters' biological mother, who complies with and upholds social conventions, rejecting the daughter who does not conform and who bears the scars of her mother's rejection. But these dancing women comfort, teach, and heal Nadine, whose scar disappears while she is among them.

The spiritual and emotional promise of this community of women, however, cannot transform either the ritual or the family life of the sisters in this novel. Instead, Katz concentrates on exposing the dichotomous tendencies toward repression, exclusion, and persecution that insulate tradition and the Jewish family from change. The novel shows that within the family traditional rituals keep alive the hope of reunion among the sisters but actually reinforce impulses that exclude and alienate them from one another. For example, Nadine returns to her family in the season of Passover. She enters the seder at the moment her sister Jane rises to open the door for Elijah—the guest who brings comfort and hope to all Jewish seders. Nadine offers both—by asking her family's forgiveness. But instead of embracing her, they turn her out into the snow. During this explusion, Jane breaks her great-grandmother's seder plate, brought from Poland to America to connect this family to its past and its spiritual tradition. It cannot be repaired. "Let it go, it's old," the grandmother sighs (181). The plot itself "lets go" in much the same way, separating the lesbian feminist sisters from one another and from their parents, refusing the possibility of reconnection.

Instead of rewarding the hope of reunion that family ceremonials al-

ways nourish, rituals in Katz's novel invariably fall short because they fail
to penetrate the self-regard of those who perform them. For example,
every year Jews cast into rivers crumbs that symbolize their own sins in
a ritual called *taschlich*. But when Nadine, burdened by sins her family
has heaped upon her, casts herself into a river, the self-righteous family
cannot see that her sins are really theirs. Thus, the wine of traditional
ritual is watered down. It persists in the vessel of this story, but its significance is no longer apparent, and it serves no redemptive end.

In a similar way, the novel both offers and frustrates hope. Its perse-
cuted protagonists are truly at home only within the vernacular of Jewish experience; its language is enriched by both Hebrew and Yiddish; its
sense of time depends upon the annual cycle of Jewish ritual; its understanding of character and event depends upon traditional assumptions
and historical associations; it contains the pain and alienation of its personae like an old kiddush cup. In that cup, the sacramental wine is still
recognizable. But it is now contaminated by impulses that make, in
Klepfisz's phrase, all Jews "*goyim* to each another."

An image of reunion appears only in a dream that highlights the need
to embrace differences that otherwise divide and alienate the sisters from
one another. As they wrestle together in her dream, Jane strenuously
embraces Nadine in an epilogue entitled "Tikkun," a Hebrew word that
means "the repair of the world." The title suggests that the work of world
repair may have to begin with the struggle to embrace what is unlike
oneself.

Actually, the possibility of repair engages all the women whose stories this chapter discusses. Whether protagonists model themselves on
their mothers or take as models the stories of disappointment their mothers cannot speak, whether they take back Yiddish, or restore to secular
Jews the option of traditional worship, or expose the resistances that, for
the moment, make change unlikely, these stories are mostly about recalling what has been lost and restorying it to repair damaged connections
among Jewish women and between them and Jewish "tradition." The
most complex version of this process appears in the work of Jewish feminists who seek to move more deeply into sacred spaces set apart from
dailiness by ritual and prayer. Among them, women who are Jewishly
learned and observant and who wish to remain faithful to traditional
Judaism write a meliorist plot that attempts to modify tradition without
betraying their feminist commitments.

In "Can a Mild-Mannered Yeshiva Girl Find Happiness among the

Feminists?" Blu Greenberg exemplifies one mode of this activist engagement with tradition. Born into a "strongly traditional family," Greenberg knew her place and liked it, never giving a thought to what she "did or didn't have as a female growing up in the Orthodox Jewish community." She sat with her friends in the separate women's section of the synagogue when the boys they knew became bar mitzvah; she gladly slept an hour later than her male friends who had to rise early to daven *shaharit,* the morning service; she "had a fine Jewish education, the best a girl could have," without envying male students whose course of study was more demanding and who could become rabbis instead of Hebrew teachers; and she married a rabbi in the late 1950s, considering herself "very lucky to have a husband to care for me."

Her "equilibrium" as an Orthodox Jewish woman remained unshaken by deprivations that merely annoyed her, until she was deeply disturbed by Betty Friedan's *Feminine Mystique* in 1963. The disturbance first provoked her to defensiveness, but gradually her "complacency" gave way, and she began to question her own satisfactions, to look more closely at her experience as a woman. In 1973, she first began to study systematically the "Jewish issues of feminism." Like millions of other women, she says, she "stumbled" her way "through this revolution," trying to preserve her love for tradition even as she confronted its failure to accord her equality with Jewish men. Making common cause with many other feminists who were "not hostile to Judaism," who "had begun to search for their roots as Jews" in the course of "searching for their roots as women," Greenberg undertook the activist work of reform. She entered a process that she calls "the interweaving of feminism and Judaism," knowing that she will never "abandon tradition" and trusting that "Judaism will have to find a way to bridge the gap" between itself and the needs of Jewish feminists (*On Women* 21–37). Having reconceived her own identity in feminist terms, she expects, like Plaskow, that traditional Judaism will also reconfigure itself to accommodate her.

In fiction as well as autobiography, Jewish feminists seek to change from within a tradition they can neither abandon nor wholeheartedly embrace. Nessa Rapoport's novel, *Preparing for Sabbath* (1981), for example, traces the progress of a protagonist who, like Greenberg, enjoys not only the best Jewish education a woman can have but also a family legacy of distinguished scholars and rabbis. The novel portrays most successfully the social pressures of the fifties and sixties that trivialized the lives of even Jewishly learned young women so that they would move toward domestic rather than spiritual quests. From the gender imbalances in what Rosellen Brown calls the "bourgeois life of her childhood," Rapoport's protagonist, Judith Rafael, develops a sense of male priority in the world that keeps her, for a long time, excrutiatingly dependent upon male regard. Of all the women she knows, only Judith's widowed grandmother seems free of that dependence, finally "content in herself" (52) and in the ordered pieties of her solitary life. The end of Judith's journey is prefigured by this grandmother, for a spiritual quest ultimately emerges for Judith, too, first from her adolescent yearning for romance and finally from her critical feminist concern with seductive male mentors (264) and the need of women for "equal rights" to an "inner life" within Judaism (148).

Unlike her grandmother, Judith will not pursue that quest alone. Aided, enlightened, and supported by other women in Israel, she readies herself at the end of the novel for a Jewish life that will be spiritually deep and intellectually rich in the way of her forefathers[20] but also hospitable to the particular wisdoms and passions of her experience as a woman. Against the intellectual stature of her father and the illustrious rabbis who preceded him, Judith's own mother has always seemed weak, soft, and indecisive: content with her secondary role in the family. Other women—both within and outside of the family—"mother" Judith more creatively when she needs them. Thus, despite the prevalence of fathers over mothers in the spiritual and intellectual traditions of Judaism, the novel offers hope that, in this generation, learned and devoted Jewish women will mother one another as they redeem tradition from the patriarchs.

American Jewish feminists like Greenberg and Rapoport are determined not only to sustain tension between apparently incoherent elements in their own identities but also to reduce that tension by working to change a religious and cultural tradition that doesn't conform to their needs as feminists. In Sylvia Fishman's view, they have "merged two commitments to produce a vigorous hybrid" (14). The merger—like the strenuous embrace of two wrestlers—articulates the disparate needs that produced it.[21]

Other feminist writers, however, reject the meliorist plot developed by feminists like Blu Greenberg. In their view, securing what Plaskow has called "equal access" for women to "all the privileges and responsibilities of Jewish men" would fail to accord women the spiritual agency and authority they seek. They are also unwilling to adopt the separatist plot of Judith Katz's story, for they desire to remain within the historical community of Jews. As they search for ways to maintain their faithfulness, these feminists discover that Jewish identity—like female identity—requires a turning backward in order to move forward. From an ancient matrix of spiritual experience capable of nourishing women's need for religious authority and agency, they recall images, rituals, and prayers that preceded patriarchal religion. Their narratives transform these ancient images and practices to restory Jewish women's spirituality.

E. M. Broner and Kim Chernin, two writers committed to that enterprise, clarify the nature of its process. For Broner, it begins in appraisal of the ways in which tradition and the community oppress Jewish women. Devalued and cast out by their families, exploited and abused by their husbands, publicly humiliated by their lovers, and unsupported by a society that views them with contempt, the women of Broner's *Weave of Women* (1978), set in Jerusalem, continue the story of women's oppression begun in her earlier novel, *Her Mothers* (1975). The family context focuses the earlier novel on one daughter's quest to recover her foremothers and her runaway daughter. In the later work this context gives way to a reading of women's lives that is collective rather than individualistic, political *and* spiritual, as well as psychological.

Like other feminist stories in the seventies and eighties that connect the personal with the political, *Weave of Women* assumes, demonstrates, and spiritually augments the power of that connection. If, as Ann R. Shapiro persuasively argues, the protagonist of *Her Mothers* learns from women of the literary and historical past only the "history of defeat and disavowal of achievement" ("Novels" 97), *Weave of Women* gives its protagonists the means both to make history and to live meaningfully within it.

A *Weave of Women* empowers its characters by giving them one another and by developing the spiritual resonance of their interactions. Though each character moves alone through her own labyrinth of work and love, all of them are supported, healed, and strengthened by the ritual life of the group.

For example, a woman beaten nearly to death by an Orthodox fanatic is restored to health by women who ritually act out the vengeance her wounds require. A mother bereaved of her infant by a vengeful Islamic fanatic is enabled to mourn and ultimately even to marry by other women who ritually dance and sing what they know of loss and letting go. A young Israeli boy, disabled both by his military service and by his sister's public humiliation, is recalled to life by the ritualized sexual generosity of women.

To be sure, these rituals of healing, mourning, and calling back into life are not "in keeping with historical Judaic attitudes." As the women dance and chant by the waters of the Dead Sea, as they shriek curses, or offer themselves in love, they perform rituals unknown to traditional Judaism. To some readers, these rituals appear to be examples of feminists "yearning back toward paganism as a naturally matriarchal, benignly female-focused epoch in human history" (Fishman 236). However, in the simultaneously backward and forward movement that constitutes individual growth in many of these feminist writings, Broner's novel seems rather to reach backward only to draw from the prebiblical matrix the rituals that can empower forward cultural movement. Her characters, like Broner herself, make "ceremony out of need" ("Honor" 236).[22] In order to "make" the ceremonies they need, they recall—from behind the disappointing mothers of *Her Mothers*—a prepatriarchal layer of female experience whose images of powerful women can nurture their self-esteem and move them toward collective spiritual autonomy.

Thus, among the "mothers" of the far past, Broner's women seek images that can empower women to move into their own futures. Unlike the Jewish feminists who work *within* the boundaries of traditional Judaism to make a place for women within a patriarchal religion, Broner chooses to work *on* the boundary of Judaism, restorying Jewish women's observances by drawing into them rituals and prayers that recall "prepatriarchal ceremonies" ("Honor" 234). Only before "modern religion" was established, Broner believes, can one find spiritually empowering images of women. Long ago, she writes, women possessed spiritual agency and authority: "Women greeted the new moon, presided at births, held forth at funerals. We selected our mates and passed property on to our daughters" ("Honor" 234). But now,

> the new moon ceremony is danced at the beginning of the Jewish month by male Chasidic Jews. The birthing ceremony in the Jewish religion welcomes only the birth of a boy child. The puberty ceremony welcomes only the maturation of the boy child. After death, it is the son who can mourn for his parents. Even the word *holy* in Hebrew has been reserved for males exclusively. . . . The prayer for the dead, *kaddesh*, another form of *holy*, is uttered only by male lips. That which is not holy is profane. Women priests were renamed temple prostitutes. ("Honor" 235)

To reclaim and restory rituals free of the contaminants that Judith Katz describes, to become agents of their own spiritual experience, Broner's women "have to know of [those ancient women], to know of that origin, of that beginning" ("Honor" 236).

In this process, the women in her novel reclaim the practices of "daughter priests" who honored the "ancient female gods" displaced, now, by modern religious tradition. These women use their voices not only to pray but also to talk back to abusers and exploiters and to story themselves. Bound together not only by their common deprivations but also by their resistance to oppressors, they become as threatening to traditionalists as if they really *were* "yearning backward" toward pagan gods.[23] But they look back only for inspiration to move forward. That movement transforms not only the patriarchal spiritual tradition but also the dichotomous tendencies common to earlier activists. As Broner's women battle civil authorities, the media, and the medical establishment, they restory the activist Jewish women who took on earlier oppressors of the poor and powerless. Now, however, their adversaries, like the women themselves, belong to a thoroughly mixed community of people. Thus, this novel sets aside the binary model on which radical revolutionary ideologies often depend. It commits itself instead to an agenda that does not dichotomize capitalists and workers, Americans and Israelis, religionists and secularists, women and men, lesbians and heterosexuals, Jews and non-Jews. It addresses, rather, the needs of people who do many kinds of work and love in many ways, who are Jews or who choose to live with Jews, according to the rhythm of the ritual Jewish year, within the sometimes problematic embrace of a Jewish culture.

The effect of this restorying upon the form of Broner's novel is itself significant, as many readers have noticed. Broner eschews here the single narrative voice that speaks in *Her Mothers*. As if to underscore the failure of individual mothers of the past to nurture individual daughters, *Weave of Women* is spoken by a group of daughters who nurse, feed and discipline, enlighten and amuse, and "mother" one another. The novel weaves their stories and their lives together, showing how likeness yields to difference and difference becomes likeness, how commonality comes and goes, how anger, alienation, and love follow one another in the endless woven pattern of the narrative. Resisting closure, Broner's story even suggests that the fabric of women's collective experience—like the process of individuation—is open always to change and new directions.

This positive emphasis on openness to change—in both oneself and one's "tradition"—is very strong in all the works discussed in this chapter. Indeed, the immigrant origins of this literature virtually mandate the readiness to change as a given of American Jewish women's experience. Some stories celebrate it; some reckon its costs; some consider the resistances that slow its progress and increase its pain. But only Kim Chernin develops explicitly the role that storying plays in the process of cultural and psychological change. Chernin's first book, *In My Mother's House* (1983), describes the devotion of a strong, nurturing, activist mother to political change and the devotion of her daughter to personal and spiritual change. The differences between them are mutually alienating. But the memoir honors and insists on them. In a narrative matrix that allows their stories to tangle and overlap, both women discover themselves by restorying their mothers.

Constructed partly by her heroic responses to her immigrant mother's weakness and partly by her readiness to sacrifice her mother to her own narrative, Rose Chernin's persona testifies to the complexity of the filial bond. When Rose's suicidal mother is imprisoned in an asylum by an abusive husband grown weary of her, Rose rescues her. "This was the first battle I won against injustice," Rose recalls. The virtual beginning of her long career as a communist organizer, this recollection of her triumph over oppression demonstrates the political significance of personal experience that distinguishes Rose's entire story of self.

For Rose Chernin as for Emma Goldman, the personal matrix of a mother's suffering opens out to embrace the plight of other women. First, Rose sees her mother simply as "a woman without a people behind her"; "that was her tragedy" (80). But ultimately she will link her mother's powerlessness and pain not only to the plight of immigrant women but also to the wider experience of Jews in the shtetl and to the historic oppression of other subordinate people. One story catches this movement toward fuller perception.

One day, Rose joins a demonstration of workers broken up by police on horseback, and the cry of one demonstrator carries her directly back to "a village and Cossacks were riding down. You could go so far back in Jewish history and always you would find that cry. Always, in the history of every people," she remembers. "That was the day I joined the Communist Party" (91); "I had fought for my mother and now I was ready to start fighting for the people." Linking always the personal to the political, Rose Chernin's narrative style makes visible the knot of female suffering and resistance that binds so many Jewish feminists to their activist "mothers" and to one another.

This heroic mother/warrior is scarred, however, not only by the battles she has fought and won for others but also by the pain of having betrayed and abandoned her own mother in order to become herself. Recalling that she left her mother to her father's dubious care so that she and her sister could break free of the family's hopeless poverty, she remembers also other betrayals of women by women in her family. Storying these episodes suddenly reveals their pattern. She says, "I understand; it seems . . . even, forgivable. One sees the social meanings; this tragedy of woman, always needing to sacrifice someone else in order to go after her own life" (108–9, ellipses in original). Thus, storying reveals to the teller the terrible logic of change among women and also turns the interpretive narrative gaze from psychology to politics as a context for understanding it. Contextualizing personal betrayal in terms of social change, the story transforms guilt into grief and rage.

This mother's story has other powers as well, for it can open up to embrace her listener. For example, through her mother's recollection Kim enters the woods near the shtetl home where her grandmother, wearing an old dark shawl, is sitting on a wooden bench (147). Kim knows this narrative power in herself: "It's called memory," she says, "but to me it seems an immense, inarticulate, rush of feeling. At first I am afraid it will eat up my words. Then, I open my lips and it makes language" (212). Like the looking glass through which Katz's women pass to find a way to one another, like the ritual circle in which Broner's daughters of Jerusalem recall the womanly images they need, like the moment of withdrawal in which Mama Gornick thinks, the act of reflection that both recalls and transforms earlier stories leads to vision and the speaking of self.

For Kim, as for Rose, its effects are personally transformative. When Kim is enabled by entering her mother's story to see from within the places where it touches and diverges from her own, she is changed. "Released" from long antagonism by the tenderness and love that "entering into" her mother's narrative has granted her, Kim can ultimately speak her own "story of how I stopped being a Communist" (262–63). This betrayal of her mother's vision inserts Kim into the narrative of the family's women. But it also transforms that pattern and offers new insight into it. Suddenly enlightened by her mother's story, Kim realizes "that the value of her [mother's] life's work did not depend upon the triumph of socialism anywhere in the world. When I am eighty years old, I shall be happy if I have managed to remain true to myself, against all the passionate contradiction that cries out in my nature" (263–64). Thus, the personal, filial drama of rejection, separation, and reconnection enacted in Jewish women's stories since the immigrant period culminates here, in an insight that is born of and released by the power of storying.

Chernin's subsequent novel, *The Flame Bearers* (1986), turns that power from personal to spiritual ends. Looking and listening backward in order to grow forward, this novel rises from what Chernin calls the longing of women in her family for "a world far off and far away" (*In My Mother's* 106)—the world of the European shtetl. That longing exposes the conflict between ethnicity and gender that haunts the stories of contemporary Jewish feminists.

Rose Chernin waged an "ancient battle against the limiting of women" (107) by shtetl culture. Like other European activists, this communist mother set aside Jewish concerns not only because they "limited . . . participation in the class struggle" ("In the House" 56) but also because Jewish culture was tainted for her by its treatment of women. For Rose Chernin, as for the European radical women who preceded her, politics replaced ethnicity and religion.

But the replacement was never wholehearted. In America, her daughter notes, Rose never quite let go of the ethnic bonds of shtetl culture. She continued to speak Yiddish to her mother and her husband; she continued to prepare and to participate in family observances of Jewish rituals; and she sent her daughter in summers to a "Jewish day camp . . . where I learned to light the candles on the Sabbath and to speak Hebrew prayers I was not allowed to repeat at home" ("In the House" 56–57). Submerged in the narrative of her mother's life, Kim discovers a countertext—the story of one mother's refusal to "sever or choose" that will furnish the plot of her daughter's story.

Kim believes that what she and her generation "long for, grew up in the shtetl in spite of hunger and dust; a sacred dimension to daily life, which held its own alongside the terror and violence" (*In My Mother's* 106). To the explicitly political longings of her mother, Kim Chernin thus adds the ethnic and spiritual longings that were submerged in her mother's story but that surface in both her own experience and the writings of nearly three decades of American Jewish feminists.

Kim identifies this longing with her sense of herself as a Jew, and she locates its origins and transformative power in her mother's and grandmother's gifts as storytellers. These women pass on no heirlooms, only stories in which they "reworked Judaism" (*In My Mother's* 57). Such women become for her the bearers of a tradition peculiar to Jewish women. It is an essentially conservative tradition: "'You know what my mother used to say?'" Rose asks; "'Through us, the women of the world, only through us can everything survive.'" But this women's tradition is also committed to change.

Kim Chernin, in her turn, takes up her mother's vision of the Jewish woman's task but reconceives it in a new image: "I see generations of women bearing a flame. It is hidden, buried deep within, yet they are handing it down from one to another, burning. It is a gift of fire, transported from a world far off and far away, but never extinguished. And now, in this very moment, my mother imparts the care of it to me. I must keep it alive, I must manage not to be consumed by it, I must hand it on when the time comes to my daughter" (*In My Mother's* 16). Drawn from the world of the shtetl and the narrative power of its Jewish women, recalled and transformed by the political militancy of one of its secular immigrant daughters, restoried again by an American feminist daughter who is still a Jew, that image becomes the seed of another novel. This novel tells the story of a family of Jewish women who hand down the stories of their mothers and who belong to a sect called the *Flame Bearers* (1986).

Honoring in this way the power of the mothers' stories, Chernin takes up the submerged Jewish and feminist, rather than the explicit communist plot of Rose's narrative. Like Gornick who tunes in to her mother's narrative power beneath her supposedly exclusive devotion to domestic love, Chernin picks up beneath her mother's doctrinal certainties the radical, subversive energies that inspire her mother's politics and storytelling. Subverting, in her own story, the dominant political motif of her mother's narrative, Chernin exercises the most vital prerogative of the storyteller. At first, she asserts this prerogative developmentally. Because she knew she was "not supposed to become a Jewish woman," she obediently turned herself into a "young Communist who knew very little about Jewish life and culture, and . . . imagined that there was no difference between me and a boy." But eventually she revises her mother's ethnic and gender imperatives; Kim refashions herself into a woman, a feminist, and a Jew. By doing so, she rejects the plot of her mother's story but carries forth its radically revisionist impulse.

This revisionist prerogative also has important narrative and ideological implications. Recalling the way her mother restoried traditional narratives, making Moses "a radical, a people's hero" and Judah Maccabee "an early Communist," Kim discovers that Rose Chernin's "reworking of Judaism was evidently a more powerful teacher than her loyalty to the

Communist world view. She wanted me to acquire her dogma; she handed down to me her rebellious daring. And no doubt because Judaism can tolerate such a stance far better than Communism, I have remained Jewish where I have ceased to read Marx." Exercising in this way the storyteller's power to revise without choosing or severing one plot from another, Kim restories in the *Flame Bearers* the spirituality of shtetl women, allowing to them as Jews *both* the ancient conservative impulse *and* the daring, innovative energies that she knows in her mother and possesses in herself.

The Jewish women who are "flame bearers" carry a hidden tradition that proposes to augment a patriarchal tradition by restoring spiritual authority to Jewish women. Believing in the power handed down to them by matriarchs, the young American women of the novel help one another to transmit it. But the dramatic center of the novel is the web of stories that drive, guide, sustain, and define them. These interlaced stories begin in Canaan where women worshipped the goddess before the Hebrews came. They tell of deep-breasted goddess figures, of seed cakes and honey ritually offered and consumed, of flight and speech with birds, of the power of fire and the even greater power of stories to ignite and warm the spiritual being.

The novel inserts these stories into a recognizably Jewish frame. In the beginning, for example, two cousins long estranged make havdalah, a ceremony that traditionally divides the Sabbath at its ending from the beginning of the new week. In their ceremony they use familiar ritual objects: a silver spice box, a goblet of dark wine, a braided candle. "It was one of the few customs they shared with the Jewish patriarchal tradition" (17). But even this "shared custom" is ritually restoried: the women perform the ceremony at the beginning rather than the end of the Sabbath—for them it celebrates reunion rather than division—and they light the candle "the way their grandmother used to, without a match" (17).

Traditionalist Jewish readers object to restorying of this kind. Anne Roiphe, for example, saw in this novel a "distressing religious problem. The instant the author posits a male and female God and several goddesses, we no longer have a Jewish experience," she said ("Daughters"). But Chernin, like Broner, believes that traditional Judaism is handicapped by its exclusion and repression of the more ancient beliefs that it replaced. Thus, against the dichotomies that the ceremony of havdalah signifies, between the holy and the mundane, the Sabbath and the week, the light and the darkness, the flame bearers assert their belief in inclusiveness and in the transformation of traditional, hierarchical dichotomies.[24]

For these women, "reality" becomes a resonant Chinese box of stories, a set of hollow Russian dolls, to use Maxine Kumin's image, that carry, enclose, and release the gifts that one time and place, one set of people, yield to another. Aware of boundaries that order experience by dividing it against itself, such women move easily across them, backward and forward, recalling and transforming what the old stories offer them. The work they undertake threatens the stability of familiar, conventional modes of human connection. Like Gornick standing on her mother's threshold at the end of her memoir, like Rapoport's women readying themselves to reenter the traditional religious community, and like Broner's daughters of Jerusalem leaving the stone house to begin their lives in other places, the protagonist of this novel comes at the end to the beginning of a journey. In some ways, she recalls the immigrant mothers with whom this study began, for she is making a journey that will change her and her connection to those who stay at home. Unlike the immigrants, however, she is conscious of the losses that women of her sect have sustained in the course of many changes; she is aware of the need to join with other women who share her beliefs; and she is explicitly critical of traditional imperatives that handicap women. She recognizes the value of *both* transmitting *and* transforming what has come before. She seeks to honor "this great tradition of female knowledge we've inherited"; she wants to "pass it on, but without trying to live it in the old way" (250). Hearing the story of her mothers, she accepts the role they assign to her, becoming herself by undertaking the task of reconnection they have laid upon her. But, as both listener and storyteller, she conceives and performs that task in her own way.

Thus, the work of restorying Jewish women and their tradition by recalling and transforming the stories of their "mothers" proceeds in feminists' writing of the eighties and nineties along dramatically different paths. Profoundly disturbing to some, encouraging to others, the process in which these Jewish daughters are engaged addresses the disjunction between traditional Judaism and feminism. As Jews, they are developing a set of responses that have been at work among Jewish women for a very long time. Rooted in different parts of an old and complex tradition that is secular *and* religious, that affects personal *and* political life, individual *and* collective experience, their responses articulate the continuing vitality of women writers who know they belong, one way or another, to that tradition. As daughters, moreover, they have learned to hear beneath a mother's certainties the courage of her confusions. No longer her translator or her mirror, they know that however distinctively they speak themselves, they are also carrying forth her story.

Notes

1. See also Sarah Cohen, "Cynthia Ozick."
2. A cursory survey of research published in the 1990s also demonstrates among American Jewish women the resurgence of interest in Jewish issues that appeared in their stories a decade earlier. See, for example, Aiken, *To Be a Jewish Woman*; Davidman, *Tradition in a Rootless World*; Fishman, *A Breath of Life*; Geffen, *Celebration and Renewal*; Grossman and Haut, *Daughters of the King*; Kaufman, *Rachel's Daughters*; Frymer-Kensky, *In the Wake of the Goddesses*; Plaskow, *Standing Again at Sinai*; and Umansky and Ashton, *Four Centuries of Jewish Women's Spirituality*.
3. The passing of narrative authority from mother to daughter creates similar conflict and ends with similar uncertainty in D. Shapiro's recent novel, *Fugitive Blue* (1993). A. Roiphe's *Lovingkindness* (1987), however, ends with a maternal narrator who imagines she will resume control of her granddaughter.
4. By abandoning the marriage plot as their central structural convention, stories by American Jewish women writers since the late seventies do not articulate the general tendency among "better educated, ambitious Jewish women" marked by Fishman, who believes they are "more likely as a group to want to get married and to want to have larger families than their less educated sisters" (94).
5. Kuzmack has demonstrated that "Jewish women played a role in nearly every major national feminist venture at the turn of the century, including campaigns for social reform, feminist trade unionism, suffrage, and welfare feminism" and also created a network of Jewish women's groups (1).
6. "The authority of radical women in the factories derived from their ability to articulate in clear and sympathetic ways ideological tenets that were part of the cultural milieu of the immigrant communities" (Glenn 184).
7. One Jewish woman, for example, speaking in Yiddish, set off a general strike among shirtwaist workers when she demanded an end "to speakers who talk in general terms" (Glenn 168).
8. "Jewish girls," Rose Schneiderman observed, "were 'always ready to strike'" (Glenn 175). In some cases even wives and mothers took to the streets not only "to support the union movement" (Glenn 205) but also as "strikers on behalf of the household economy" (Glenn 196).

9. Fishman refers to this arrangement as "sequencing" (84, 92).

10. Fishman explains that "feminism with a specifically Jewish focus be-came distinct" from the movement as a whole "rather early" in its evolution. The celebration of ethnic differences encouraged by the protest movements of the 1960s, the pride in Israel felt by many Americans after the 1967 Arab-Israeli war, and the cultural self-esteem that accompanied the postwar upward mobility of American Jews all contributed, in Fishman's view, to the tenden-cy of Jewish feminists in the seventies to turn "their attention inward" (6).

11. Sara Horowitz considers Anne Roiphe, Nessa Rapoport, Vanessa Ochs, and Allegra Goodman as writers who dichotomize Orthodoxy and secularism "with no mediation" (35–36).

12. Since "The Pagan Rabbi," Ozick's stories have demonstrated brilliant-ly this tendency of traditional Jewish thought to insist upon the need to make distinctions and to oppose values to one another. As Kauvar has re-cently noted, Ozick's stories "afford contrasting views, they impart dispar-ate perspectives; they illumine the ambivalence coextensive with truth" (75).

13. It may be worthwhile to note briefly some of the ways in which les-bian autobiographical narratives resemble those by other Jewish feminists. First, lesbian narratives, like others by feminists, highlight the nature of the process in which women both become and declare themselves. For lesbians, that emphasis arises from the experience of "coming out." "Becoming a les-bian," Zimmerman points out, "requires a continual process of coming out through which identity is claimed and embraced" ("Politics" 668). For other feminists as well, however, as Gornick's and J. Greenberg's stories suggest, this process is not only "continual" but also both retrospective and transfor-mative, affecting ethnic as well as gender identity. Second, lesbian autobio-graphical narratives recall experience distinctively, "outside the contours and narrative constraints of conventional models," Zimmerman observes, because they attend closely to events and feelings that appear "insignificant . . . when a life is organized in terms of the trajectory toward adult heterosexuality, marriage, and motherhood" (quoted in Martin 85). Alienation from the heterosexual romance plot, however, has also become a feature of many fem-inists' stories regardless of their sexual orientation.

14. Beck's mother "faithfully spouted what she believed to be her truths: Love men, they are our only salvation. Fear men, they are the dangerous enemy" ("Daughters" 5).

15. Mason describes this process as a "delineation of identity by alteri-ty," a process of self-definition in relation to significant others that is "the most pervasive characteristic of the female autobiography" (Brodzki and Schenck, Introduction 8).

16. They assume, like Evi B and her daughter, that "political work" it-

self has a "particularly Jewish cast to it," that "Jewish culture" is somehow associated with "progressive socialist politics" (Beck, "Mother" 24, 19).

17. Kaye/Kantrowitz's grandparents "had come to this country from Eastern Europe, Poland and Russia. None had been political. Yet, as a teenager in the Depression, my father had belonged to the Young Communist League; and, even as an adult, his major hero remained his dead friend Aaron, a Communist who had spoken on street corners and fought in Spain. My mother had circulated petitions against the Korean War, walking up to people on the streets of Flatbush during the peak McCarthy period, and she had been spat on. Later she became president of the PTA at Walt Whitman Jr. High, and fought to bring blacklisted performers to sing at the annual PTA meeting" ("To Be" 297–98).

18. When she was young, Paley says, only her grandmother ever went to shul. Her parents were "very anti-religious[;] they laughed at religion" and rebelled against it. Growing up in an entirely Jewish neighborhood, Paley believed that "the stranger is the one to be remembered. . . . This seemed to me very much a part of being Jewish. And it wasn't a matter of hospitality. . . . It was a normal sense of outrage when others were treated badly, and along with that the idea that injustice not be allowed to continue" (quoted in Kaye/Kantrowitz and Klepfisz 323). Like Gornick, Beck, and Kaye/Kantrowitz, Paley inherits through her secular Jewish parents a sense of what "Jewish" means that emphasizes social activism rather than religious observance and that countenances political work by Jewish women as well as men.

19. Dawidowicz argues that Judaism's symbolic theology, which conceives the Torah as female, and God and Israel as male, renders "perverse" the calling of women to read from the Torah or to embrace or dance with it as men do (50–52).

20. Baris describes beautifully the ways in which Rapoport's novel employs Jewish devices and conventions to strengthen the novel's connection to traditional understandings.

21. Fishman notes, however, that their task will be extremely difficult because "feminism is by definition a political movement which aims to transform society so that gender does not define behavior or limit opportunities. It requires widespread and ideally rapid changes, either through augmented evolution or through revolution, to accomplish its goals. Orthodox Judaism, on the other hand, is by its nature very resistant to change, because it is committed to the *halakhah,* which governs every aspect of human behavior" (159).

22. Like the women characters in her novel, Broner creates what she calls "corrective ceremonies" that restory their originals from women's point of view. Her women's seder, for example, writes "women into the festival of freedom" from which they had for generations been excluded ("Honor" 238). The very act of restorying ritual in this way looks in several simultaneous

directions for Broner and her characters: toward political, psychological, and spiritual empowerment.

23. As a group, such women inspire particular malaise in traditionalists, because "fear of the disorder that might be brought on society by women in groups is an ancient one" among traditional Jews, as Fishman observes; thus, rabbinical authorities have always rejected "the concept of a group prayer for women," preferring to "keep women isolated from each other" (165). Broner annuls that isolation.

24. Some of them, Chernin's novel acknowledges, rebel violently against patriarchal tradition, going "underground" (*Flame* 80–95) like the women who live beyond the looking glass in Katz's novel. But the sect as a whole is nonviolent, preferring rather to preserve its ancient wisdom as companion to traditional Judaism.

Glossary

The following definitions are based on those in *The Encyclopedia of the Jewish Religion*, ed. R. J. Zwi Werblowsky and Geoffrey Wigoder (New York: Holt, Rinehart, and Winston, 1965).

agunah: A married woman in danger of remaining in permanent "widowhood" owing to the disappearance of her husband and the lack of decisive evidence establishing his death.

Ashkenazi: Generally applied to all Jews of European origin and customs.

bar mitzvah: The ceremony at which a thirteen-year-old boy "becomes an adult member of the community for ceremonial purposes."

bat mitzvah: The ceremony at which an adult female Jew "becomes obligated to perform the commandments."

bima: Raised platform in the synagogue on which is situated the desk for reading the Torah.

daven: Common word among Ashkenazim meaning "to pray."

galut: Exile, the enforced dwelling of the Jews outside the Holy Land.

goyim: Although in the Bible the term "goy" is used for any nation including Israel, it subsequently came to mean the non-Jewish nations in general and finally a member of any such nation (i.e., a non-Jew or gentile).

halacha: The part of Jewish literature that deals with religious, ethical, civil, and criminal law.

havdalah: From the Hebrew meaning "differentiation"; prayer recited at the conclusion of Sabbaths and festivals to indicate the distinction between the sacred day that has ended and the weekday that is beginning.

kaddish: Doxology recited at the conclusion of each principal section of every service; it has become best known as a mourner's recitation.

kashrut (kosher): The dietary laws that determine what foods may be eaten and that forbid any mixture of meat and milk.

kiddush: A ceremony and prayer by which the holiness of the Sabbath or a festival is proclaimed, recited over a cup of wine.

minyan: Minimum quorum of ten adult males required for liturgical purposes. Now, in some cases, ten adults satisfy the requirement.

mitzvah (pl. *mitzvoth*): Denotes individual injunctions, both biblical and rabbinic in origin.

Sephardi: Generally applied to all Jews of Oriental countries.

shaharit: Morning prayer, recited daily.

shul: Yiddish for synagogue.

tallith: Four-cornered cloth with fringes used by males as a prayer shawl.

tante: Yiddish for "aunt."

taschlich: A custom that symbolizes "the casting of sins into the sea."

tikkun: From the Hebrew word for "repair"; a term with its origin in the kabbalistic idea of a spiritual catastrophe that once occurred on a cosmic level. Man [*sic*] can help mend or "repair" this condition by his behavior.

Torah: In general understanding, the guidance and teaching imparted to Israel by divine revelation; also applied to scripture as a whole.

treyf: Not kosher.

Selected Bibliography

Abel, Elizabeth, ed. *Writing and Sexual Difference*. Chicago: University of Chicago Press, 1982.

Adler, Marjorie Duhan. *A Sign upon My Hand*. New York: Doubleday, 1964.

Adler, Rachel. "The Jew Who Wasn't There: Halakhah and the Jewish Woman." In *On Being a Jewish Feminist*, ed. Heschel. Pp. 12–18.

Adler, Ruth. "Mothers and Daughters: The Jewish Mother as Seen by American Jewish Women Writers." *Yiddish* 6.4 (1987): 87–92.

Aiken, Lisa. *To Be a Jewish Woman*. Northvale, N.J.: Jason Aronson, 1992.

Alpern, Sara, Joyce Antler, Elisabeth Israels Perry, and Ingrid Winther Scobie, eds. *The Challenge of Feminist Biography: Writing the Lives of Modern American Women*. Urbana: University of Illinois Press, 1992.

Alpert, Judith L., ed. *Psychoanalysis and Women: Contemporary Reappraisals*. Hillsdale, N.J.: Analytic Press, 1986.

Alter, Robert. *After the Tradition: Essays on Modern Jewish Writing*. New York: Dutton, 1969.

Ammons, Elizabeth. *Conflicting Stories: American Women Writers at the Turn into the Twentieth Century*. New York: Oxford University Press, 1991.

Anderson, Kathryn, and Dana C. Jack. "Learning to Listen: Interview Techniques and Analyses." In *Women's Words*, ed. Gluck and Patai. Pp. 11–26.

Anderson, Nancy. "No Angel in the House: The Psychological Effects of Maternal Death." *Psychohistory Review* 11.1 (Fall 1982): 20–46.

Antin, Mary. *The Promised Land*. 1912. Salem, N.H.: Ayer, 1987.

Antler, Joyce. *America and I: Short Stories by American Jewish Women Writers*. Boston: Beacon Press, 1990.

Arcana, Judith. *Grace Paley's Life Stories: A Literary Biography*. Urbana: University of Illinois Press, 1993.

———. *Our Mothers' Daughters*. Berkeley, Calif.: Shameless Hussy Press, 1979.

———. "Truth in Mothering: Grace Paley's Stories." In *Narrating Mothers*, ed. Daly and Reddy. Pp. 195–208.

Baba, Minako. "Faith Darwin as Writer-Heroine: A Study of Grace Paley's Short Stories." *Studies in American Jewish Literature* 7 (1988): 40–54.

Bakhtin, Mikhail M. *The Dialogic Imagination: Four Essays.* Ed. Michael Holquist. Trans. Caryl Emerson and Michael Holquist. Austin: University of Texas Press, 1981.

Baris, Sharon Deykin. "Nessa Rapoport." In *Jewish American Women Writers,* ed. Shapiro. Pp. 314–23.

Barker-Nunn, Jeanne. "Telling the Mother's Story: History and Connection in the Autobiographies of Maxine Hong Kingston and Kim Chernin." *Women's Studies* 14.1 (1987): 55–63.

Barrett, Michele, and Mary McIntosh. "Narcissism and the Family: A Critique of Lasch." *New Left Review* 133 (1982): 35–48.

Baruch, Elaine Hoffman, and Lucienne J. Serrano. *Women Analyze Women in France, England, and the United States.* New York: New York University Press, 1988.

Baskin, Judith R., ed. *Jewish Women in Historical Perspective.* Detroit, Mich.: Wayne State University Press, 1991.

———. "Jewish Women in the Middle Ages." In *Jewish Women in Historical Perspective,* ed. Baskin. Pp. 94–114.

———, ed. *Women of the Word: Jewish Women and Jewish Writing.* Detroit, Mich.: Wayne State University Press, 1994.

Bassin, Donna, Margaret Honey, and Meryle Mahrer Kaplan, eds. *Representations of Motherhood.* New Haven, Conn.: Yale University Press, 1994.

Baum, Camille. *A Member of the Tribe.* New York: Lyle Stuart, 1971.

Baum, Charlotte, Paula Hyman, and Sonya Michel. *The Jewish Woman in America.* New York: New American Library, 1976.

Baym, Nina. *Woman's Fiction: A Guide to Novels by and about Women in America, 1820–70.* 1978. Urbana: University of Illinois Press, 1993.

Beck, Evelyn Torton. "Daughters and Mothers: Three Generations." In *Nice Jewish Girls,* ed. Beck. Pp. 5–13.

———. "Mother and Daughter, Jewish and Lesbian." In *Nice Jewish Girls,* ed. Beck. Pp. 16–30.

———, ed. *Nice Jewish Girls: A Lesbian Anthology.* 1982. Boston: Beacon Press, 1989.

Bell, Bernard W. *The Afro-American Novel and Its Tradition.* Amherst: University of Massachusetts Press, 1987.

Benjamin, Jessica. "The Alienation of Desire: Women's Masochism and Ideal Love." In *Psychoanalysis and Women,* ed. Alpert. Pp. 113–30.

———. *The Bonds of Love: Psychoanalysis, Feminism, and the Problem of Domination.* New York: Pantheon, 1988.

———. "The Omnipotent Mother: A Psychoanalytic Study of Fantasy and Reality." In *Representations of Motherhood,* ed. Bassin, Honey, and Kaplan. Pp. 129–46.

Berger, David, ed. *The Legacy of Jewish Migration: 1881 and Its Impact.* New York: Columbia University Press, 1983.

Berman, Saul. "The Status of Women in Halakhic Judaism." In *Jewish Woman*, ed. Koltun. Pp. 114–28.

Bloom, Harold, ed. *Cynthia Ozick: Modern Critical Views.* New York: Chelsea House Press, 1986.

Boose, Lynda E. "The Father's House and the Daughter in It." In *Daughters and Fathers*, ed. Boose and Flowers. Pp. 19–74.

Boose, Lynda E., and Betty S. Flowers, eds. *Daughters and Fathers.* Baltimore, Md.: Johns Hopkins University Press, 1989.

Brandimarte, Cynthia Ann. "Fannie Hurst and Her Fiction: Prescriptions for America's Working Women." Ph.D. diss., University of Texas at Austin, 1980.

Braude, Ann. "The Jewish Woman's Encounter with American Culture." In *Women and Religion in America*, ed. Ruether and Keller. Pp. 150–92.

Braxton, Joanne M. *Black Women Writing Autobiography: A Tradition within a Tradition.* Philadelphia, Pa.: Temple University Press, 1989.

Breines, Wini. *Young, White, and Miserable: Growing Up Female in the Fifties.* Boston: Beacon Press, 1992.

Brodzki, Bella, and Celeste Schenck. Introduction. In *Life/Lines*, ed. Brodzki and Schenck. Pp. 1–15.

———, eds. *Life/Lines: Theorizing Women's Autobiography.* Ithaca, N.Y.: Cornell University Press, 1988.

———. "Mothers, Displacement, and Language in the Autobiographies of Nathalie Sarraute and Christa Wolf." In *Life/Lines*, ed. Brodzki and Schenck. Pp. 243–59.

Broner, E. M. *Her Mothers.* 1975. Bloomington: Indiana University Press, 1985.

———. "Honor and Ceremony in Women's Rituals." In *Politics of Women's Spirituality*, ed. Spretnak. Pp. 234–44.

———. *A Weave of Women.* New York: Bantam, 1978.

Brooks, Peter. *Body Work: Objects of Desire in Modern Narrative.* Cambridge, Mass.: Harvard University Press, 1993.

Brown, Dorothy M. *Setting a Course: American Women in the 1920s.* Boston: Twayne, 1987.

Brown, Lyn Mikel, and Carol Gilligan. *Meeting at the Crossroads: Women's Psychology and Girls' Development.* Cambridge, Mass.: Harvard University Press, 1992.

Brown, Rosellen. *The Autobiography of My Mother.* New York: Doubleday, 1976.

Burstein, Janet. "Cynthia Ozick and the Transgressions of Art." *American Literature* 59.1 (1987): 85–101.

———. "In the Twilight of Tradition: Trying the Myths in Jewish-American Short Stories." *YIVO Annual* 19 (1990): 105–32.

————. "Jewish American Women's Literature: The Long Quarrel with God." *Studies in American Jewish Literature* 8.1 (Spring 1989): 9–25.

————. "Lost Children in Contemporary American Jewish Literature." *Studies in American Jewish Literature* 9.1 (Spring 1990): 9–19.

————. "Mother at the Center: Jewish American Women's Stories of the 1920s." In *Women of the Word*, ed. Baskin. Pp. 182–96.

Carby, Hazel V. *Reconstructing Womanhood: The Emergence of the Afro-American Woman Novelist*. New York: Oxford University Press, 1987.

Chametzky, Jules. "Main Currents in American Jewish Literature from the 1880s to the 1950s (and Beyond)." *Ethnic Groups* 4.1–2 (1982): 85–101.

Chernin, Kim. *Crossing the Border: An Erotic Journey*. New York: Fawcett Columbine, 1994.

————. *A Different Kind of Listening: My Psychoanalysis and Its Shadow*. New York: HarperCollins, 1995.

————. *The Flame Bearers*. New York: Random House, 1986.

————. *The Hungry Self: Women, Eating and Identity*. New York: Harper and Row, 1985.

————. *In My Mother's House: A Daughter's Story*. 1983. New York: Harper and Row, 1984.

————. "In the House of the Flame Bearers." *Tikkun* 2.3 (1987): 55–59.

Chesler, Phyllis. *With Child: A Diary of Motherhood*. New York: Thomas Y. Crowell, 1979.

Chodorow, Nancy. *The Reproduction of Mothering: Psychoanalysis and the Sociology of Gender*. Berkeley: University of California Press, 1978.

Chyet, Stanley F. "Three Generations: An Account of American Jewish Fiction, 1896–1969." *Jewish Social Studies* 34 (1972): 31–41.

Cohen, Rose. *Out of the Shadow*. New York: Doran, 1918.

Cohen, Sarah Blacher. "Cynthia Ozick: Prophet for Parochialism." In *Women of the Word*, ed. Baskin. Pp. 283–98.

Cohen, Steven M., Susan Dessel, and Michael Pelavin. "The Changing (?) Role of Women in Jewish Communal Affairs: A Look into the UJA." In *Jewish Woman*, ed. Koltun. Pp. 193–201.

Cohen, Steven M., and Paula E. Hyman, eds. *The Jewish Family: Myths and Reality*. New York: Holmes, 1986.

Collins, Patricia Hill. "The Meaning of Motherhood in Black Culture and Black Mother-Daughter Relationships." *Sage* 4.2 (Fall 1987): 3–10.

Daly, Brenda O., and Maureen T. Reddy, eds. *Narrating Mothers: Theorizing Maternal Subjectivities*. Knoxville: University of Tennessee Press, 1991.

Davidman, Lynn. *Tradition in a Rootless World: Women Turn to Orthodox Judaism*. Berkeley: University of California Press, 1991.

Davidson, Cathy, and E. M. Broner, eds. *The Lost Tradition: Mothers and Daughters in Literature*. New York: Ungar, 1980.

Davies, Carole Boyce. "Mothering and Healing in Recent Black Women's Fiction." *Sage* 2.1 (Spring 1985): 41–43.

———. "Mother Right/Write Revisited: *Beloved* and *Dessa Rose* and the Construction of Motherhood in Black Women's Fiction." In *Narrating Mothers*, ed. Daly and Reddy. Pp. 44–57.

Dawidowicz, Lucy S. "On Being a Woman in Shul." In *The Jewish Presence: Essays on Identity and History*. New York: Holt, Rinehart, and Winston, 1977. Pp. 46–60.

Dearborn, Mary V. *Love in the Promised Land: The Story of Anzia Yezierska and John Dewey*. New York: Free Press, 1988.

———. *Pocahontas's Daughters: Gender and Ethnicity in American Culture*. New York: Oxford University Press, 1986.

Dinnerstein, Dorothy. *The Mermaid and the Minotaur: Sexual Arrangements and Human Malaise*. New York: Harper, 1977.

Donovan, Josephine. *After the Fall: The Demeter-Persephone Myth in Wharton, Cather, and Glasgow*. University Park: Pennsylvania State University Press, 1989.

Douglas, Ann. *The Feminization of American Culture*. New York: Doubleday, 1988.

Duncan, Erika. "Coming of Age in the Thirties: A Portrait of Tillie Olsen." *Book Forum* 6.2 (1982): 207–22.

———. "The Hungry Jewish Mother." In *Lost Tradition*, ed. Davidson and Broner. Pp. 231–41.

DuPlessis, Rachel Blau. *Writing beyond the Ending: Narrative Strategies of Twentieth-Century Women Wrtiters*. Bloomington: Indiana University Press, 1985.

Ehrenreich, Barbara, and Deirdre English. *For Her Own Good: 150 Years of the Experts' Advice to Women*. 1978. Garden City, N.Y.: Anchor Books/ Doubleday, 1979.

Ewen, Elizabeth. *Immigrant Women in the Land of Dollars: Life and Culture on the Lower East Side*. New York: Monthly Review Press, 1985.

Falk, Candace Serena. *Love, Anarchy, and Emma Goldman*. New Brunswick, N.J.: Rutgers University Press, 1990.

Federman, Raymond. "Displaced Person: The Jew/The Wanderer/The Writer." *Denver Quarterly* 19.1 (Spring 1984): 85–105.

Ferber, Edna. *Cimmaron*. 1930. Boston: G. K. Hall, 1981.

———. *Fanny Herself*. Chicago: Grosset, 1917.

———. "The Girl Who Went Right." In *America and I*, ed. Antler. Pp. 57–71.

———. *The Girls*. 1921. New York: Doubleday, 1936.

———. *A Peculiar Treasure*. New York: Doubleday, Doran, 1938.

———. *Show Boat*. Garden City, N.Y.: Doubleday Page, 1926.

Ferraro, Thomas J. *Ethnic Passages: Literary Immigrants in Twentieth-Century America*. Chicago: University of Chicago Press, 1993.

Fisch, Harold. "The Crisis in the Jewish Family: Its Literary Reflection." *Jewish Book Annual* 41 (1983–84): 24–34.

———. "Fathers, Mothers, Sons and Lovers: Jewish and Gentile Patterns in Literature." *Midstream* 18.3 (Mar. 1972): 37–45.

Fishman, Sylvia Barack. *A Breath of Life: Feminism in the American Jewish Community*. New York: Free Press, 1993.

Flynn, Elizabeth A., and Schweickart, Patrocinio P., eds. *Gender and Reading: Essays on Readers, Texts, and Contexts*. Baltimore, Md.: Johns Hopkins University Press, 1986.

Friedman, Melvin. "Jewish Mothers and Sons: The Expense of Chutzpah." In *Contemporary American-Jewish Literature*, ed. Malin. Pp. 156–74.

Frymer-Kensky, Tikva. *In the Wake of the Goddesses: Women, Culture, and the Biblical Transformation of Pagan Myth*. New York: Free Press, 1992.

Gafni, Isaiah M. "The Institution of Marriage in Rabbinic Times." In *Jewish Family*, ed. Kraemer. Pp. 13–30.

Gallop, Jane. "Reading the Mother Tongue: Psychoanalytic Feminist Criticism." *Critical Inquiry* 13.4 (1987): 314–28.

Gardiner, Judith Kegan. "On Female Identity and Writing by Women." *Critical Inquiry* 8.2 (Winter 1981): 347–61.

———. "A Wake for Mother: The Maternal Deathbed in Women's Fiction." *Feminist Studies* 4.2 (June 1978): 146–65.

Garner, Shirley Nelson. "Constructing the Mother: Contemporary Psychoanalytic Theorists and Women Autobiographers." In *Narrating Mothers*, ed. Daly and Reddy. Pp. 76–93.

Garner, Shirley Nelson, Claire Kahane, and Madelon Sprengnether, eds. *The (M)other Tongue: Essays in Feminist Psychoanalytic Interpretation*. Ithaca, N.Y.: Cornell University Press, 1985.

Geffen, Rela M. *Celebration and Renewal: Rites of Passage in Judaism*. Philadelphia, Pa.: Jewish Publication Society, 1993.

Gilbert, Julie Goldsmith. *Ferber: A Biography*. New York: Doubleday, 1978.

Gilligan, Carol. *In a Different Voice: Psychological Theory and Women's Development*. Cambridge, Mass.: Harvard University Press, 1985.

Ginsburg, Faye, and Anna Lowenhaupt Tsing, eds. *Uncertain Terms: Negotiating Gender in American Culture*. Boston: Beacon Press, 1990.

Gitenstein, R. Barbara. "The Temptation of Apollo and the Loss of Yiddish in Cynthia Ozick's Fiction." *Studies in American Jewish Literature* 3 (1983): 194–201.

Glenn, Susan. *Daughters of the Shtetl: Life and Labor in the Immigrant Generation*. Ithaca, N.Y.: Cornell University Press, 1990.

Gluck, Sherna Berger, and Daphne Patai, eds. *Women's Words: The Feminist Practice of Oral History*. New York: Routledge, 1991.

Gold, Herbert. "The Heart of the Artichoke." In *Jewish American Stories*, ed. Irving Howe. New York: New American Library, 1977. Pp. 270–300.

Goldman, Emma. *Living My Life*. 1931. New York: New American Library, 1977.

Gollin, Rita K. "Understanding Fathers in American Jewish Fiction." *Centennial Review* no. 18 (1975): 273–87.

Golub, Ellen. "Eat Your Heart Out: The Fiction of Anzia Yezierska." *Studies in American Jewish Literature* 3 (1983): 51–61.

Goodheart, Eugene. "*Trust*." In *Cynthia Ozick*, ed. Bloom. Pp. 11–14.

Gornick, Vivian. *Fierce Attachments*. New York: Farrar, Straus, Giroux, 1987.

———. "The World and Our Mothers." *New York Times Book Review*, Nov. 22, 1987, 52–54.

Greenberg, Blu. *On Women and Judaism: A View from Tradition*. Philadelphia, Pa.: Jewish Publication Society, 1981.

Greenberg, Joanne. *A Season of Delight*. New York: Holt, Rinehart, and Winston, 1981.

Grossman, Susan, and Rivka Haut. *Daughters of the King: Women and the Synagogue*. Philadelphia, Pa.: Jewish Publication Society, 1992.

Harap, Louis. *Creative Awakening: The Jewish Presence in Twentieth Century American Literature, 1900–1940s*. New York: Greenwood Press, 1981.

Hartmann, Susan M. *The Home Front and Beyond: American Women in the 1940s*. Boston: Twayne, 1982.

Hasanovitz, Elizabeth. *One of Them*. Boston: Houghton, 1918.

Heilbrun, Carolyn. *Hamlet's Mother and Other Women*. New York: Ballantine, 1990.

———. "Non-Autobiographies of 'Privileged' Women: England and America." In *Life/Lines*, ed. Brodzki and Schenck. Pp. 62–76.

———. *Writing a Woman's Life*. New York: Ballantine, 1988.

Heinze, Andrew R. *Adapting to Abundance: Jewish Immigrants, Mass Consumption, and the Search for American Identity*. New York: Columbia University Press, 1990.

Henriksen, Louise Levitas. *Anzia Yezierska: A Writer's Life*. New Brunswick, N.J.: Rutgers University Press, 1988.

Hertzberg, Arthur. *The Jews in America: Four Centuries of an Uneasy Encounter: A History*. New York: Simon and Schuster, 1989.

Heschel, Susannah. Introduction. In *On Being a Jewish Feminist*, ed. Heschel. Pp. 3–11.

———. "Jewish Feminism and Women's Identity." In *Seen but Not Heard*, ed. Siegel and Cole. Pp. 31–40.

———, ed. *On Being a Jewish Feminist: A Reader*. New York: Schocken, 1983.

Hirsch, Marianne. *The Mother/Daughter Plot: Narrative, Psychoanalysis, Feminism*. Bloomington: Indiana University Press, 1989.

Homans, Margaret. *Bearing the Word: Language and Female Experience in Nineteenth-Century Women's Writing*. Chicago: University of Chicago Press, 1986.

Horney, Karen. *The Neurotic Personality of Our Time*. New York: Norton, 1937.

Horowitz, Sara R. "Portnoy's Sister—Who's Complaining?: Contemporary Jewish-American Women's Writing on Judaism." *Jewish Book Annual* 51 (1994): 26–41.

Horowitz, Steven P., and Miriam J. Landsman. "The Americanization of Edna: A Study of Ms. Ferber's Jewish American Identity." *Studies in American Jewish Literature* 2 (1982): 69–80.

Hoy, Nancy Jo. "Of Holy Writing and Priestly Voices: An Interview with Esther Broner." *Massachusetts Review* 24 (Summer 1983): 254–69.

Hunter, Dianne. "Hysteria, Psychoanalysis, and Feminism: The Case of Anna O." In *(M)other Tongue*, ed. Garner, Kahane, and Sprengnether. Pp. 89–115.

Hurst, Fannie. *Anatomy of Me: A Wonderer in Search of Herself*. New York: Doubleday, 1958.

———. *Anywoman*. New York: Harper and Brothers, 1950.

———. *Back Street*. New York: Cosmopolitan. 1930.

———. *Family!* New York: Doubleday, 1960.

———. *Five and Ten*. New York: Harper, 1929.

———. *Humoresque*. New York: Knopf, 1919.

———. *Imitation of Life*. New York: Harper, 1933.

———. *The Lonely Parade*. New York: Harper, 1942.

———. *Lummox*. New York: Harper, 1923.

———. *Mannequin*. New York: Knopf, 1926.

———. *The Man with One Head*. New York: Cape, 1953.

———. *Star Dust: The Story of an American Girl*. New York: Harper and Brothers, 1921.

Hyman, Paula E. "Culture and Gender: Women in the Immigrant Jewish Community." In *Legacy of Jewish Migration*, ed. Berger. Pp. 157–68.

———. "Gender and the Immigrant Jewish Experience in the United States." In *Jewish Women in Historical Perspective*, ed. Baskin. Pp. 222–42.

———. "The Modern Jewish Family: Image and Reality." In *Jewish Family*, ed. Kraemer. Pp. 179–96.

———. "The Other Half: Women in the Jewish Tradition." In *Jewish Woman*, ed. Koltun. Pp. 105–13.

Isaacs, Neil D. *Grace Paley: A Study of the Short Fiction*. Boston: Twayne, 1990.

Jelinek, Estelle C., ed. *Women's Autobiography: Essays in Criticism*. Bloomington: Indiana University Press, 1980.

Jong, Erica. *Fear of Flying*. 1973. New York: Signet, 1974.

Juhasz, Suzanne. "Maxine Hong Kingston: Narrative Technique and Female Identity." In *Contemporary Women Writers*, ed. Rainwater and Scheick. Pp. 173–90.

———. "Texts to Grow On: Reading Women's Romance Fiction." *Tulsa Studies in Women's Literature* 7.2 (1988): 239–59.

Kaledin, Eugenia. *Mothers and More: American Women in the 1950s*. Boston: Twayne, 1984.

Kamel, Rose. "Literary Foremothers and Writers' Silences: Tillie Olsen's Autobiographical Fiction." *Melus* 12.3 (1985): 56–72.

Katz, Judith. *Running Fiercely toward a High Thin Sound*. Ithaca, N.Y.: Firebrand, 1992.

Kaufman, Debra. *Rachel's Daughters: Newly Orthodox Jewish Women*. New Brunswick, N.J.: Rutgers University Press, 1991.

Kauvar, Elaine M. *Cynthia Ozick's Fiction: Tradition and Invention*. Bloomington: Indiana University Press, 1993.

Kaye/Kantrowitz, Melanie. *The Issue Is Power: Essays on Women, Jews, Violence and Resistance*. San Francisco: Aunt Lute, 1992.

———. "Some Notes on Jewish Lesbian Identity." In *Nice Jewish Girls*, ed. Beck. Pp. 34–50.

———. "To Be a Radical Jew in the Late 20th Century." In *Tribe of Dina*, ed. Kaye/Kantrowitz and Klepfisz. Pp. 297–320.

Kaye/Kantrowitz, Melanie, and Irena Klepfisz, eds. *The Tribe of Dina: A Jewish Women's Anthology*. 1986. Boston: Beacon Press, 1989.

Kazin, Alfred. *A Walker in the City*. New York: Harcourt, Brace, 1951.

Kessler-Harris, Alice. Introduction. *Bread Givers*, by Yezierska. Pp. v–xviii.

Klein, Marcus. *Foreigners: The Making of American Literature, 1900–1940*. Chicago: University of Chicago Press, 1981.

Klepfisz, Irena. "Secular Jewish Identity: Yiddishkayt in America." In *Tribe of Dina*, ed. Kaye/Kantrowitz and Klepfisz. Pp. 32–50.

Kohut, Rebekah. *My Portion*. 1925. New York: Arno Press, 1975.

Koltun, Elizabeth, ed. *The Jewish Woman: New Perspectives*. New York: Schocken, 1976.

Koppelman, Susan, ed. *Between Mothers and Daughters: Stories across a Generation*. New York: Feminist Press, 1985.

———. "The Educations of Fannie Hurst." *Women's Studies International Forum* 10.5 (1987): 503–16.

Kraemer, David, ed. *The Jewish Family: Metaphor and Memory*. New York: Oxford University Press, 1989.

Kramer, Sydelle, and Jenny Mazur, eds. *Jewish Grandmothers*. Boston: Beacon Press, 1976.

Krause, Corinne Azen. *Grandmothers, Mothers and Daughters: Oral Histories of Three Generations of Ethnic American Women*. Boston: Twayne, 1991.

Kuzmack, Linda Gordon. *Woman's Cause: The Jewish Woman's Movement in England and the United States, 1881–1933.* Columbus: Ohio State University Press, 1990.

Lacan, Jacques. *Écrits: A Selection.* Trans. Alan Sheridan. New York: W. W. Norton, 1977.

Lang, Lucy Robbins. *Tomorrow Is Beautiful.* New York: Macmillan, 1948.

Lasch, Christopher. *The Culture of Narcissism: American Life in an Age of Diminishing Expectations.* New York: W. W. Norton, 1978.

Lazarre, Jane. *The Mother Knot.* New York: McGraw-Hill, 1976.

Lerner, Gerda. *The Female Experience: An American Documentary.* Indianapolis: Bobbs-Merrill, 1977.

Lester, Elenore. "The Riddle of Tillie Olsen." *Midstream* (Jan. 1975): 75–79.

Lichtenstein, Diane. "Fannie Hurst and Her Nineteenth-Century Predecessors." *Studies in American Jewish Literature* 7.1 (1988): 26–39.

———. *Writing Their Nations: The Tradition of Nineteenth-Century American Jewish Women Writers.* Bloomington: Indiana University Press, 1992.

Liebowitz, Herbert. *Fabricating Lives: Explorations in American Autobiography.* New York: Knopf, 1989.

Linden-Ward, Blanche, and Carol Hurd Green. *American Women in the 1960s: Changing the Future.* New York: Twayne, 1993.

Lionnet, Francoise. "Metissage, Emancipation, and Female Textuality in Two Francophone Writers." In *Life/Lines,* ed. Brodzki and Schenck. Pp. 260–80.

List, Shelley Steinmann. *Did You Love Daddy When I Was Born?* New York: Saturday Review Press, 1972.

Lomas, Peter, ed. *The Predicament of the Family: A Psychoanalytical Symposium.* London: Hogarth Press, 1972.

Lukas, Susan. *Fat Emily.* New York: Stein and Day, 1974.

Lyons, Bonnie. "Tillie Olsen: The Writer as a Jewish Woman." *Studies in American Jewish Literature* 5 (1986): 89–102.

MacCannell, Juliet Flower, ed. *The Other Perspective in Gender and Culture: Rewriting Women and the Symbolic.* New York: Columbia University Press, 1990.

Malin, Irving, ed. *Contemporary American-Jewish Literature: Critical Essays.* Bloomington: Indiana University Press, 1973.

Margolis, Maxine L. *Mothers and Such: Views of American Women and Why They Changed.* Berkeley: University of California Press, 1984.

Martin, Biddy. "Lesbian Identity and Autobiographical Difference[s]." In *Life/Lines,* ed. Brodzki and Schenck. Pp. 77–106.

Mason, Mary G. "The Other Voice: Autobiographies of Women Writers." In *Life/Lines,* ed. Brodzki and Schenck. Pp. 19–44.

Meier, Joyce. "The Subversion of the Father in the Tales of Grace Paley." *Delta* 14 (May 1982): 115–27.

Merkin, Daphne. *Enchantment.* 1984. New York: Harcourt Brace Jovanovich, 1986.

Meyerowitz, Joanne J. *Women Adrift: Independent Wage Earners in Chicago, 1880–1930.* Chicago: University of Chicago Press, 1988.

Miller, Alice. *Thou Shalt Not Be Aware: Society's Betrayal of the Child.* 1981. New York: New American Library, 1986.

Miller, Nancy K., ed. *The Poetics of Gender.* New York: Columbia University Press, 1986.

———. "Writing Fictions: Women's Autobiography in France." In *Life/Lines*, ed. Brodzki and Schenck. Pp. 45–61.

Miner, Madonne A. "Guaranteed to Please: Twentieth-Century American Women's Bestsellers." In *Gender and Reading*, ed. Flynn and Schweickart. Pp. 187–209.

———. *Insatiable Appetites: Twentieth-Century American Women's Bestsellers.* Westport, Conn.: Greenwood Press, 1984.

Mintz, Jacqueline A. "The Myth of the Jewish Mother in Three Jewish, American, Female Writers." *Centennial Review* 22.3 (1978): 346–55.

Molodowsky, Kadia. "Women Songs." Trans. Adrienne Rich. In *A Treasury of Yiddish Poetry*, ed. Irving Howe and Eliezer Greenberg. New York: Schocken, 1969. P. 284.

Moore, Deborah Dash. *At Home in America: Second-Generation New York Jews.* New York: Columbia University Press, 1981.

Morton, Leah [Elizabeth G. Stern]. *I Am a Woman—and a Jew.* New York: Harper, 1926.

Munt, Sally, ed. *New Lesbian Criticism: Literary and Cultural Readings.* New York: Columbia University Press, 1992.

Newton, Judith, and Deborah Rosenfelt, eds. *Feminist Criticism and Social Change: Sex, Class and Race in Literature and Culture.* New York: Methuen, 1985.

O'Barr, Jean F., Deborah Pope, and Mary Wyer, eds. *Ties that Bind: Essays on Mothering and Patriarchy.* Chicago: University of Chicago Press, 1990.

Olsen, Tillie. *Silences.* New York: Delacorte Press, 1978.

———. *Tell Me a Riddle.* 1961. New York: Dell, 1978.

Ozick, Cynthia. *Art and Ardor.* New York: Knopf, 1983.

———. *Bloodshed and Three Novellas.* New York: Knopf, 1976.

———. *The Cannibal Galaxy.* New York: Knopf, 1983.

———. "Eureka." *Lilith* 19.3 (Fall 1994): 11.

———. "Notes toward Finding the Right Question." In *On Being a Jewish Feminist*, ed. Heschel. Pp. 120–51.

———. *Trust.* 1966. New York: Dutton, 1983.

Paley, Grace. *Enormous Changes at the Last Minute.* New York: Farrar, 1974.

———. *Later the Same Day.* 1985. New York: Penguin, 1986.

————. *The Little Disturbances of Man: Stories of Women and Men at Love.* 1959. New York: Virago, 1980.

Parent, Gail. *Sheila Levine Is Dead and Living in New York.* New York: Putnam, 1972.

Pearlman, Mickey, ed. *Mother Puzzles: Daughters and Mothers in Contemporary American Literature.* New York: Greenwood, 1989.

Personal Narratives Group, ed. *Interpreting Women's Lives: Feminist Theory and Personal Narratives.* Bloomington: Indiana University Press, 1989.

Pesotta, Rose. *Days of Our Lives.* Boston: Excelsior, 1958.

Piercy, Marge. *Small Changes.* New York: Fawcett, Crest, 1973.

Plaskow, Judith. "The Jewish Feminist: Conflict in Identities." In *Jewish Woman,* ed. Koltun. Pp. 3–10.

————. *Standing Again at Sinai: Judaism from a Feminist Perspective.* San Francisco: Harper and Row, 1990.

Pratt, Norma Fain. "Culture and Radical Politics: Yiddish Women Writers in America, 1890–1940." In *Decades of Discontent,* ed. Scharf and Jensen. Pp. 131–52.

————. "Transitions in Judaism: The Jewish American Woman through the 1930's." *American Quarterly* 30 (Winter 1978): 681–702.

Prell, Riv Ellen. "The Begetting of America's Jews: Seeds of American Jewish Identity in the Representations of American Jewish Women." *Journal of Jewish Communal Service* 69.2–3 (1993): 4–23.

————. "Rage and Representation: Jewish Gender Stereotypes in American Culture." In *Uncertain Terms,* ed. Ginsburg and Tsing. Pp. 248–68.

Radway, Janice A. *Reading the Romance: Women, Patriarchy, and Popular Literature.* Chapel Hill: University of North Carolina Press, 1984.

Rainwater, Catherine, and William J. Scheick, eds. *Contemporary American Women Writers: Narrative Strategies.* Lexington: University of Kentucky Press, 1985.

Rapoport, Nessa. *Preparing for Sabbath.* 1981. New York: Biblio Press, 1988.

Reddy, Maureen T. "Maternal Reading: Lazarre and Walker." In *Narrating Mothers,* ed. Daly and Reddy. Pp. 222–38.

Regenbaum, Shelly. "Art, Gender, and the Jewish Tradition in Yezierska's *Red Ribbon on a White Horse* and Potok's *My Name Is Asher Lev.*" *Studies in American Jewish Literature* 7.1 (1988): 55–66.

Reich, Tova. "Hers: My Mother, My Muse." *New York Times Magazine,* Nov. 6, 1988, 30, 32.

————. *Mara: A Novel.* New York: Farrar, Straus, Giroux, 1978.

Reimer, Gail Twersky. "Revisions of Labor in Margaret Oliphant's Autobiography." In *Life/Lines,* ed. Brodzki and Schenck. Pp. 203–20.

Rich, Adrienne. *Of Woman Born: Motherhood as Experience and Institution.* 1976. New York: Bantam, 1977.

————. *On Lies, Secrets, and Silence: Selected Prose, 1966–1978*. New York: W. W. Norton, 1979.

————. *Sources*. Woodside, Calif.: Heyeck Press, 1983.

————. "Split at the Root." In *Nice Jewish Girls*, ed. Beck. Pp. 73–90.

Roiphe, Anne. "Daughters of the Israelites" (review of *The Flame Bearers*). *New York Times Book Review*, Nov. 9, 1986, 12.

————. *Lovingkindness*. New York: Summit Books, Simon and Schuster, 1987.

————. *Up the Sandbox!* New York: Simon and Schuster, 1970.

Rosenfelt, Deborah. "From the Thirties: Tillie Olsen and the Radical Tradition." *Feminist Studies* 7.3 (Fall 1981): 370–406.

Roth, Philip. *Portnoy's Complaint*. 1969. New York: Vintage, 1994.

Rudnick, Lois. "The Life of Mabel Dodge Luhan." In *Challenge of Feminist Biography*, ed. Alpern, Antler, Perry, and Scobie. Pp. 116–38.

Ruether, Rosemary Radford, and Rosemary Skinner Keller, eds. *Women and Religion in America: The Nineteenth Century*. New York: Harper and Row, 1981.

Rupp, Leila J., and Verta Taylor. *Survival in the Doldrums: The American Women's Rights Movement, 1945 to the 1960s*. New York: Oxford University Press, 1987.

Sachs, Emanie. *Red Damask*. New York: Harper, 1927.

Sayers, Janet. *Mothers of Psychoanalysis: Helene Deutsch, Karen Horney, Anna Freud, Melanie Klein*. New York: W. W. Norton, 1991.

Schaeffer, Susan Fromberg. *Falling*. New York: Macmillan, 1973.

Scharf, Lois, and Joan M. Jensen. *Decades of Discontent: The Women's Movement, 1920–1940*. 1983. Boston: Northeastern University Press, 1987.

Schenck, Celeste. "All of a Piece: Women's Poetry and Autobiography." In *Life/Lines*, ed. Brodzki and Schenck. Pp. 281–305.

Schneider, Susan Weidman. *Jewish and Female: A Guide and Sourcebook for Today's Jewish Woman*. New York: Simon and Schuster, 1984.

Schneiderman, Rose. *All for One*. New York: Paul S. Erickson, 1967.

Schoen, Carol. *Anzia Yezierska*. Boston: Twayne, 1982.

Schwab, Gabriele. "The Multiple Lives of Addie Bundren's Dead Body: On William Faulkner's *As I Lay Dying*." In *Other Perspective*, ed. MacCannell. Pp. 209–41.

Schwartz, Adria E. "Some Notes on the Development of Female Gender Role Identity." In *Psychoanalysis and Women*, ed. Alpert. Pp. 57–82.

Schwartz, Lynne Sharon. *Leaving Brooklyn*. Boston: Houghton Mifflin, 1989.

————. *The Melting Pot and Other Subversive Stories*. Harmondsworth, U.K.: Penguin, 1987.

————. "The Two Portraits of Rembrandt: A Memoir." *Moment* 11.8 (Nov. 1986): 35–41.

Seligman, Dee. "Jewish Mothers' Stories: Rosellen Brown's *The Autobiography of My Mother.*" In *Mother Puzzles*, ed. Pearlman. Pp. 115–22.

Shapiro, Ann R., ed. *Jewish American Women Writers: A Bio-Bibliographical and Critical Sourcebook.* Westport, Conn.: Greenwood, 1994.

———. "The Novels of E. M. Broner: A Study in Secular Feminism and Feminist Judaism." *Studies in American Jewish Literature* 10.1 (Spring 1991): 93–103.

Shapiro, Dani. *Fugitive Blue.* New York: Doubleday, 1993.

Sharistanian, Janet. Afterword. In *Unpossessed*, by Tess Slesinger. 1934. New York: Feminist Press, 1984. Pp. 359–86.

Shepherd, Naomi. *A Price below Rubies: Jewish Women as Rebels and Radicals.* Cambridge, Mass.: Harvard University Press, 1993.

Showalter, Elaine. "Feminist Criticism in the Wilderness." In *New Feminist Criticism*, ed. Showalter. Pp. 243–70.

———, ed. *The New Feminist Criticism: Essays on Women, Literature, and Theory.* New York: Pantheon, 1985.

Shulman, Alix Kates. *Memoirs of an Ex-Prom Queen.* New York: Knopf, 1972.

———, ed. *Red Emma Speaks: An Emma Goldman Reader.* New York: Schocken, 1983.

Siegel, Rachel Josefowitz, and Ellen Cole, eds. *Seen but Not Heard: Jewish Women in Therapy.* New York: Harrington Park Press, 1991.

Simon, Kate. *Bronx Primitive: Portraits in a Childhood.* New York: Harper, 1982.

———. *Etchings in an Hourglass.* New York: Harper, 1990.

———. *A Wider World.* New York: Harper, 1986.

Sinclair, Jo [Ruth Seid]. *Anna Teller.* New York: McKay, 1960.

———. *The Wasteland.* 1946. Philadelphia, Pa.: Jewish Publication Society, 1987.

Slesinger, Tess. "Mother for Dinner." In *Between Mothers and Daughters*, ed. Koppelman. Pp. 141–60.

———. *The Unpossessed.* 1934. New York: Feminist Press, 1984.

Smith, Adrienne J. "Reflections of a Jewish Lesbian-Feminist Activist-Therapist; or, First of All I Am Jewish, the Rest Is Commentary." In *Seen but Not Heard*, ed. Siegel and Cole. Pp. 57–64.

Smith, Sidonie. *A Poetics of Women's Autobiography: Marginality and the Fictions of Self-Representation.* Bloomington: Indiana University Press, 1987.

Sochen, June. *Consecrate Every Day: The Public Lives of Jewish American Women, 1880–1980.* New York: SUNY Press, 1981.

———. "Identities within Identity: Thoughts on Jewish American Women Writers." *Studies in American Jewish Literature* 3 (1983): 6–10.

Sollors, Werner. *Beyond Ethnicity: Consent and Descent in American Culture.* New York: Oxford University Press, 1986.

Spacks, Patricia Meyer. "Selves in Hiding." In *Women's Autobiography*, ed. Jelinek. Pp. 112–32.

Spieler, Susan. "The Gendered Self: A Lost Maternal Legacy." In *Psychoanalysis and Women*, ed. Alpert. Pp. 33–56.

Spretnak, Charlene, ed. *The Politics of Women's Spirituality: Essays on the Rise of Spiritual Power within the Feminist Movement*. New York: Doubleday, 1982.

Stein, Hana. *The Wedding*. New York: A. A. Wyn, 1950.

Stone, Laurie. *Starting with Serge*. New York, Doubleday, 1990.

Strandberg, Victor. "The Art of Cynthia Ozick." *Texas Studies in Literature and Language* 25.2 (1983): 266–312.

Sullivan, Ralda Meyerson. "Anzia Yezierska, an American Writer." Ph.D. diss., University of California at Berkeley, 1975.

Taylor, Jacqueline. *Grace Paley: Illuminating the Dark Lives*. Austin: University of Texas Press, 1990.

Thorne, Barrie, and Marilyn Yalom, eds. *Rethinking the Family: Some Feminist Questions*. New York: Longman, 1982.

Tompkins, Jane. *Sensational Designs: The Cultural Work of American Fiction, 1790–1860*. New York: Oxford University Press, 1985.

Trebilcot, Joyce, ed. *Mothering: Essays in Feminist Theory*. Totowa, N.J.: Rowman, 1984.

Umansky, Ellen M. "Females, Feminists, and Feminism: A Review of Recent Literature on Jewish Feminism and the Creation of a Feminist Judaism." *Feminist Studies* 14.2 (Summer 1988): 349–65.

———. "Representations of Jewish Women in the Works and Life of Elizabeth Stern." *Modern Judaism* 13.2 (May 1993): 165–76.

———. "Spiritual Expressions: Jewish Women's Religious Lives in the Twentieth-Century United States." In *Jewish Women in Historical Perspective*, ed. Baskin. Pp 265–88.

Umansky, Ellen M., and Diane Ashton. *Four Centuries of Jewish Women's Spirituality*. Boston: Beacon Press, 1992.

Wade-Gayles, Gloria. "The Truths of Our Mothers' Lives: Mother-Daughter Relationships in Black Women's Fiction." *Sage* 1.2 (Fall 1984): 8–12.

Wald, Alan M. "The Menorah Group Moves Left." *Jewish Social Studies* 38.3–4 (1976): 289–320.

Walters, Suzanne Danuta. *Lives Together/Worlds Apart: Mothers and Daughters in Popular Culture*. Berkeley: University of California Press, 1992.

Wandersee, Winifred D. *On the Move: American Women in the 1970s*. Boston: Twayne, 1988.

Ware, Susan. *Holding Their Own: American Women in the 1930s*. Boston: Twayne, 1982.

Wasserstein, Wendy. "Sister Wasserstein's Chronicle." *Forward*, Mar. 19, 1993, 11–19.

Waugh, Patricia. *Feminine Fictions: Revisiting the Postmodern.* New York: Routledge, 1989.

Wegner, Judith Romney. "The Image and Status of Women in Classical Rabbinic Judaism." In *Jewish Women in Historical Perspective,* ed. Baskin. Pp. 68–93.

Weinberg, Sydney Stahl. *The World of Our Mothers: The Lives of Jewish Immigrant Women.* New York: Schocken, 1988.

Weingarten, Violet. *Mrs. Beneker.* New York: Simon and Schuster, 1967.

Westkott, Marcia. *The Feminist Legacy of Karen Horney.* New Haven, Conn.: Yale University Press, 1986.

Wexler, Alice. *Emma Goldman: An Intimate Life.* New York: Pantheon, 1984.

Wilentz, Gay. "White Patron and Black Artist: The Correspondence of Fannie Hurst and Zora Neale Hurston." *Library Chronicle* 25 (1986): 21–43.

Winnicott, D. W. "Mirror-Role of Mother and Family in Child Development." In *Predicament of the Family,* ed. Lomas. Pp. 26–33.

Wolk, Merla. "Uncivil Wars: The Reproduction of Mother-Daughter Conflict and Rosellen Brown's *Autobiography of My Mother.*" *American Imago* 45.2 (1988): 163–85.

Wyatt, Jean. *Reconstructing Desire: The Role of the Unconscious in Women's Reading and Writing.* Chapel Hill: University of North Carolina Press, 1990.

Yezierska, Anzia. *All I Could Never Be.* New York: Brewer, Warren, and Putnam, 1932.

———. *Bread Givers.* New York: Persea Books, 1975.

———. *Red Ribbon on a White Horse.* New York: Scribners, 1950.

———. *Salome of the Tenements.* New York: Boni and Liveright, 1923.

Zack, Michele. "Deification and Disdain: A Literary View of Black and Jewish Mothers." *Journal of Psychology and Judaism* 3 (1979): 268–77.

Zimmerman, Bonnie. "Lesbians Like This and That: Some Notes on Lesbian Criticism for the Nineties." In *New Lesbian Criticism,* ed. Munt. Pp. 1–16.

———. "The Politics of Transliteration: Lesbian Personal Narratives." *Signs* 9 (Summer 1984): 663–82.

Index

JANET HANDLER BURSTEIN is a professor of English at Drew University, Madison, N.J., where she teaches Victorian literature and American Jewish literature. The author of articles in a number of journals, including *American Literature*, *Studies in American Jewish Literature*, and *Victorian Studies*, she continues to research American Jewish women writers, particularly those of the 1920s and 1930s.